Baghdad

UNDERGROUND RAILROAD

Advance Praise
"Baghdad Underground Railroad"

Steve Miska provides a riveting, vivid description of the mutual trust, shared sacrifice, and extraordinary bonds between U.S. servicemembers and their foreign interpreters on the battlefield.

General David Petraeus, US Army (Ret.),
former Commander of the Surge in Iraq, former Director of the CIA

"Absolutely riveting. Tells the story of the harrowing escape from sectarian violence of many interpreters working alongside Americans. Through the eyes of soldiers and the interpreters, the reader learns to better understand the risks of collaborating with deployed military and diplomats in conflict zones."

General Barry McCaffrey, U.S. Army (Ret.),
former Commander Southern Command, NBC News commentator

"The soldiers of Task Force Justice displayed the same determination in fighting al-Qaeda and Shia militias, as they did in battling the US bureaucracy to get visas for their interpreters whose lives were in danger. This book is a testament to the commitment and values of the U.S. military who determined that their creed of "no man left behind" extended to those Iraqis who had shed blood with them and deserved the opportunity to build new lives in America."

Emma Sky, Author, "The Unraveling: High Hopes and Missed
Opportunities in Iraq"; Director, Yale World Fellows Program

Baghdad

UNDERGROUND RAILROAD

Saving American Allies in Iraq

— A Memoir —

Steve Miska
Colonel, U.S. Army (Ret.)

ONWARDPRESS.ORG

LOS ANGELES

Published in the United States by Onward Press, an imprint of United States Veterans Artists Alliance, a 501-c-3 educational non-profit organization.
5284 ½ Village Green
Los Angeles, CA 90016

www.onwardpress.org
www.usvaa.org

Edited by Christina Hoag
Cover Art by Jamie Peterson
Cover design by Teddi Black
Formatted and designed by Megan McCullough

ISBN Hard Cover: 978-1-954988-03-3
ISBN Paperback: 978-1-954988-04-0
ISBN E book: 978-1-954988-05-7

Library of Congress Control Number: 2021937253

Author's note

Due to the sensitive nature of information provided from interviews and the author's experience, names and details of some incidents have been altered to protect the identities of the people portrayed, and their families. Some are still in harm's way. Several have returned to combat as U.S. servicemembers. Those interviewed volunteered to contribute to the story. Given the raw emotional nature of the experiences, interviews created the possibility of revisiting painful memories and triggering post-traumatic stress. Despite those risks, many did not hesitate to step forward and tell their stories. Their hope is that this work might help influence U.S. policy or at least stand as a beacon of light against those very dark times.

Contents

Part Two: America

Foreword

Steve Miska has written a stunning book on the Iraq war. It is as powerful as it is disturbing. *Baghdad Underground Railroad* is the story told by a US infantry officer with multiple Iraq tours. Miska occupies a unique space: he was a tactical commander with strategic vision. He describes how Presidential initiatives translated into action on the ground. How lives are put at risk and often lost in efforts to carry out the intentions of policy makers who have no concept of the complexities of execution where the proverbial rubber reaches the proverbial road.

Absolutely crucial to this process in Iraq and Afghanistan are interpreters. They are essential for any hope of success. They translate not just words but cultures, histories, intentions. Without them, our losses would be far greater and our achievements much less. This book is their story, brilliantly told.

Miska uses his own experiences on the battlefield to illustrate the work interpreters do and the risks they run. He opens with the murder of an interpreter, a young husband gunned down by his Iraqi countrymen because of his service to Miska's unit. His story is all too common. But the main story is what happens to these heroes after their service. In theory, they are eligible for Special Immigrant Visas, allowing them and their families to travel to the United States. A reward for hazardous duty performed well, certainly. But also, a literal lifesaver as many are hunted down and executed because they facilitated our mission.

As the American Ambassador, I was an architect for these programs in Iraq and Afghanistan. But the programs do not function as intended. Fathoms of red tape and multiple, redundant security checks delay issuance for years. Miska is unblinking in illustrating the consequences of these delays—living on the run in their own countries and dying when there is no place left to run. He forced us to look as well. It is not comfortable reading, nor should it be. What it should be is mandatory reading for policy makers: their actions and inactions cause the entirely avoidable deaths of those who stepped forward to support our missions. We betray them and we betray our own values as Americans.

Miska's epigraph for the book threads its way throughout his narrative. It is drawn from an early American Abolitionist: You may choose to look the other way, but you can never say again that you did not know. May this book and Miska's message reach many in our country who once they know, will not look away.

The Honorable Ryan C. Crocker
United States Ambassador to Iraq
March 31, 2007 – February 13, 2009

Preface

We lived in hell. In 2006, Baghdad broke out in intense waves of sectarian cleansing. Extremists on both the Sunni and Shia sides inflicted terrible brutality upon innocents of each population. In our sector of Northwest Baghdad, Dagger Brigade discovered, on average, 275 bodies per week at the height of the violence. Those were just the dead Iraqis that brigade patrols found. There were scores of other corpses that went unreported, bodies found by civilians, Iraqi police, and others who delivered them to urban morgues, where the needle-in-a-haystack task of attempting to identify the victims began.

The Dagger Brigade had deployed to Iraq from tranquil Bavaria in Germany, a corner of the planet where genocide had fomented seven decades earlier as the world turned a blind eye. Most academics who study conflicts use the benchmark of 1,000 deaths per month as the threshold to mark the existence of civil war. We experienced more than that number of deaths per month in one quadrant of the Iraqi capital city. "Civil war" was not authorized by the U.S. government as a term to describe the situation in Iraq back then. So, as soldiers, we lived *our* reality and tried to use the words that were more in line with Washington, D.C.'s aspirations. Put another way, those of us who served in the U.S. Armed Forces in Baghdad in those days were surrounded by unbearable human misery on every side.

Amidst that backdrop, the Iraqis who worked alongside us, interpreters and suppliers, most contracted by U.S. firms, experienced extreme risk. Adversaries went after their families; they hunted the "collaborators" who betrayed their country by working with the occupation. As our closest Iraqi colleagues were killed, injured, or forced to quit, we realized we had to try to do something to help them. We couldn't function without their linguistic skills and logistical knowledge. We would be culturally blind without them. More importantly, we would fail to live up to our ethos of "leave no one behind" if we abandoned them upon redeployment. As a result, we began the process of helping them escape.

Journalists became natural allies in our effort to help interpreters. Intrepid reporters spotlighted the tragedy of partnering alongside Americans. Given the lethality of the environment, the press couldn't get to the story without the military. Sometimes, they used stringers, Iraqis hired to report on news in areas too dangerous for Western journalists. Other times the media used fixers, Iraqis who helped with security and safety. When the locals who assisted journalists came under threat, which happened frequently, reporters sometimes helped them move out of harm's way. Thus, when military troops looked for people who knew how to protect Iraqis, journalists became logical partners.

The first step to keep our interpreters and other partners safe was to protect their identities. We learned this the hard way. Many of our partners understood that wearing a face mask, growing a beard, and staying incognito were their only means of protection. If they failed with a disguise, they could forfeit not only their own lives but those of loved ones and friends. We Americans made mistakes, such as taking an interpreter on patrol through his own neighborhood. If that interpreter had to dismount and interact with the population, they risked discovery. Word traveled fast among locals, and the ramifications were swift.

As a result, many of our interpreters set out on what we called the Baghdad Underground Railroad. It was a path fraught with peril from Baghdad to Amman, Jordan, and ultimately the United States. The fortunate ones were those lucky few who qualified for a Special Immigrant Visa, or SIV. They had to run the gauntlet to travel to

Amman because the U.S. Embassy in Baghdad had closed its doors to Iraqis citing "security concerns." To make matters worse, Jordan closed its Iraqi border because of the refugee crisis ignited by the war. As a result, the official U.S. policy had a built-in catch-22. Even for those who qualified for a SIV, it seemed next to impossible to get one.

This is their story. It's also my story, one about trying to maintain some semblance of humanity in an extremely violent environment.

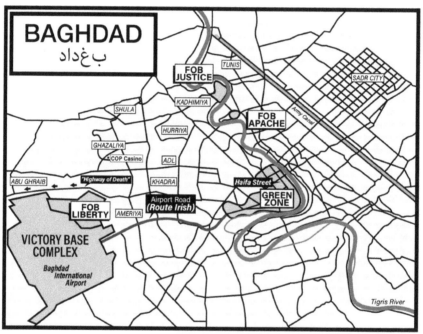

Graphic produced by: Zoe Knepp

"Highway of Death"

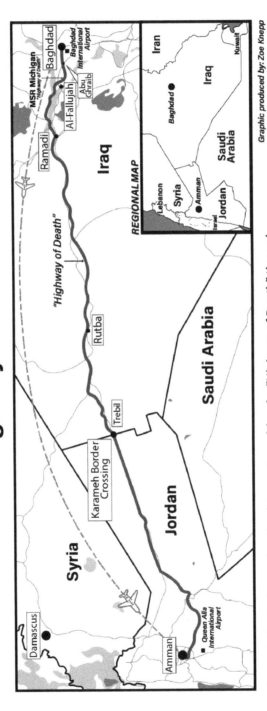

Above is the choice confronting interpreters: drive the "Highway of Death" through Anbar Province to Jordan or risk capture and torture/death by militia at the Baghdad International Airport.

Graphic produced by: Zoe Knepp.

7

Part One

Iraq

Chapter One

Awakening

"You may choose to look the other way,
but you can never say again that you did not know."

~ William Wilberforce, British abolitionist, 1759-1833

AKEEL WAS NOT a traitor. That's what Ahmed Hassan al-Baydi thought of his son as he looked at his wife in the kitchen of their modest home in the city of Balad, eighty kilometers north of Baghdad. He wrung his hands. Paced. Their son had returned from the capital where, he told his parents, he was enrolled at the police academy. That justified his lengthy absences, sometimes months at a time. However, neighbors whispered rumors that Akeel had taken a job with the Americans. That might explain his moderate increase in wealth. Everyone knew the police were not paid well. On the other hand, they were known to extort people for cash. Whichever, it was clear Akeel couldn't bring home enough pay as a policeman to account for his newfound ability to care for his family.

The last time he'd visited, two months earlier, armed men approached him with the frightening accusation that he collaborated with the Americans. His father and a friend intervened. They convinced him to swear on the Holy Koran that he was not employed by the Americans in the Green Zone, the seat of Iraqi government, the U.S. Embassy and military command. Akeel acquiesced and swore on the Koran. His father had breathed a sigh of relief.

The next trip, Akeel returned home to visit his young wife, Wafa. She'd given birth to stillborn twins and was distraught. Akeel told his family he'd taken a leave of absence from his training. Overcome with grief and loss, he cried with his parents and sat with Wafa. Unable to comfort her, he said, "I need some air."

"Too dangerous," said Ahmed. "Neighbors can't be trusted."

Akeel understood. The rumors and whispers were true. He was a translator for the Americans but would never admit to his parents. He did all he could to hide the truth. He never carried his U.S. translator identification and depending on the neighborhood, he pretended to be Sunni or Shia. Collaborators were not welcome in any quarter.

Akeel was torn between a desire to be with Wafa and the danger his presence created for his family. Despite his father's pleas, he walked out the front door, glanced back, and saw his father struggle to light a cigarette. The flame shook. It took two tries.

He left the traditional, walled compound of his parent's home and walked along a dark street. Only two streetlights still functioned. Night shadows grew long. Some moved. Akeel lost his thoughts over ways to ease his wife's grief. He sucked a drag off a cigarette, looked up and noticed a car with no headlights. It turned the corner a couple of blocks ahead and drifted towards him. The hair on his neck stood up.

"Traitor," a silhouette said from across the street. "Where are you going this time of night?"

Akeel squinted into the darkness. His mind raced. Run or stay? The streets were barren except for another shadow that emerged from an alley and blocked his escape. He recognized a former accuser. The car coasted to a halt. The doors opened and two men stepped into the street.

"What do you want?" Akeel said. Beads of sweat popped out on his forehead. "I already swore on the Koran."

"We know you've been lying to us," the shadow stated matter-of-factly. "And now you've lied to Allah. You need to pay for your blasphemy."

The three men closed in. He never saw the pistol aimed by the passenger from the car. The shooter fired the weapon from a meter away. The bullet punctured Akeel's skull and knocked him to the ground. Five more shots rang out as the insurgent emptied the magazine into Akeel's torso.

"Fucking traitor," the shooter yelled. "That's what you get for joining the occupation and working with the American pigs. Maybe they'll come take care of your wife now."

"Leave the message," the shadow ordered.

The shooter reached into a pocket and dropped a piece of paper on Akeel's bloody body.

Ahmed heard the gunfire. He ran outside.

His wife screamed, "No! Stay! Don't go!"

He ignored her, pushed open the courtyard gate and peered down the street. He saw three men jump into a car a block away. Headlights flicked on, exposing a crumpled body in the middle of the road. The car backed up and turned, tires screeching as it drove away.

Ahmed ran toward the limp form, a recognizable shape on the dirt. Akeel was much taller than most Iraqis. He had dark hair and a thin frame. Ahmed saw his son's body riddled with bullet wounds. Blood spilled onto the street. He grabbed his son's shoulders but realized he was dead. A round had penetrated the left temple and exploded out the other side. Bullet holes punctured Akeel's chest. Blood, almost black in the moonlight, saturated his white dishdasha and pooled under his body.

Ahmed picked up the paper that had been dropped on his son's corpse and read: "By way of Allah's will this infidel has been punished for being a traitor. Let this be a lesson to all who would seek to collaborate with the occupiers." Ahmed dropped to his knees and wept. Nobody from the neighboring homes came outside.

Hassan Benkato poked his head around my open office door to see if he could get my attention. If I seemed too busy, he might come back another time. He was an absolute gentleman and always exercised impeccable discretion. If the issue was pressing, Hassan would ask if I had a minute. A U.S. citizen with a security clearance, Hassan had worked at a Jaguar dealership in Houston for twenty-five years before volunteering to support the U.S. effort in Iraq.

"Colonel Miska? We've got a problem, boss," he said. His body language indicated he was reluctant to tell me. "Jack's father just phoned me from Jack's cell phone. He was killed in the street in Balad." Jack was Akeel's American name. Almost every interpreter used a nickname, which was easier for us to pronounce and made it more difficult for other Iraqis to identify them.

I stared at Hassan. I was inured to bad news. It was my second combat deployment to Iraq. Things had gone from bad to worse in the sixteen months between my tours. I was deputy commander of the 2nd Brigade, 1st Infantry Division, known as the Dagger Brigade, based in Schweinfurt, Germany. I'd deployed ahead of the brigade, leading a small team that received units flowing into Kuwait and helped push them into theater, ready for combat.

Violence in Iraq had spiked after al Qaeda blew up the al Askiri Shrine in Samarra in April 2006. The brigade sent units into various sectors, then built a provisional task force of just over one hundred soldiers around the nucleus of my small team. As a lieutenant colonel with sixteen years' experience in the Army, I was assigned to lead Task Force Justice.

We deployed to Khadamiyah, Baghdad, with orders to maintain watch over one of the most politically sensitive areas of the country. The imposing Khadamiyah Shrine dominated that portion of the city. It served as a beacon to millions of pilgrims who marched to pay homage during Shia religious holidays each year.

With dozens of small training teams, an Iraqi Army brigade, and a National Police Division headquarters, our team occupied Forward Operating Base (FOB) Justice. I was beginning to appreciate how dangerous the situation was for our closest Iraqi partners, the thousands of interpreters and other local nationals who risked their lives and families to support the American war effort.

When I arrived for my second tour, Baghdad was a killing field. After the fall of Saddam Hussein and his capture in 2004, the country drifted inexorably toward civil war. Al Qaeda in Iraq (AQI) pursued an intentional strategy to push the country in that direction. When the terror group blew up the al Askiri Shrine, a major Shia religious site, they achieved their aim. The country spiraled into violence.

Michael Holmes of CNN did an embed with our task force in January 2007. His producer contacted me to describe the story. They titled it *Month of Mayhem*. I took issue with the title but later realized they were right. Those of us who experienced that January did indeed live through a month of mayhem. Unfortunately, it seemed to extend into the following months. So, it was hard for me to be rattled when one of my closest interpreters was killed, even though his loss had a significant impact. I learned not to be emotional in the heat of the moment. The time for grieving came later.

"Sunni insurgents killed him," Hassan said. "They were probably the same insurgents who made him swear on the Koran that he was not working with the Americans the last time he went home."

I didn't know what to think other than Sunni insurgents pissed me off. So did the Shia militias, the different elements of Jaysh al Mahdi, the militia loyal to Muqtada al Sadr, and the al Qaeda in Iraq terrorists. All of them slaughtered innocent people with the aim of inciting violence and further destabilizing the already unstable Iraqi government. Baghdad, and Iraq more generally, was a mess. And we owned it because we broke it in the first place. Damn Bush. I said to Hassan, "Tell me what happened in detail. Anyone else know?"

"No. I wanted to let you know first. I figured the boys would take it hard, and you might have some guidance or want to tell them yourself." Hassan had a gentle manner and waited for me to mull over the situation. I felt fortunate to have him as a friend and colleague.

"Let's get the chain of command together. I'll tell them, then we can break it to our patrol. Round up the interpreters and inform them, too. Everyone needs to know about the threats."

Hassan nodded. My heart sank as I let the news soak in. Jack had started his job with a platoon from Alpha Battery, 1-7 Field Artillery, the Brigade's artillery battalion. He had a quiet demeanor and always seemed in a good mood. The soldiers loved him and had nicknamed him the Black Cat because of his black hair and dark complexion. We all had nicknames. It was a sign of affection. The interpreters also had nicknames, in addition to their western monikers. It let them know they were part of the team.

Nicknames were also a security measure to ensure that people couldn't identify the interpreters, or their neighborhoods and cities of origin. In Iraq, if a person's full name were known, you could figure out where their family lived. That was dangerous since it exposed relatives to threats, intimidation or worse. Jack, as we knew him, had been at FOB Justice for some time and performed well on patrol. Many interpreters didn't want to leave the relative safety of the base and go on patrol due to the risk of being wounded or identified.

Jack was fearless and proved himself invaluable when he shifted to my patrol. He attended all patrol briefs. That was part of the job. Interpreters needed to know what was going on as much as every U.S. soldier. They were our cultural eyes, ears, and mouthpieces. They might be able to spot a problem and help the unit if they understood the mission. However, many units didn't allow their interpreters to participate in briefs. Commanders claimed the need for operational security, or OPSEC. I believed it was better to have everyone armed with both information and weapons to defend themselves, and in turn, the overall unit. That's what teamwork was all about; training and investing in each teammate to allow them to achieve their potential and allow the unit to achieve its mission.

When Jack traveled home to his family, the risks were extreme. He had to pass as either Sunni or Shia depending on the area he was transiting. When he approached a checkpoint, he needed to recognize the telltale signs of who manned it, either the Mahdi Militia or Sunni insurgents. Even sectarian-minded members of the Army or police could be dangerous. Until his final trip, Jack had managed to outwit the insurgents, the militia, and even the police who stopped and questioned him.

"Jack is dead," I said to the chain of command, a few officers and half a dozen noncommissioned officers. They nodded, used to daily setbacks and bad news. We had lost soldiers, engaged in fire fights, had vehicles blown off roadways and responded to assist other U.S. and Iraqi units in contact with militia. "Hassan will coordinate with

Jack's family and let the other interpreters know. Please ensure all your people get the info." Many of the leaders hung their heads. The losses, whether American or Iraqi, were disheartening, even if the soldiers were stoic about the news.

"Nick, contact brigade and see whether GLS can get a replacement for Jack," I said, referring to Global Linguistic Solutions, the defense contractor that located and hired interpreters.

Nick Kron, our intelligence officer, was always responsive and would probably have the solution before day's end, or midnight since we worked shifts around the clock. While it was important for individuals to get sleep and be alert, the military always developed shifts to ensure the unit never slept. Our enemies didn't respect the clock. They felt time was on their side.

The insurgent strategy was to wait out the Americans. It was enough for the rebels not to lose. They could wait out the impatience of U.S. democracy, which could bring in a new administration every four years and last at most eight years. They would then have a chance to reestablish their power base after the occupiers, the Coalition forces, departed. Of course, the insurgents weren't the only ones who struggled for power in Iraq. Militias like Jaysh al Mahdi, the Shia militia aligned with Muktadar al Sadr, were also active.

In June 2003, George, one of the Iraqi contractors on base, began working with Americans. He was an English major in his final year at the University of Baghdad. George thought he could improve his language ability by seeking out Americans at police stations, checkpoints and other places. He was offered a job with a unit from the 82nd Airborne Division. His family lived three miles from FOB Justice.

A couple of years later, George was at work when his brother called. George never told anyone who he worked for because he didn't want his family to be at risk. His brother said, "I was backing the car out of the garage today. Mother came after me, waving a paper. She thought I had dropped it. The message came from bad people. They claimed you work for the Americans and they instructed our family to disown you."

"I'm sorry this happened," George said.

"You're lucky that mother can't read. I think she realized that something was wrong by my expression. I'm not going to tell you what to do, but you've got to be careful."

"I can't come home anymore. It's too dangerous for the family."

"We don't want to see anything happen to you, brother. These guys are ruthless. The letter was written in eloquent Arabic and directed us to hang a sign from our home stating 'Repent! Repent! Repent!' to warn all the neighbors of the dangers of collaboration."

"Thank you, little brother. I'll be in touch."

"Please be careful and go with Allah."

Two years later, George was working as a contractor on FOB Justice. He handled projects big and small for us and the Iraqi Army. For safety, we allowed him to live on the base. He hadn't been home again but had worked out careful ways to see his family, to assure them he was okay and give them money. He instructed them to tell neighbors and anyone who asked that he had gone away on business. George believed that if he stayed away, he could protect his family from the violence that percolated throughout the country.

Ronnie began his job with the Americans when he was eighteen. The son of a university English professor, he'd learned the language well and became proficient by practicing with his father and watching American movies. He wanted to make Iraq a better place, and the Americans paid well. However, he knew better than to tell anyone about his employment, not even his own family.

Eight months after he started work at a base called Camp Banzai, Ronnie was home one evening. His mother called that dinner was ready. Ronnie walked into the kitchen and found her folding a pile of laundry.

"What's this?" his father asked in English, holding Ronnie's U.S. military base access badge.

Ronnie stared at it, stunned.

"Your mother found it in the laundry. Luckily, she was not sure what it was."

"I can explain."

"You don't need to. Your mother and I just want to make sure that you're safe. What would we do without you?"

"Of course, I'm safe. I translate documents in an office all day. Very mundane work, but they pay well." All a lie, of course.

At that time, the Americans didn't issue interpreters body armor or helmets, and Ronnie patrolled every day. He was so naïve to the risks that he wore his college clothes, white pants and a nice shirt, on his first patrol. He learned in a hurry from other interpreters how to mask his identity. In 2004, when the Americans asked him to replace an interpreter named Sameer, they didn't tell him how Sameer had died. Ronnie thought it happened on a patrol but felt it prudent to ask. Only then did he learn that Sameer had been killed leaving his house.

Ronnie's father said, "We appreciate that you help provide for the family. Please be safe." It was impossible to tell if his father knew he was lying, but Ronnie understood he had to make changes.

He attended nursing school in the evenings. He wore his hospital scrubs to and from work, a useful alibi. People who had time on their hands to observe his comings and goings could plausibly believe that a hospital employee worked long hours. The disguise allowed him to leave early in the morning, change on base, and patrol with the Americans. After his shift, he'd change into scrubs and go to nursing school, and late at night, return home.

Ronnie arrived on the base one day and found his lieutenant in distress. The previous day the officer had made a severe mistake while reversing his Bradley armored vehicle. He'd crushed a minivan loaded with Iraqi civilians. People died. Others were seriously injured and evacuated to a hospital. The interpreters were all talking about it. One of them described the incident to Ronnie so when the lieutenant asked Ronnie to come with him, he surmised it had something to do with the accident.

"I've been ordered to compensate the families of those who were killed or injured," the lieutenant said. "We're going to the hospital. You know where it is?"

Ronnie hesitated then said, "Can I make a suggestion? That's a very bad idea." He wasn't sure how his input would be received. He was new on the job. The Americans were just getting to know him.

"I know it's a crappy situation." The lieutenant was angry and pacing. "I don't want to go to the hospital and deal with wailing families, but I have to give the families blood money to keep them from seeking revenge." The U.S. military made frequent solatia payments to compensate grieving families for injury and loss.

"I understand blood money," Ronnie said. "And you are right about that. However, Iraqis are very emotional people. If you go to the hospital, they might go crazy on you right there. Let me call and get the information on the families. That way we can settle in the privacy of their homes when emotions calm down."

Ronnie had walked the lieutenant back from a possible cultural disaster. It was one of the many ways he and the other interpreters kept us from causing unnecessary damage and escalating a situation from bad to worse.

Three years later, Ronnie had long hair and a beard. He wore a mask on all patrols and translated meetings on the streets of Baghdad from behind a handkerchief over his mouth. He looked like Jesse James in an old western movie as the Americans attempted to keep an endless stream of tense situations from unraveling. Ronnie also wore a helmet and body armor. Things were kinetic, as his American colleagues liked to say.

Ronnie had quit nursing school and lived on FOB Justice. During Saddam's time, average Iraqis avoided the compound that became FOB Justice because it had been the dictator's secret police headquarters. People heard rumors about a human meat grinder and other accounts of torture and death. Ronnie became a permanent resident . A trip to his neighborhood risked not only his life, but the lives of his entire family. He dared not do it.

It hadn't always been that way. In 2003 and 2004, before the insurgency picked up, visiting FOB Justice was almost therapeutic for Iraqis. The city was safe, and people relished visiting areas they had avoided during the dictator's reign. Ronnie searched the prison walls for written messages, or any indicators of what Saddam's prisoners thought. He wondered if the prisoners dreamt of escaping, similar to his own dreams of a better life for his country.

Nadal, bald with a laurel of salt-and-pepper hair around his head and a neat, trim mustache, was an Iraqi businessman who scored a gold mine working with the Americans. He ran a convenience store in the basement of the main U.S. building on FOB Justice. Our soldiers loved him. Nadal figured out ways to acquire shampoo and soap, the typical sundries, but also chewing tobacco and items difficult to find in the ailing Iraqi economy. The products were not the brands American soldiers were used to back home, but they seemed to do the trick.

I had briefly considered opening an Army and Air Force Exchange Service (AAFES) shop, called the post exchange, (PX for short), on the base. We would have an AAFES mobile store similar to dozens of other bases across Iraq. The shops, built in converted truck trailers, carried a selection of products from home that soldiers desired. It would make FOB Justice a little bit more comfortable. So, I initiated the bureaucratic process to explore whether the size of our troop contingent warranted a store on our little base.

Hassan approached me one day about the PX. "Hey, boss."

"Yes, Old Dog," I said, using Hassan's patrol nickname, which he loved. He had amazing stamina for his age and bragged that he could keep up with the young soldiers while goading them to greater effort, part of the relentless teasing that occurred on patrol.

"The Iraqi shopkeepers are concerned about this AAFES shop idea," he said. "They think it's going to drive out their business with the soldiers."

I sat back in my chair. "That's a good point and one we should probably consider."

"Some of the storeowners came to me, very worried. Nadal goes all over Baghdad to find the soldiers what they need. He takes a lot of risks, but he loves the soldiers and is willing to get them what they want."

"I don't believe anyone wants our Iraqi partners to go out of business, especially when our purpose is to help reinvigorate the economy," I said.

Over the next few days, Task Force Justice leadership explored the ramifications of not bringing in an AAFES facility, which had never been guaranteed anyway. It would cost us valuable political capital, which we were willing to spend to take care of our soldiers. But at the end of the process, I decided to cancel the plan because the storeowners promised to obtain whatever the soldiers needed to maintain quality of life. Not everyone agreed with my decision, but they accepted it on the rationale that our mission was to provide security, which would allow the Iraqis to regain economic footing. In turn, that would allow us to go home. We were playing the long game.

Several times a week, Nadal drove through multiple Iraqi Army checkpoints in Khadamiyah on his way to Shula, a Shia neighborhood in northwest Baghdad. He would buy deodorant, cigarettes, socks, and other sundries. Not only was Shula a good place for him to stock up, but his family lived there. As a Shia, he could avoid the Sunni-controlled neighborhoods where al Qaeda in Iraq and other Sunni insurgent groups dominated the population. The Shia areas still carried risks, even for him. Jaysh al Mahdi, commonly known as JAM by both Americans and Iraqis, ruled many of the Shia neighborhoods. Khadamiyah, the location of Task Force Justice, was a JAM-controlled area. Shula was another.

Nadal had a modest car and would return to the American base with his trunk and backseat stuffed with new items for his shop. Given that the small American base was tucked inside a larger Iraqi base, Nadal had plausible deniability with the militia. He managed his inventory daily, kept track of which items sold and fielded new requests from customers. Every two to three days he would make a trip to Shula or to markets in central Baghdad for more difficult-to-find items.

Nadal stopped at the first Iraqi Army checkpoint. A soldier waved him over and demanded identification. "*Gensia*, Mister."

The soldier wore American sunglasses, either received from an American or purchased on the black market. The Iraqi soldiers had smart uniforms and typical body armor, but this soldier did not have the protective plates. Many Iraqis removed them because of the weight. That reduced the ability to stop a bullet, but many cared more about surviving the intense heat when they manned checkpoints on the streets of Baghdad. Their officers often didn't check equipment, and some soldiers sold the protective plates for their own profit. Nobody made a big deal about the lack of proper body armor.

Nadal, used to the routine, presented his identification. Often, Iraqi soldiers threw in Shia religious questions to test whether a Sunni was trying to infiltrate the neighborhood. Since Nadal was headed out of Khadamiyah, the scrutiny would be much lighter.

"Where are you going?" the soldier said.

"Home to my family in Shula." That was a lie. While it was true Nadal was headed to Shula, he wasn't going home. He planned to purchase a few special requests then return to Khadamiyah before sunset.

"Proceed." The soldier returned Nadal's identification.

"Thank you." Minutes later he entered Shula. Nadal kept an eye out, knowing that JAM watched the checkpoints. They often sent their own fighters to question people as they passed in and out of the area. JAM might send a car to follow him or have men approach him when he stopped to shop. That day he didn't notice anything unusual.

The hours wore on. He was able to find a couple dozen cartons of cigarettes, razor blades, and soap at his usual stops, but needed one more item. Nadal decided to check a final place that might carry special "sensitive skin" shaving cream a soldier had requested. Nadal was proud of his reputation as a businessman who delivered what his customers wanted.

He found the shaving cream at his last stop and drove out of Shula as dusk fell upon the city. The day's shopping had taken longer than he expected. As with most Iraqis, Nadal moved on the streets of Baghdad with a high degree of paranoia. He glanced at a vehicle on the road then looked beyond it for men who might be watching from streets and alleyways.

Without warning, a car raced past him and careened through the left lane. No oncoming traffic was visible, so it seemed like a typical crazy driver. Then it slowed. Nadal tapped his brakes and noticed another set of headlights in his rearview mirror. The car in front swerved again but cut into his lane and came to an abrupt halt. Nadal skidded his vehicle to a stop.

The car behind him rammed his bumper. Without a seatbelt, Nadal slammed into the steering wheel and had the wind knocked out of him, cutting his lip and forehead. Two men jumped out of the front vehicle. Another approached from the trail car.

"You are a traitor," a masked man yelled into Nadal's open window. Dazed, all he could manage was to stare as the man waved a pistol.

"I am Shia," said Nadal. That was his typical response to prove he was supportive of the Shia-led government.

"Enough, old man," the gunman said. "You work with Americans. You are an apostate. We're going to make sure that everyone knows your family collaborates with the infidels."

"My family has nothing to do with this." Nadal never saw the gunman at the rear of his vehicle. The stealthy militiaman squeezed the trigger. He fired a round point blank into the back of Nadal's head.

"That will be a lesson," the shooter said. "Take the message to his family."

Hassan knocked on my door. I could see he was rattled. He shook his head. "Hey, boss. Just got a call from Nadal's family. Jaysh al Mahdi killed him between Shula and Huriyah."

It was just two weeks after Jack was killed.

Hassan was especially upset. He and Nadal had struck up a friendship born of the wisdom of their years. They were about the same age and commanded the same respect from everyone. Of course, Nadal took risks, but he seemed adept at navigating Shia checkpoints. Since Shia leadership controlled the Iraqi military forces and the militia that operated in areas Nadal frequented, he developed the right relationships and paid *baksheesh*, bribes, to operate.

Nadal was kind and venerated and he was dead. I said, "Let's find out more of the details and inform the chain of command."

"Okay, boss. I'll go let the other store owners and interpreters know as well."

"I know you were close. I'm sorry. We all loved Nadal."

"A good man. Damn Jaysh al Mahdi." Hassan was a pious follower of Islam. Swearing was rare for him. Soldiers, both leaders and rank-and-file, exercised cursing as an art form and the F-word flowed freely around base. Hassan, however, maintained his bearing and faith. He remained calm and introduced a measure of civility in an otherwise insane and violent milieu. "Damn" was the extreme end of Hassan's temperament.

I knew Nadal had a wife and four children. I looked at the photos on my desk. My wife of seventeen years and my two kids, a son, eleven, and daughter, nine. They were safe in Germany, a feeling of both comfort and guilt. Most of my Iraqi colleagues didn't have the luxury of knowing their families were safe.

My office was a small hole-in-the-wall in a building where many soldiers lived and worked. A cot occupied one corner behind the door. It served to let me power nap when I had the chance or sleep in my office if I needed to be close to the command post.

One day, George Packer, a writer for *The New Yorker,* came in to speak with me. We had recently met. We spent time in an operational overview briefing, and he later interviewed several Iraqi interpreters on base.

We were interrupted when he received a call on his cell phone. Reporters always carried them, though most military commanders, myself included, believed they violated security protocols. Our unit banned cell phones during missions. The signal could be intercepted and give away important details—such as the location of an operation—that could get people killed. There was enough death in Baghdad, and we didn't need to add phones to the mix as the cause of stupid deaths. That said, in a few months I, too, would start using a cell phone to communicate with reporters and key Iraqi leaders. I realized they could inform me faster and more accurately than our intelligence officers about important events as they occurred.

Packer's call was from his wife, who told him she'd just gone into labor with their first child. He ended his embed and flew home. I didn't spend much time thinking about his visit, other than I wished it had been longer. I was impressed with George's book, *Assassin's Gate*, which outlined the absurdity of much of the American effort in Iraq. Given the short time he'd spent with us, I couldn't imagine he had enough material to write anything substantial about this visit. I was wrong.

His article "Betrayed" was published in *The New Yorker* a couple months later. It had a huge impact on many of us in Iraq, both soldiers and diplomats. The article was a scathing indictment of the lack of U.S. policy to protect Iraqis who worked side-by-side with Americans. For me, the article was particularly powerful as it was published on the heels of the deaths of Akeel and Nadal.

Before I finished George's lengthy piece, I had to put it down. I was choked with emotion. It took me several tries before I made it through to the end. The accuracy and insight of George's observations wrenched my soul:

> *"In Mosul, insurgents circulated a DVD showing the decapitations of two military interpreters. American soldiers stationed there expressed sympathy to their Iraqi employees, but, one interpreter told me, there was 'no real reaction': no offer of protection, in the form of a weapons permit or a place to live on base. He said, 'The soldiers I worked with were friends and they felt sorry for us—they were good people—but they couldn't help. The people above them didn't care. Or maybe the people above them didn't care.' This story repeated itself across the country: Iraqi employees of the U.S. military began to be kidnapped and killed in large numbers, and there was essentially no American response."*

I took immediate issue with the aspersions George's article cast on all Americans involved with the effort to bring some level of normalcy to this insane environment. Couldn't he see how hard this was? Couldn't he understand that we had countless things to do, not the least of which was to try to keep American soldiers alive in this incredibly lethal country? The parents of America's talented military members had a certain expectation that their leaders would keep them safe and not take unnecessary risks. Even though I took that obligation seriously, I allowed all interpreters to live on the base with my soldiers. I balanced the humanitarian imperative to do the right thing with being able to look myself in the mirror every day.

I knew I had a different view about interpreters than some of my contemporaries. I also had a different view of winning. For me, winning wasn't just about engaging in firefights or avoiding casualties. It was about making incremental progress each day toward returning the city to a level of normalcy. *Normal* meant interpreters wouldn't need to sleep on the base; they could go home to their families without fear of retribution. They wouldn't have to take multiple taxis, or duck out of one cab and into another after passing through a building like a spy in a James Bond movie. Packer's article described such measures:

> *"Ahmed took two taxis to the Green Zone, then walked the last few hundred yards, or drove a different route every day. He carried a decoy phone and hid his Embassy phone in his car. He had always loved the idea of wearing a jacket and tie in an official job, but he had to keep them in his office at the Embassy—it was impossible to drive to work dressed like that. Ahmed and the other Iraqis entered code names for friends and colleagues into their phones, in case they were kidnapped. Whenever they got a call in public from an American contact, they answered in Arabic and immediately hung up. They communicated mostly by text message. They never spoke English in front of their children. One Iraqi employee slept in his car in the Green Zone parking lot for several nights because it was too dangerous to go home."*

Maybe it was a naïve pipedream that our Iraqi partners could go home at night to their families, but we had to establish expectations of a future they could live with. One where we could say we did enough, where the next generation of our children wouldn't have to finish this godawful conflict that my generation started. Maybe that was the grist of fiction. The nonfiction stories didn't include anything that resembled a bright future. George Packer's story didn't:

> *"It's as if the Americans never imagined that the intimidation and murder of interpreters by other Iraqis would undermine the larger American effort, by destroying the confidence of Iraqis who wanted to give it support. The problem was treated as managerial, not moral or political."*

Heartbroken, I immediately emailed George. My desire was to balance his harsh critique with some of our other responsibilities, such as safeguarding America's sons and daughters who I sent every day into hell. Beyond simple force protection issues, we were also trying to win the conflict. The situation in Baghdad had such complexity and nuance that it was like playing three-dimensional chess. Once we thought we had something figured out, we should probably have been scared because it was getting ready to change. Soldiers learned to turn aside optimism lest it only led to deeper disappointment and misery.

Plus, there were the other stories of those who'd tried to keep interpreters and local national partners safe but failed. Jack. Nadal. There would probably be others. Of course, situations would arise, like the day Jack received the call from home informing him of the loss of his babies. That caused a family to lose a son and a significant source of income. It caused Jack's wife to become a widow. It caused our unit to lose a key contributor and a friend. We had to minimize those incidents.

Packer's article cut me to the bone because of Jack. Because of Nadal. Because of the damned immensity of the mission and the number of expectations everybody placed on us. Who the hell was a journalist to place one more expectation on us? A third of the way through my second go at reading the article, I read George's rendition of the first interpreter cleansing campaign. It began in 2004 and was led by Sunni insurgents. I remembered it from my first deployment to Tikrit, Saddam Hussein's hometown.

My unit recognized the threat to local Iraqis and developed what we considered an innovative approach to counter it. In our area of operation, the insurgents delivered threats via taxi. We received reports of insurgents getting in taxis and delivering threats to locals or forcing the drivers to deliver messages.

Half-orange, half-white taxis were ubiquitous on the streets of Tikrit and most of Iraq. Our task force began what we dubbed Operation Orange Crush. For a week, our units partnered with local police and pulled over every cab in traffic stops. We took photos of all drivers and license plates, then stuck a military shipping label on the windshield.

The shipping label had no value and meant nothing, but the enemy didn't know that. What the insurgents surmised was that we were interested in taxis. The threats dried up. That vignette provides some insight into the psychology of insurgency. Insurgents seek to avoid drawing attention to themselves. They want to remain in the shadows. Attention generates uncomfortable questions, potential detention or worse. The insurgents who had perplexed us by intimidating taxi drivers went underground as they tried to figure out what we were doing. I heard reports that some thought we could track the taxis by satellite. In reality, we bought a couple months for our local nationals to transit back and forth to work threat-free via the orange cabs. Orange Crush would have a temporary effect while we waited for the next chess move.

George's article reminded me that at the time, we considered our operation in Tikrit quite clever. We outwitted the insurgents, if only for a few months. What dawned on me three years later was the clinical approach we had taken to the problem. Like doctors with no bedside manner, we assessed what was ailing the patient and prescribed a remedy. I couldn't recall a single individual I knew who was saved or helped by Operation Orange Crush. It was a professional accomplishment, albeit without the sense of purpose that comes from serving in a way that makes a difference in someone's life. It wasn't personal. In 2007, I needed to do something different for our Iraqi partners in Baghdad.

I recalled a time my wife and I lived in Panama. It was the early '90s. She befriended several biology teachers and others interested in bird watching. We lived in a small community nestled within the rain forest called Gamboa, which was adjacent to the Panama Canal. It was a bird watcher's paradise. Our neighbors regaled us with stories of identifying hundreds of different bird species while they walked through the jungle on a trail next to a pipeline. Occasionally, I accompanied my wife and her friends. They'd look to the trees and with excitement describe a brilliantly colored bird.

I couldn't share their excitement. It was frustrating, but my eyes were untrained. I rarely saw the birds even when my wife pointed right at them. If we scared the bird, I would catch a glimpse as it flew away through the jungle canopy. It was a revelation to discover that proper training was needed to see birds right in front of you. Biologists and enthusiasts like my wife studied the birds. They knew where in the trees the birds perched and the sounds that identified their species. They knew the different hues that distinguished males from females and knew their mating habits. I, as an uninformed walker, didn't have the benefit of knowing how to look, where to look, or what to listen for. I was blind to what was in plain sight.

Six months into what became a sixteen-month tour, I was blind to the plight of our interpreters until Packer did the great service of writing "Betrayed." I had not fully understood the risks that Jack and Nadal took. My eyes, maybe even my soul, hadn't been trained to see the problem from the perspective of my Iraqi colleagues. Once George opened my eyes, I could no longer accept the status quo. I had to do something. My inner jihad had begun. It would, at times, feel like a jihad against elements of my own government. Journalists, whose mission it was to hold government accountable, became natural partners in this effort.

I could not close my eyes to the problem anymore. I had to help interpreters stay alive and eventually find their way to safety. From that point on, this goal became a large part of not only the burden of leadership, but also my personal challenge in this crazy, complex country.

Chapter Two

Back to Iraq –
Task Force Justice

*Always I try to keep my work focused on the people
most impacted by these conflicts: the Iraqis and
Afghans themselves, caught in the cauldron of post-
9/11 geopolitics, and the American servicemen and
servicewomen sent into harm's way in unfamiliar lands.*

~ the late Chris Hondros,
Getty Images war photographer and friend

AUGUST 2006 OPPRESSED us like Cerberus guarding the gates of hell.
I decided that the purpose of Camp Buehring, our staging base in Kuwait,
was to make soldiers *want* to deploy to Iraq. Temperatures at the camp,
located sixty miles northwest of Kuwait City, averaged well over one
hundred degrees during the day and dropped to a balmy mid-eighties at
night. We spent two months as the strategic reserve, then had two weeks
to move the brigade to Baghdad, the most dangerous city in the world.

Commanded by Colonel J.B. Burton, brigade leadership deployed to Taji, just north of Baghdad. We attended a mandatory week of counterinsurgency (COIN) education. The COIN Academy provided many classes, one on human intelligence, or HUMINT. Instructors spoke about protecting sources, emphasizing that we needed to prevent units from establishing patterns that would put good people at risk. Not once during the discussion did the instructors broaden the idea of "good people" beyond the intelligence sources we cultivated and relied upon to feed the targeting process. The result was that we neglected the risks to other good people, our "soft networks"—the Iraqi interpreters, merchants and contractors who supported our efforts.

We did not delve into the complexities of protecting soft networks. Instead, we focused on more mundane tasks: moving equipment and personnel, tactical preparations for patrolling, base security, and the myriad other military activities required to accomplish our mission. Had someone warned us that our adversaries would target those Iraqis closest to us, we might have thought through the challenge and come up with innovative ways to protect those good people. As it stood, we rushed into a situation that grew deadlier by the day for us and our trusted partners.

One of the last presentations at the COIN Academy was delivered by a British two- star who served as the Deputy Commanding General, Multi-National Forces—Iraq. Major General Graeme Lamb spoke about the situation in both Baghdad and the entire country. We had analyzed the current situation and couldn't make strategic sense of it. U.S. units had boundaries that did not align with Iraqi Army boundaries. Iraqi Army boundaries did not align with Iraqi police jurisdictions. As a result, there was so much turbulence with unit transitions that it was impossible to develop the relationships with Iraqi security force and civilian leaders needed to drive sustainable progress. That violated a key tenet of counterinsurgency—relationship building—which was a primary focus of the brigade during our train-up and a must preached by the COIN Academy.

After Lamb's briefing, COL Burton said, "Sir, looking at the map of Baghdad and boundaries between the police, army, our forces, and civilian administrative districts, it doesn't seem to make strategic sense. We can't focus on developing strong relationships when our units rotate in and out as fast as the Iraqis and the boundaries keep changing. How did it get this way?"

General Lamb reflected for a moment: "It was a series of short-term decisions. They all probably made sense at the time, but I agree the situation doesn't make overall strategic sense now."

We, the officers and NCOs of Dagger Brigade, were stunned. After seeing his sincere delivery and the look on his face, we knew the general was serious. We would inherit this scenario in a matter of days. Little did we realize the situation would turn out to be even more complicated than described.

Another layer of complication involved U.S. transition teams, small groups of Americans partnered with the Iraqi army and police. These teams operated on different deployment schedules than the Iraqis and other American units. That made the development of relationships even more difficult. The constant personnel changes, unit rotations, and shifting boundaries created a menagerie of actors and friction. It created a system that made sustainable progress impossible. We were defeating ourselves before we even thought about how our adversaries' actions would impact us.

FOB Justice, or FOB Adalah in Arabic, had two gates on the outer wall guarded by Iraqis. Our small base within the main compound had one gate, guarded by U.S. soldiers. The Iraqi base housed three different detention centers and was nestled inside a bend in the Tigris River. The base stood on the north side of the city in the Khadamiyah neighborhood, a Shia-dominated area controlled by the Jaysh al Mahdi militia and home to the Khadamiyah Shrine. Tens of thousands of pilgrims visited each year. Given its religious importance, our units were required to exercise a high degree of sensitivity.

One of the first decisions I made after arrival at FOB Justice was to change the weapons control status. It required all soldiers to remove magazines and clear their weapons when they entered the U.S. portion of the base, meaning soldiers carried their weapons but not ammunition. This was standard practice at most U.S. facilities in Iraq. It was standing policy for soldiers to always have their weapon on their person unless they secured it in their room or another location. I made the decision to increase our weapon control status to amber. That meant soldiers would always have ammunition with their weapon. My concern centered on signaling the strength of our discipline and unit cohesion to our enemy while ensuring our soldiers understood the level of discipline necessary to keep them alive. It would help protect against any possible insider attacks from enemies catching our teams off guard. We would hold our Iraqi colleagues to the same standard.

Lieutenant Nick Kron knocked on my door. "Sir, I have Hassan Benkato here to speak with you."

Nick was the newly minted task force intelligence officer. He had no military intelligence experience but had been designated to the job because he was scheduled to become an intelligence officer in the future. The Army called this method of career management "branch detailing." The intent was to fill the high demand specialties in combat arms with junior officers and then transition them to fields that required more senior officers at higher ranks.

"Sir, brigade is telling Hassan that he is their asset, and they will bring him back to FOB Liberty."

"That's what the S2 is telling you?" The S2 is the intelligence officer at brigade and battalion levels.

"Yes, sir. We only have about six Cat II's in the entire brigade, so S2 will manage them from that level."

Cat II was military intelligence jargon for Category Two linguist, a translator with a secret security clearance. My previous deployments in Iraq and Bosnia taught me that good interpreters were combat gold. They improved our understanding of the environment, our bargaining power with key counterparts, and simply our ability to get things done. Good interpreters were action figures who added substantial value to any effort, whether kinetic, like raids, or sitting in meetings with sheiks, police chiefs and governors. Those with security clearances were even more valuable because they were trusted with sensitive information. However, some with security clearances were young. They enlisted in the Army to become linguists and were excellent at translating but tended not to have the *wasta*—Arabic for influence—to establish credibility with elders in power positions.

Hassan was not only a CAT II, but also an older linguist who looked as if he could add value to complex and difficult situations. He'd been with the artillery unit we replaced when we took over the mission in late 2006. Hassan reminded me of an elderly interpreter my unit employed in Tikrit in 2004. That man had added great value to our understanding of the mosaic of diverse people who lived in a violent city. There was no way I would let Hassan return to FOB Liberty. It was a super-FOB, a large U.S. base with thousands of troops. It had resources we didn't. No way I'd allow brigade S-2 to abandon my small contingent of soldiers who lived in the middle of an Iraqi base. We needed every bit of cultural understanding possible.

"Good afternoon, sir," Hassan said as Nick Kron showed him into my small office.

"Nick tells me that you want to quit the team already, and we just got here." Hassan Benkato was about six feet tall and thin. He had trim, grey hair, which suggested a younger look than his true age. He projected an aura of wisdom combined with a lightheartedness that hinted he enjoyed life and those around him.

"Brigade is telling me that I need to return to FOB Liberty because I am a brigade asset."

"I am the brigade, so you're going to stay right here." I explained that not only was I the Task Force Justice Commander, I was also the Deputy Brigade Commander.

"I'm just telling you what the brigade S2 shop told me."

"I don't doubt that, but you've got to remember that the brigade S2 shop is filled with staff officers who technically all report to me. As a matter of fact, I rate the brigade S2 himself, so I think he'll want to work with us if I tell him you really need to stay here and support this incredibly important mission." I rarely thought about rank and rating chains that indicated who was the boss of whom, but it was one of those times when pulling rank was necessary to achieve a vital aim.

Hassan didn't seem upset. "I'll be sure to inform them."

"Nick will follow up with them, too. That way we don't put you in the middle of things. Feel free to notify them through your channels, also. I believe in using multiple means of communication to ensure that everyone gets the word."

Hassan and Nick headed out. In months to come, Hassan would recount this tale and laugh about it with me and others. "I am the brigade," he proclaimed as he regaled members of the task force with our first encounter. He confided to me that he felt it would be the start of a lifelong friendship. Hassan became my closest confidant in the most difficult situations at the height of sectarian violence in Baghdad. He was with me through firefights, meetings at the Prime Minister's office, interviews with *The New York Times* and *CNN*. He informed and supported me during private discussions of how to deal with issues with interpreters. Hassan was by my side for fourteen months of the most difficult times in combat.

Hassan was of Libyan decent from Benghazi. That helped him understand tribal norms. He easily broke the ice in meetings with senior tribal sheiks, imams, military commanders, police chiefs, and others. His judgement proved invaluable. Hassan provided both expert linguist capability and wise counsel about the nature of our complicated environment. In addition, he would become the "grandfather" figure to many of the Iraqi interpreters. He understood their concerns and helped us shape responses that balanced our security requirements with the humanitarian imperatives of taking care of our closest Iraqi partners.

It was SOP that most patrols took only one interpreter outside the wire. I insisted on two. That provided our soldiers the ability to interact with the populace. They would learn about the culture. Interpreters like Ronnie and Hassan were more than mouthpieces hired to help us interact. They taught soldiers, explaining things they didn't understand. They also made us laugh at the absurdity of our situation.

My leadership style centered on building an environment of inclusion where everyone felt welcomed, including our local nationals and other people attached to the unit. Over the course of the deployment, Task Force Justice would either control or be in support of hundreds of different people from various organizations and agencies including the National Guard, Marines, Navy, Department of Justice, civilian contractors, and various other elements affectionately referred to as "cats and dogs." My first couple of months on that small compound, I often ran into people I'd never met and discovered they lived on base. And I was supposed to be in charge.

I made it a point to sit with different groups of soldiers at each meal. It helped communicate that all team members mattered, regardless of rank. One morning I sat with a couple soldiers in the dining facility and ate my usual scrambled eggs and bacon. We made small talk. I asked them about things going on with their duties or how their families were back at our home base in Schweinfurt, Germany.

"I thought I'd find you here," Hassan said as he approached the table.

"What's up, Old Dog?" I said.

"I had a really interesting conversation with some guys you should meet. We have four contractors from the Department of Justice on base."

I wasn't sure about his point. "Guess I'll have to meet them."

"That's not the interesting part. They live on the other side of the wall. Close to the Ministry of Justice facility."

"You mean outside our perimeter?"

"I figured you would want to know."

Hassan took me to meet the four civilian contractors, and we examined their living arrangement. Technically, they didn't work for me. However, I felt compelled to extend protection to anyone who needed it.

On my previous tour, people often got in trouble when they operated "on their own FTX," as we said in military jargon. FTX stands for field training exercise. The term indicated that an individual or an entire unit might be operating in someone else's area without coordination. The arrangement had the potential for all sorts of bad things to happen, and not just to those individuals. For example, the four DOJ contractors could be killed or kidnapped, and we might not find out for days. Minutes, even seconds, could spell the difference between a thwarted and successful kidnapping or assassination.

They were allowed do what they wanted because we had no direct authority over them. However, and it was a big however, it would fall to us to deal with the repercussions of an incident.

A drive through Baghdad was different from driving in the open desert or through Tikrit as I did during my first tour. Tikrit was a small, peanut-shaped city, narrow in width. It ran east to west for about one to two miles, and seven miles on the north-south axis. Nestled against the Tigris River, Tikrit offered a bypass route to the west that avoided city traffic. Patrols could transit east to west in a matter of minutes. As soon as a patrol escaped the city confines, a suburb or two popped up along the main north-south route. East or west led to open desert. Our forays into the desert brought a dramatic change of environment. All we saw for miles was flat, barren land. Many times, as we moved west toward the Thar-Thar reservoir, we saw walled off homes with farm equipment scattered around the surrounding area. The road, the only defining feature, disappeared where the sand met the horizon.

Baghdad, on the other hand, sprawled for miles in all compass directions. The Tigris River wound through the city from north to south. It interrupted areas where grids of homes formed Sunni or Shia neighborhoods. Pedestrians and cars moved everywhere. Roadways were congested. Throngs of people crowded into outdoor shopping markets ringed with street vendors, chai shops, and stores that sold cheap electronics. Soldiers patrolled, many on sensory overload. Some of us, however, had lost a formerly keen sense of smell because of the burning trash, diesel fumes, and other toxic smoke that permeated our routes. Up-armored Humvees were never far from foot patrols. Gunners' heads protruded from turrets. They wore bandanas over their faces that shielded them from the incessant dust kicked up by everything that moved, human, animal, and machine. Sights and sounds pierced our imaginations and heightened our anxiety about when and from where the next threat would come.

Baghdad was dangerous for soldiers, but even more so for Iraqis. The people bore the brunt of sectarian violence fomented by al Qaeda and the militias. At any moment their lives could be interrupted by suicide bombers. Some drove cars rigged with explosives into marketplaces. Others delivered bombs detonated by remote control where large groups of people congregated. To put it in context, Iraq suffered carnage on the level of the 9/11 attacks every month. Much of the violence stemmed from Shia militia retaliation against the Sunnis for al Qaeda bombing attacks.

We cleared the gates of FOB Justice and headed for FOB Liberty. I had a meeting at Brigade Headquarters. The team would run logistics while I was tied up in the conference. We would also attend a memorial service for a soldier who'd been killed by a roadside bomb.

Between the brigade meeting and the memorial service, we spent six hours on base. Most of the soldiers were ready to get off the super-FOB and back to Justice, the place we called home. We headed out the gate that bordered Ameriyah, a Sunni-dominated neighborhood that had seen intense fighting. The Iraqi police, mainly Shiites, had abandoned Ameriyah and left it to the mercy of al Qaeda and the insurgents. From time to time, the Iraqi Army would venture there at the behest of American units. The Iraqis were happy to leave the neighborhood to its own misery. Many Shiite leaders believed the Sunnis had brought their fate upon themselves.

We cleared the main gate and wound along the dirt road between the base and Ameriyah. Given the proximity to Sunni areas, we worried about conventional IEDs. These bombs could be modified artillery shells hidden on the side of the road or deep-buried bombs that could flip a tank. Any debris could be used to hide IEDs. Every person in the patrol, even interpreters, scanned trash bags, animal carcasses, even potholes for signs of danger.

Hassan leaned forward and glanced out the front window of the Humvee. "Looks like normal atmospherics today in Ameriyah," he said over the vehicle communications network.

"I guess, Old Dog," I said. "I wouldn't know what normal looks like for Ameriyah."

"I'm not sure anyone who lives here knows either. They've been under al Qaeda's thumb for so long. I think most people just want the violence to stop."

"I'll sign up for that," said Specialist Woods, the driver.

We cleared the danger zone, although there had been relatively few IEDs this close to the base. Our guard towers provided good fields of observation. We turned onto Route Irish, the highway between Baghdad International Airport and the Green Zone, the seat of governance, if you believed that Iraq had any governance. To those of us on the street every day, the idea that this place had anything resembling a government that administered rule of law was pure fantasy. The only authority we saw rested in bullets and dollar bills. Any other influence faded from view as soon as we left the gate.

We picked up speed to fifty miles per hour. Only months before, Route Irish had been a deadly, dangerous highway. At one point, it was the highest density IED zone in Iraq. Highway signs flew by as we moved along the route. Every mile, we saw National Police armored personnel carriers that had changed the security dynamic on the roadway. Until the National Police manned checkpoints along the route, IEDs were common. Now, the IED emplacement teams had migrated elsewhere, in search of easier targets. Most of the bombs on Route Irish had come from Sunni insurgents. The sectarian, predominantly Shiite National Police provided an effective deterrent.

As part of my brain scanned the road for anything unusual, other thoughts ran through my mind. Ideas I'd pondered during the COIN Academy. Family issues back in Schweinfurt. Problems that came up at the last brigade meeting. I recited the mantra about figuring out how to win this conflict, so my kid's generation didn't have to fix my generation's failure.

The lead vehicle veered to the left and came to a sudden halt. My mind snapped back as my vehicle, second in the patrol, veered to the right and established a fishbone pattern as we called it in the military.

Lieutenant Kronick called over the radio, "Dagger Six Mike, looks like we have an accident up ahead." Dagger Six Mike was my radio call sign.

"Roger," I said and flipped a switch to communicate with only those inside the vehicle. "We may need to get out and help. What do you think, Hassan?"

"It's probably a good idea," he said. "Looks like a lot of people are hurt."

I radioed the patrol. "Let's get out and help."

About ten men exited vehicles, including Hassan, and walked toward the accident scene. Gunners and drivers stayed put. Their job was to scan for any threats. Jack hustled and met Lt. Kronick at the head of the patrol. He'd been in the third vehicle.

People ripped bodies out of a mangled van and dragged or carried them to cars and drove off. Bystanders yelled at us, shaking their fists.

Smoke bellowed from the van's engine. Jack ran up and asked locals if we could provide assistance. Before anyone answered, one of our soldiers aimed a fire extinguisher and sprayed the engine with foam.

Jack and Lt. Kronick attempted to speak with frantic people who ripped the van apart to remove bodies. Bystanders dragged more victims onto the street in hopes some had survived. Most were unresponsive. Another soldier brought body bags that angry Iraqis grabbed.

Lt. Kronick and Jack hurried to where Hassan and I stood surveying the carnage. "Jack said the people don't want us here," Kronick said. "They called us Jews. Said that we're the cause of all their problems."

"They've lost so much," Hassan said.

"Things have definitely gotten worse since my last time in country," I said.

We stood by as the last of a dozen bodies were dragged into the street. Some people threw the dead over their shoulders and ran to nearby cars. Other victims were carried off by two people, one lifting feet, the other shoulders. Traffic backed up as bodies disappeared. Road closures were a normal part of the Baghdad environment. Drivers found detours and bypassed south of us while oncoming traffic, separated by a median, slowed to rubberneck. People glared at us. Seeing the military vehicles, they probably blamed us for the accident, the traffic jam, or both.

Lt. Kronick radioed, "People are all evacuated."

I said, "We can tow that wreck out of the middle of the highway. The least we can do is open the roadway."

The lieutenant wrangled his crew, hitched a strap to his vehicle and dragged the wreck out of the way.

"Those people were traveling to celebrate the end of Ramadan," Jack said. "I think everyone died. I found out they got hit by a drunk driver."

What could I say to that? I nodded and directed everyone to mount up. We returned to our vehicles and drove north again.

That night, reeling from the hostile reception we received when attempting to help, I wrote in my journal:

> *I was saddened by the hatred and loss of humanity. Things have slipped so far since I was last in Iraq. The battlefield has become much more lethal, the people more callous, the insurgents more determined and ruthless.*

The next day at FOB Liberty, the patrol waited outside the headquarters building. I'd been inside for hours. Jack stayed with the soldiers. Hassan accompanied me into HQ but didn't attend the meetings in COL Burton's office. Instead, he popped his head into the S2 shop. He liked to touch base with the intelligence analysts and give them updates on what we saw on the streets. Many of the analysts were young and looked up to him as a father figure. Since many of the analysts didn't get out on the streets, talking to Hassan provided context to their assessments.

In the meeting, COL J.B. Burton, MAJ Brynt Parmeter, COL Tom Felts, and I discussed the dynamics of JAM infiltration of the 1st Brigade, 6th Iraqi Army Division. We were getting a more focused picture of how bad loyalty had been contorted by the mafia-like racketeering of the militia. Tom Felts led the transition team partnered with the Iraqi Army brigade. He had three teams under him that partnered with the Iraqi battalions. The worst corruption was in 3rd Battalion. Intelligence confirmed rumors that indicated it was heavily infiltrated. Some reports hinted that the battalion commander and intelligence officer participated with JAM. Worse, the brigade commander, COL Felts's counterpart, either looked the other way or was complicit. Tom took everything in stride. He had developed good rapport with the Iraqi commander and chose to give him the benefit of the doubt.

Burton said, "Sure have yourself a pickle, Tom."

"It's a tough situation," Felts said. "My 3rd battalion team has the worst of it. We'll keep our eyes open and try to provide the Iraqis with plausible deniability."

"Guess that's all you can do. These local politicians keep meddling in the Army's affairs, pressuring them to release militia leaders and probably a lot of other things we have no idea about."

"Yeah. I wouldn't trade places with them. Our families are safe and sound. Most of these guys have wives and kids exposed to these thugs."

"That's why I make sure my wife drives the Astro van," Brynt Parmeter said. He wanted a laugh and got several.

Burton shook his head. "You and your Astro van. And we've got Miska over here who tried to counsel me about driving a big SUV in Germany when I first arrived. What am I going to do with these jokers, Tom?"

Felts laughed. "Guess you're gonna have to keep the band together. You've got a good team, J.B. You'll need every one of them given the mess we find ourselves in."

"Speaking of which," J.B. looked at his watch and changed the subject. "We have an early day tomorrow and it's late. You guys," indicating Tom and me, "probably need to get back to Justice before the boogeyman comes out."

"Hell, sir," I said, "Hassan's out there rounding up the boogeyman so he can ride along with us."

COL Burton shot me an incredulous look. "Miska, just wear your damn seatbelt and stay out of trouble."

"But you know the Iraqis gave me a new nickname. *Abu Mashakel.*"

"What's that mean?"

"Father of all trouble." I grinned.

J.B. shook his head. "Get out of here." Then he gave me our traditional brigade hug with a couple slaps on the back.

On my way out I glanced at Tom Felts as he showed Brynt on a map the route his team would take home. Felts had decided to do a little battlefield circulation and check out a notoriously dangerous route that had suffered numerous JAM IED attacks.

On the return patrol to Justice, thoughts raced through my mind. What if my family lived in Baghdad? Would I be as cavalier on patrol everyday with the knowledge that someone could threaten my wife or follow my kids home from school? Our Iraqi colleagues had a lot to worry about.

We arrived at FOB Justice and rolled through the Iraqi gates. It had been an uneventful trip down Route Irish, skirting the Green Zone, then up to Khadamiyah. The patrol secured all our equipment and prepped the vehicles for the next day. I went into my office and figured I'd get in a workout. The pace had been extreme lately, so I'd managed only two or three workouts a week, often in the late evening. After, I'd shower and fall asleep.

I changed into my work-out gear, which I kept in my office, and headed to the gym in the same building. I put on earphones and listened to hard-rock tunes. I had about forty favorite songs. It was the MP3 player's second deployment, too, and strapped to my arm it played *Linkin Park, AC/DC,* and *Led Zeppelin.* As I ran on the treadmill, I slipped into a zone and my thoughts wandered.

Soldiers generally left me alone when I worked out. It was rare that someone interrupted. When First Sergeant Tony Pryor and Hassan stepped in front of me, both with serious expressions, I turned off the machine and stepped off. Dripping sweat, I grabbed a towel. "What's up?"

Tony said, "Sir, we just got a call from the brigade MTT team. They've got a medevac on site flying away Colonel Felts and another soldier."

"What's the status of the patrol? Do they need assistance?"

"We're sending DuPerre and the wrecker out to help recover their vehicle," Tony said. "We're getting the battle roster numbers and other information to start the casualty notification process."

Each soldier had a unique battle roster number. Instead of calling names over the radio, transmissions would maintain a calm professionalism with an alpha-numeric code. There was no emotion tied to a number, whereas, transmitting the name of an individual could upset listeners. Battle rosters kept emotional reactions off the radio.

"Damn," I said.

"We've got confirmation that both casualties are dead," Tony said.

Hassan shook his head, mourning yet more losses.

About an hour later, the patrol arrived. I went outside to meet Lieutenant Colonel Bill Payne, the Deputy Commander for the transition team, who had been in a vehicle behind Felts. Bill looked shell-shocked. He didn't say much. He was clearly exhausted from the ordeal of flying out the casualties and recovering the damaged vehicle.

"Felts wanted to do battlefield circulation," Bill said.

I looked at him, not sure what to say. Sometimes the best response was to listen. Our losses mounted.

Specialist Justin Garcia was also killed that night. He was an augmentee sent to bolster the transition team. Garcia's unit was a stateside battalion attached to our brigade when we entered Baghdad. His loss was tragic on many levels, not the least of which was that his chain of command, and potentially other units, might push back against sending their soldiers to augment the small transition teams.

Other units understood the mission but didn't like sending a couple soldiers to supplement the transition teams, which had only ten men. They were vulnerable to any disruption that took a member out of the fight: sickness, casualties, R&R. When the brigade issued an order to send soldiers to bolster vulnerable squads, many commanders resisted. They worried their soldiers wouldn't receive the same care as those in the parent unit. When a detached soldier was killed conducting operations with a transition team, that made the argument salient.

Later that evening, Hassan and I walked off the little American base to Iraqi Brigade headquarters, accompanied by a female Iraqi interpreter and Bill Payne. The interpreter was filling in for the transition team's normal interpreter, Ali. He'd been injured in the blast and sent to the Combat Support Hospital, or CSH (pronounced "cash" in military jargon). That evening, Ali had returned from R&R in the United States. He was an American citizen with a security clearance, like Hassan. Felts's patrol picked Ali up at FOB Liberty. It was his first night back and his last mission. He never returned to the team after getting blown up.

It was late. We each carried a pistol and chambered a round as we passed the soldiers at the sentry post. We spoke to an Iraqi as we entered the building to let them know we wanted to see Brigadier General Abdullah.

As we entered the office, Abdullah sat at his desk. The Iraqi Command Sergeant Major for the brigade also greeted us.

Abdullah seemed to know an attack had occurred and waited for me to speak. We had a tense relationship due to lack of trust. Our side suspected militia infiltration and collusion between his brigade and JAM and applied pressure to end it. He expected me to accuse him of being involved.

"Tom Felts is dead," I said.

His face turned white. My guess was he knew Felts's patrol had been attacked, but not about the casualties. Most Iraqis, including generals, found out about U.S. losses from their American counterparts or media reports. I imagined Abdullah had suspected bad news, but not that severe. Later, Hassan confirmed that Felts's death was a complete shock to the general.

Tears streamed down his cheeks. "Colonel Felts was my friend." He cried for ten minutes, time Hassan used to step out and speak with the Iraqi Sergeant Major about why his commander was upset. Abdullah was either the best actor in the world, or experienced Tom's loss on a deep level. Felts had an amazing presence and combined a rare level of patience with his drive to serve and make a difference. Maybe that was the straw that broke the camel's back for the Iraqi commander. We all experienced tremendous stress, but Abdullah, as commander of one of the most scrutinized brigades in the country, faced nearly intolerable daily pressure.

He composed himself. We spent a little time remembering Tom.

"Colonel Miska," Abdullah said, "can I speak at his memorial service? He was my friend, and I would like to honor his memory."

I felt compassion. Tom had spent a lot of time with Abdullah. However, to allow an Iraqi to speak on behalf of a fallen American soldier was an unusual request. Abdullah was lucky our brigade inhabited a world of nonstandard thinking, at least by military standards.

"I'll have to ask Colonel Burton and see about the procedures. We have some time as it usually takes three to five days to schedule a service and coordinate the details."

Abdullah nodded. Hassan stepped back in with the Sergeant Major and we departed. I excused the party from the office. Hassan and I stopped by the command center to check in.

Each time we ventured into headquarters, I made a point to spend at least a few minutes with the guys in the building. Their shifts were monotonous and dangerous. Sometimes, only two men occupied the room with a staff of Iraqis. Though not far from our small U.S. base, they were vulnerable to an insider attack. We spent a lot of time emphasizing the need to maintain discipline and stay alert. They were never allowed to sleep. Their weapons were always within arm's reach.

Sergeant First Class Rodney Stanfield was there with another soldier. They had heard about Colonel Felts and Specialist Garcia. We greeted each other with a hug and talked about the lethality of the environment.

"Sir, that just confirms it for me," Stanfield said. "As much as this job here is painful because it's every day, I don't have a desire to go running around out there on the highways with you. Unless you order me to, of course."

"I don't believe in needless patrolling," I said. "Every patrol outside the gate has a purpose. If we have a need for you out there, I'll tell you, but I value your experience here. Soldiers need your leadership and guidance. You'll get off the base enough to have a feel for the city. It only makes you better inside the command post when you know what it's like outside the wire, but no need to make it a habit."

"Thanks, sir. I'm going through some stuff at home, so this gives me a chance to work through it, too."

Abdullah was the last speaker at Tom Felts's memorial on FOB Liberty. We had to coordinate access for him to enter the heavily guarded base. This came a couple days after the memorial for Corporal Justin Garcia, who was posthumously promoted to corporal by his unit. His battalion, 1-23 Infantry, had done the coordination for his memorial, which was standard procedure.

The memorials continued. They made our traditional Thanksgiving celebration more poignant, especially with a table off to the side with a place-setting for one. A single rose adorned the lone table, a military custom of honoring the fallen. When I was a cadet at West Point, the tradition had seemed eccentric, like the military was trying to keep a tradition alive for tradition's sake. That was a peacetime Army in the late 1980s. In 2006, every military member entering that dining facility in Baghdad took note and quietly paid respects.

Tradition also dictated that senior ranking members served the soldiers their holiday meals. Colonel Burton and Command Sergeant Major John Fortune came to visit us that day. We donned chef hats while company-grade officers—lieutenants and captains—and NCOs pulled guard duty to allow more soldiers time to enjoy their meal. We had turkey, stuffing, mashed potatoes, green beans, and all the fixings. The unit made sure that every soldier rotated in from duty or patrols to celebrate. Leaders also made time for soldiers to communicate with loved ones back home.

Celebration of American holidays helped soldiers deal with the lengthy separations from friends and family. We broke deployments into discrete blocks of time by celebrating something every four to six weeks. The next holiday would be Christmas. Since it was only about a month away, soldiers could focus on making it through the next month. It helped manage the isolation from family.

Concurrent with the Thanksgiving meal, we hosted a "turkey shoot" at the range on base. The task force engineer had constructed a range where soldiers could shoot at twenty-five-meter targets to zero weapons, adjust sights and scopes, and check other aspects of their firearms. SFC Stanfield, a master gunner, developed a fun competition with targets that looked like turkeys. We invited the Iraqis to attend. American soldiers shot AK-47s on the range and Iraqis fired our M4s. It was a fun activity that helped to make the day special beyond a good meal. It was our intention to craft positive memories to populate the Task Force Justice yearbook. Combined with memorial pages, they would provide a mix of important memories. The hope was that the soldiers would always remember fallen comrades but wouldn't dwell on the losses and negative experiences. They could also flip a couple of pages and remember friends, colleagues, and the good times they shared.

Tom Felts's loss had a significant impact. He'd exercised great patience, skill and nuance interacting with one of the most perplexing Iraqi Army organizations, which suffered from heavy militia infiltration. Tom's team, and their subordinate teams, kept tabs on the Iraqis, and at the same time helped build their indigenous capacity. The relationship between Iraqis and Americans was fraught, yet Tom managed it with sophistication. His team was devastated by his loss.

As a result of Tom's death, the Iraqi Army Brigade received the message from JAM: cooperate or face the same consequences as the Americans. The month between Thanksgiving and Christmas saw an American attempt to rebuild our team's morale and to pressure Iraqi senior leaders to hold their subordinates and JAM accountable.

In the U.S., Tom's family asked people to consider donating gifts for soldiers to dispense to the Iraqi people in honor of Tom's efforts to make a difference in Baghdad. His widow served Gold Star families when she later moved to the Fort Bragg area. Tom's legacy of service wouldn't die with him, but the holiday season would be very different that year, for everyone.

Chapter Three

Month of Mayhem

"One simply cannot engage in barbarous action without becoming a barbarian...one cannot defend human values by calculated and unprovoked violence without doing mortal damage to the values one is trying to defend."

~ J. William Fulbright, *The Arrogance of Power*

BAGHDAD WAS ONE of the deadliest places in the world, not just for our soldiers, but for anyone on the streets. Trips to the hospital had turned into the movie *Groundhog Day*. We made so many trips, we combined them with other patrol requirements. For example, we'd check on troops at a combat outpost or attend a meeting at one of the major bases. On the way home, we'd swing by the hospital in the Green Zone because a soldier we knew was injured the evening prior. Lt. Kronick and his patrol became experts at navigating the Green Zone gates and roadways for quick arrivals at the hospital. While I went inside, most times with Hassan and one or two others, the patrol would reorient for a quick exit, resupply, and prepare to move. Most of my visits to the hospital lasted about thirty minutes. They were longer if we had to seek out doctors and nurses for input on a patient's status, such as when they would be evacuated or whether they might return to duty. From the soldier's perspective, a thirty-minute visit was relatively brief compared to many of the meetings I attended.

Our patrol pulled into the usual parking spot in front of the hospital one day.

"Who are we going to see this time?" Hassan said.

"You stay here, Old Dog," I said. "Stray Dog is gonna go with me. We both know this guy from 1-18."

"Don't let him get you into any trouble."

Stray Dog, also known as Sergeant First Class Michael Glancy, had been the sniper team leader when I served as the operations officer in 1-18 Infantry, the Vanguards, in Tikrit. Glancy and I had a history of working together. He had been assigned to Baghdad on a transition team and clashed with his chain of command. They didn't value his operational experience, so he'd been frustrated during the yearlong deployment. When I found out he was in Baghdad, I reached out to him. He described his circumstances and asked to join our small post at FOB Justice. We gave it a try. He was a great asset, and we had him extended for a few months on a volunteer basis.

I keyed my mic. "Stray Dog, where you at?"

"Out of the vehicle and waiting for you," he said in his trademark raspy voice.

"Roger. This should be quick, guys," I said to the entire patrol. "We'll be right back."

"Likely, sir," said one of the soldiers with a smile.

"Yeah, sir, where have we heard that before?" Woods said over the intercom.

"We'll be here for hours," groaned Neyer, the gunner.

"Enough," Kronick cautioned.

I laughed. I deserved the jibes. I often took a long time in meetings. Hassan and I would be stuck in hours-long discussions with Iraqis over numerous glasses of chai, or at brigade headquarters. I rarely set expectations as to how long it would take. I'd learned my lesson. This meeting would be quick, though. Mike and I were just checking on the soldier. As if to prove we'd be fast, we didn't bother to take off our body armor. Many times, at a secure area, we'd leave it in the vehicles.

Stray Dog and I walked through the main door that opened into a foyer. On the far side of the entry, a corridor extended into the hospital. We walked in that direction. I noticed there were some unusual people in the hall. On a normal visit, we saw doctors and nurses and maybe the occasional group of leaders or soldiers. That day, there were several women in the corridor who seemed out of place. One wore a civilian jacket with a huge star on the back.

"Who the heck are these people?" Glancy said.

"Maybe we got caught up with a Dallas Cowboy cheerleader visit or something," I said.

"We can hope."

"Yeah, right. Like we would really get that lucky."

We continued along the hallway and found our way upstairs. A nurse directed us to a room where the soldier rested, his head swathed in bandages. After about ten minutes with him, we knew that the young man would be fine. He might be sent to Schweinfurt for a couple of months, but he'd be okay.

Mike and I wished him luck, excused ourselves and walked into the corridor. We confirmed with a nurse that the soldier would be evacuated in a couple of days. It was December 22. Depending on priority and aircraft availability, some patients spent days and some only hours at the hospital. That guy wouldn't make it to Germany in time for Christmas, but he'd be there to see in the New Year.

Downstairs we turned into the corridor and walked toward the foyer. We saw several beautiful young women wearing jackets with the Dallas Cowboys star emblazoned on the back. They didn't wear the traditional white boots, but everything else fit their signature attire.

"Damn, sir, you were right." Glancy kept his voice low.

So did I. "Every once in a while, a blind squirrel finds a nut."

We entered the foyer and two of the cheerleaders stared at us.

"Are you guys combat soldiers?" said a blonde.

We stood out in our body armor since almost nobody wore it at the hospital. Doctors and nurses usually wore medical scrubs over fatigues and looked as if they belonged there.

"I'm not sure what you mean by combat soldiers," Mike said. "I thought everyone was supposed to be a soldier in combat."

"Were you fighting somewhere? Why are you wearing all that stuff?" another, a brunette, asked.

"Oh, this stuff? That's so when we get blown up, they bring us here instead of the morgue."

"I'm Tiffany," said the blonde. "And this is Jeanette. Have you been blown up?"

"Not recently. But it happens out there quite a bit."

"That looks *really* heavy," Jeanette said, pointing to our body armor.

"It is," said Mike.

I enjoyed watching him try to parry the flirtatious inquiries.

"Can we try it on?" Jeanette said. Tiffany nodded.

Mike looked at me.

"I don't see why not."

We took off our body armor and set it on the floor. With all the ammunition, equipment, and protective plates, the armor stood upright like the upper torso of a mannequin. Mine weighed over fifty pounds, but it distributed the weight across the shoulders.

Jeanette moved toward us and attempted to pick up my armor. Tiffany grabbed Mike's, which was heavier. They struggled and couldn't lift them.

"Why is it so heavy?" Tiffany asked.

"We carry a lot of ammunition, water, and other supplies," I said. "When you need it in a hurry, you have it right there."

"You guys are so brave," she said.

"Can you help us put it on?" Jeanette asked.

Mike and I glanced at each other again with a "what have we gotten ourselves into" look.

"Sure," I said. I lifted my armor up and helped Jeanette get into it. I showed her how to Velcro the front shut so it would stay seated properly. Mike did the same for Tiffany. Doctors and the occasional nurse wandered through, peeped at the spectacle, and smiled.

"Wow," said Tiffany. "You guys wear this stuff all the time?"

"We don't need to do cartwheels and handstands in it," Mike joked.

"We wouldn't be doing much of that if we wore all this stuff," said Jeanette.

A nurse passed through the area. The cheerleaders asked him if they could get photos with us and the equipment. He took several shots with Mike's camera and then the cheerleader's camera. "Our guys are never gonna believe this," I said.

The cheerleaders mentioned that they were performing for the soldiers at Victory Base that evening and invited us to attend. They would wear their boots for the show.

Mike could tell that I wanted to return to our patrol. "We gotta boogie, ladies," he said. "Have to get back outside the wire where the bad guys are."

The cheerleaders seemed disappointed that we were leaving but didn't protest. We walked out of the building, laughing. Mike said, "You know the soldiers are gonna rib you about the 'we'll be right back stuff.'"

"They're used to me," I said. "And when was the last time you got to meet a couple of Dallas Cowboy cheerleaders?"

"Never."

"Exactly."

A couple of the soldiers waited outside our vehicles and mounted up when they saw us. Mike and I got in. I put my headset on.

"That wasn't exactly a be-right-back moment," Neyer, the gunner said. He was such a wiseass. I loved him for that. He usually wouldn't even include a "sir" in his commentary. If he did, he would drawl it out and add a few syllables, like a mother chiding a naughty kid.

"Yeah, sir," Woods added. "We never believe you anymore. Why do you try to get our hopes up, anyway?"

"Guys, if you were wounded, I'd come spend time with you in the hospital, too. Plus, it wasn't like we were hanging out with the Dallas Cowboys cheerleaders or anything."

"Hah, in your dreams," Hassan said and laughed.

"Yeah, right, sir," said Woods. "What's the likelihood of that happening?"

"'Nother lame excuse," Neyer said.

"What if I told you that I wasn't making that up? And, what if I told you that Stray Dog and I took care of you guys, too. We got you an invitation to see the cheerleaders' show tonight."

"Whatever, sir," Woods said. "Nice try."

"Look, sir," Rodin, the driver said. "We know you have all this *responsibility* and we're just the guys doing the legwork. No need to try and make up stories for us."

This discourse inside my vehicle poured out over our open microphone. I decided to call in support. "Stray Dog, are you telling your guys about what happened inside the hospital?"

"Roger," he said. "I showed them some of the photos we took."

"That sounds like a story you both made up," Hassan said. "I knew I should've gone in there to keep you out of trouble."

"Whatever, old man," Neyer said. "You'd a been checking out the girls with the two of them."

"Umm, your body armor smells good." Hassan laughed as he leaned over my seat.

The teasing continued all the way back to FOB Justice. When we returned to base, the guys huddled around SFC Glancy, who validated the story with the photos. Charlene, our female 240B gunner, shook her head and removed her machine gun from the vehicle to clean it.

Later that evening Lt. Kronick stopped by my office. Hassan and I were drinking chai and talking about the week's events.

"I let the guys know about the cheerleader show on Liberty," Kronick said, "but they decided not to go. They didn't think it was worth the risk of another patrol today just to see a show."

"Makes sense, although the guys would've got to see them in their boots."

"They wanted me to thank you, though, for thinking about them."

"Just trying to help you take care of the guys."

"Thanks, sir. Anything else we need to worry about today? I've already looked at the intel for tomorrow's patrol."

"Nope. Just another day in this wacky country."

"Roger," he said and walked out.

"Dallas Cowboy Cheerleaders. Never know what we're gonna run into in this crazy place," said Hassan.

We sang Christmas carols and folk songs on the rooftop lounge Corporal Huffman had constructed. It was Christmas. With so much misery and drama playing out every day, singing allowed us to escape some of the tragedy for a little while.

Chaplain David Mikkelson brought a support team to hold a holiday service for the soldiers. The Dagger Quartet accompanied him. They were a group of talented vocalists, all soldiers, who added richness to the Task Force Justice holiday observance. After the service and special meal in the dining facility, we went up to the roof. Someone brought a guitar and played. While waiting for their helicopter to arrive, members of the quartet, Chaplain Mikkelson, and I sang along as the guitarist alternated between Christmas carols and familiar songs from back home. *O Come, All Ye Faithful*; *Jingle Bell Rock*; *We Wish You a Merry Christmas*; the *Twelve Days of Christmas*; and other favorites.

As we walked to the landing pad, the chaplain said, "Steve, this was one of the more meaningful ways I've spent Christmas. Your team is doing great work."

"You brought the quartet and guitarist. They made all the difference."

As they flew off, my thought was how this day almost seemed normal. The soldiers enjoyed themselves. We let our hair down a bit, sang, drank chai and eggnog with cinnamon. I felt good about what we'd accomplished by creating some semblance of normalcy for the soldiers. We brought a bit of holiday tradition into the chaos of Baghdad. As I walked to my office, I hummed a carol and decided to call Amy. We'd celebrated fifteen years of marriage two days prior and had traveled a long way from our dreamy days of bird watching in Panama.

A few hours later a different call came into the command cell. Jaysh Al Mahdi hit an explosive ordnance disposal (EOD) team with an EFP, an explosively formed penetrator bomb. Men were dead. Some were evacuated. The bomb shredded the Buffalo, a specialized engineer vehicle used for disposing ordnance. The Buffalo had a V-shaped hull to withstand mine strikes from underneath. Soldiers inside used cameras and a thirty-foot mechanical arm to disable potential roadside bombs. Designed in South Africa, this type of vehicle did a great job protecting against mines that exploded underneath vehicles. Designers never envisioned EFPs angled from the side of the road.

Nick Kron was in the command cell with First Sergeant Pryor.

"It's bad, sir. They flew out casualties but were unable to get two of the bodies out of the burning vehicle."

"Damn it. Any assessment or other info?"

"Ninety-nine percent sure it's JAM using an EFP. Typical attack for them in that area. Brigade called and asked if we could send a QRF, the military acronym for quick reaction force. Even though the attack site isn't far from the Green Zone, the unit down there refused to send a QRF."

"Are you fucking kidding me?"

Kron stared back at me.

Hassan entered. "Sir, the boys are ready to go."

We strategized how to get to the scene without attracting other attacks. We jumped on some old railroad tracks for part of the route. Our assessment was that the enemy would not place an IED there. We'd never used that route before, which meant no pattern for the enemy to target but uncertainty whether the tracks were navigable. Lt. Kron stared at me wide-eyed when I voiced the decision. It was more important to avoid an attack. The team moved with stealth and had great situational awareness. I was proud of them. They'd grown in battlefield savvy over the months.

My anger cranked when we arrived at the attack scene. We saw dark vehicles and no activity. I was pissed at fucking JAM, who undoubtedly was behind the assault. Pissed at a sister unit that didn't want to leave the safety of the freaking Green Zone with its massive Embassy, smoothie bars, and fucking swimming pools. Pissed at the officer and NCO leadership of the engineer patrol who allowed their men to hunker in their vehicles, damn near inviting another attack.

I knew these men had experienced a horrible night. It was Christmas. Three soldiers were dead. Two burned inside the vehicle, unable to be recovered. But a leader could not afford to wallow in pity while still exposed to the enemy. No number of military platitudes could teach this lesson. *False motivation is better than no motivation. Never quit. Hooah!* That was garrison bullshit.

On the streets of Baghdad, leaders needed to compartmentalize the loss, otherwise risk more tragedy. If JAM knew they could continue to hit the engineer patrol, they could set IEDs along the egress route, send in RPG teams or figure out ways to inflict further pain.

The soldiers needed to wait for a wrecker to evacuate the burning vehicle. However, their inactivity invited more attacks. I needed to get them into the nearby buildings to search for scouts or shooters. That type of action generally scared the enemy off. If we showed no presence, they might get curious again.

Hassan said, "I'll go with some of the guys to inspect the blast sight." Woods and a couple of others joined him. Several more fanned out to pull security. I knocked on vehicle doors.

"Who's in charge?" I said to a soldier in a turret. He was hunkered down and popped his head up.

"Lieutenant's over there." He pointed at an armored vehicle.

I walked to it and banged on the outside door. It slowly opened. "Who's in charge?" I said again.

Squinting into the darkness, a young lieutenant said, "I am." He appeared shell- shocked.

"Why aren't your guys pulling security?"

He looked at me, eyes adjusting to the darkness.

"I know it sucks. You lost good guys tonight. Others are wounded, but you have men out here right now who need your leadership. My guys are pulling security for you. They've been searching for the blast site. Do you know where you were hit?"

"No, sir."

"How is the EOD team going to do forensics here if you haven't done an initial investigation?"

I've never understood why emotional suppression came naturally to me. Maybe it was experience. I had to do it the first night we assumed mission in Tikrit in 2004 when Sunni insurgents killed a company commander and another soldier. The second in charge of the company was close friends with the commander. I found him distraught and crying in the battalion command center.

"You don't have time for grief right now. There are 130 other men out there who need your leadership. That's what Hans would expect." Hans Kurth was the commander killed.

I'm sure I could have showed more empathy at the time, but it didn't feel as if that was what he needed. Maybe I'm able to more easily put losses aside than most. The counterinsurgent environment felt natural to me. Being on patrol felt natural to me. The streets of Baghdad fed my spirit. Patrolling gave the impression we were trying to change things for the better. The super-FOBs were claustrophobic, stifling of any initiative, like bureaucracy gone amuck in combat. Why go to war to sit on a base for a year and get shot at by rockets or mortars? It was much better to take the fight to the enemy and attempt to protect the populace.

Hassan returned to our vehicle and lifted himself inside. "The rims on the Buffalo kept reigniting because it was some type of magnesium alloy."

I had no idea how he knew this or if it was even right. Maybe one of the NCOs told him. Nothing surprised me anymore. Bad shit continued to happen. We attempted to stay unpredictable to keep from being an easy target.

Merry Christmas.

Five days later, Chaplain David Mikkelson pulled me aside as I walked into the chapel. I was numb. I'd lost track of how many memorial services we had attended.

"Steve, that lieutenant from the other night and his soldiers are pretty angry. They said some lieutenant colonel showed up to their patrol in the middle of the night, chewed their asses and disappeared into the darkness."

"That's one version of the story," I said. I was a little defensive. I understood their frustration. They drove at a snail's pace, at night, hunting for bombs to disable. "I'll talk to them. Maybe that'll help."

David placed his hand on my shoulder with compassion. "I'll set it up." His eyes held sadness. He knew that to some extent we were all broken. He often told me that he prayed for me.

At a memorial service, it was okay to show soldiers compassion and acknowledge their loss. They were safe on base. Many times, a patrol hit that bad was removed from the mission cycle for a couple of days. The command had combat psychologists interview the soldiers. NCOs and officers, if they led by example, sat in on group therapy sessions or even led them with the psychs in support.

I spoke to the guys, explained my perspective on the evening and why I responded that way. I stayed and answered their questions. After the session with the engineers, we were back on patrol with our game faces. We left the massive FOB Liberty complex and headed across Baghdad back home to FOB Justice.

We were swamped with embed requests from journalists. Chris Hondros, a Getty Images war photographer, returned. Chris was known to many of the soldiers. He hailed from Fayetteville, North Carolina, home of Fort Bragg, where I had served in the 82nd Airborne Division as a company commander from 1995 to 1997. He was always low maintenance, and I welcomed his company. We would sip chai in the upstairs lounge and share experiences.

Cassidy Eaves, our task force engineer and de facto public relations guru, stopped by my office. I stared at a small chessboard. My eleven-year-old son, Rob, and I played long-distance chess to maintain our relationship during the separation. Games took weeks with only one or two moves per day.

"CNN just reached out for another embed," Eaves said.

"Is it Arwa?" I said. Arwa Damon was a CNN reporter who had interviewed some of our interpreters after George Packer's story. I liked her fearlessness.

"No, some guy named Michael Holmes. I still need to do the research on him, but they want to bring a camera crew and go see Ashura."

"That's interesting. Wonder when the last time Western media got to cover Ashura in Iraq?" Ashura was a big Shia religious holiday where thousands of pilgrims marched to the most sacred shrines and sites. Hassan had told me we could expect tens of thousands to visit the Khadamiyah Shrine.

"I think that's the thing," Eaves said. "I talked to his producer. She said it's been years since they had access. They were hoping we might be able to provide it."

"Can you tell Hassan to come see me? We might need to ask Sheik Sami for assistance on this one."

Sheik Sameer al Dulaymi was the leader of the Dulaymi tribe in Baghdad. We called him Sheik Sami, pronounced Sammy, for short. He was a powerbroker in Khadamiyah and helped us keep a finger on the pulse of various factions and players. I was still attempting to gauge how much influence the sheik had, but Hassan believed he was influential.

Hassan called Sheik Sami and told him we'd like to arrange an interview with CNN. We often appealed to ego when we attempted to move things along. Hassan also informed the sheik that CNN would visit during the time of Ashura and hoped to shoot some footage. Sheik Sami didn't think it would be a problem.

Three days later the crew arrived. I liked Michael Holmes. An Australian, he wielded a sharp sense of humor, a critical quality for survival in the darkness of Baghdad. We sat in the conference room for a couple of hours going over dynamics of the city. He asked a lot of questions. His producer sat and listened.

"What else can we line up for you?" I said.

"Nothing, mate," Holmes said. "We're very excited. You guys are amazing. We'll check out Ashura, interview the sheik, and see what other kind of trouble we can get into."

"You've definitely come to the right place then."

Hassan, who sat near the producer, laughed. "His Iraqi nickname is *abu Mashakel*, so trouble will follow."

"What's that mean?" Holmes said.

"Father of all trouble."

"Don't worry," Hassan said. "We'll come up with a nickname for you, too."

"Feel free to chat with any of the soldiers or interpreters," I said. "You can speak to the Iraqi soldiers, too, if you want. See you tomorrow morning."

The next day, our patrol met thirty minutes prior to departure. The CNN crew was ready to roll. Lt. Kronick led the briefing, and we went around the group to ask questions.

"All right guys." I began what had become a familiar stump speech. "A free press is critical in our society. Not only that, but our families greatly appreciate the reporting that makes it back home, whether to Germany or the U.S. Your moms and dads want to hear the news and read the stories."

Good or bad, our families were hungry for any news about their soldiers. They loved to watch CNN footage that helped fill in some gaps about our mission and our progress.

Michael accompanied me on the short ride downtown. He sat behind the driver, Rodin, the seat Woods usually occupied.

"You have a new nickname, Michael," I said.

Hassan did the honors. "Down Under Dog."

"I like it, mate."

"Liking your nickname doesn't really matter," I said.

It was a quick drive. We took the four-person CNN crew and six soldiers to the sheik's interview. The rest of the team stayed with our vehicles. I wanted to maintain a light signature, so we levied the least disruption possible during the celebration.

The streets were mobbed by pilgrims dressed in white robes. Security forces attempted to control the crowds. Street vendors provided all manner of food and drink. One of the amazing aspects of Iraqi celebrations was that vendors supplied the pilgrims with food, chai, and water for free, a testament to Iraqi hospitality. Within minutes, Sheik Sameer found us. Hassan followed the necessary tribal mores, said the Muslim greetings, and they kissed cheeks.

The sheik opened his arms wide for an embrace and approached me. We kissed three times, alternating cheeks. Stubble from his beard scratched a little on my face. I thought about how my wife always complained when I grew a beard.

Woods looked at the guys in the patrol vehicles and smirked. Following Iraqi customs always earned me a good bit of ribbing from the guys. They'd bring up the kissing or the fact that most sheiks held my hand. That was a normal Iraqi custom but weird for young American men. They always looked for things they could use to give me a hard time.

I introduced Sheik Sami to the CNN crew. He greeted them with a nod and spoke about what they would see. Hassan translated.

We wandered the streets toward Adan Square, a place on the west side of Khadamiyah that afforded access toward the shrine. Thousands of people thronged the streets.

"This is incredible," Holmes said.

Our small group stared in amazement as a procession unfolded in front of us. Units of twenty or thirty men marched. They wore white robes and carried what looked like small, cat-o-nine-tail whips and used them to flagellate their own heads and backs. Blood trickled down their faces and shoulders, spreading crimson onto their white robes. On the sidelines stood men who had already completed the parade, red droplets still fell from their foreheads. Young boys also participated. Hundreds continued marching through the streets in groups. The crowd cheered their sacrifice.

We watched the procession for twenty minutes and decided to move. Nerves twitched. We couldn't see the vehicles. We had four civilians, not counting Hassan, and only six of us had weapons. However, Sheik Sami provided our security for the excursion. He guaranteed our safe passage.

We returned to the vehicles and promised Sami we would see him soon at his residence for the interview. As we mounted up, the CNN crew was ecstatic.

Michael said, "Do you realize the last time we had that type of coverage of Ashura? Saddam had shut down most of the Shia celebrations."

"I had no idea what we were getting ready to witness," I said. "That was definitely…different."

We drove the few blocks to Sheik Sami's dwelling, where we were met by his son, Abdullah, and ushered into the home. The sheik offered us seats in the living room. He asked about chai, which Hassan said we would appreciate.

"Thank you for taking us to see Ashura," I said. "Michael was very excited about the coverage. He was hoping to ask you some questions."

The sheik nodded. "You see," he said, addressing Holmes and his producer. "This is why Iraq will never be a great country again. All those idiots beating themselves in the streets."

Hassan chuckled before he translated to let us know a joke was coming. That was a tactic used by experienced interpreters to help bridge cultural understanding.

Michael asked questions about the sheik, the current state of security in the country, and what was needed to secure the future.

Sheik Sami said, "Things were bad under Saddam, but at least people had security. They had food and water, electricity. Many people suspect that the Americans could fix the situation but they just don't want to. Iraq needs a Pinochet or a Franco, someone who could rule with a strong hand."

We had heard this before, which seemed bizarre coming from Shia leaders. It was as if they were nostalgic about the good old days under Saddam.

We spent an hour with the sheik and returned to base. Holmes and his crew departed later that evening, on to their next assignment. A few weeks later, the producer reached out to me again. She sent a link to a piece they had titled, "The Month of Mayhem." I took issue with the title. It seemed to be a typical editorial exaggeration of events. For me, January had been an extension of the previous months of violence. However, in hindsight, I realized they were right. January 2007 was a cruel month.

Chapter Four

Bureaucratic Jiu-Jitzu

*"Rules are mostly made to be broken and
are too often for the lazy to hide behind."*

~ General Douglas MacArthur

THE LEVEE BROKE in April 2006 when al Qaeda blew up the al Askiri Shrine in Samarra. It was a significant Shia place of worship and pilgrimage. Waves of sectarian violence erupted in Iraq and later around the Middle East. The upheaval was aggravated by state and nonstate sectarian actors: Iran, the Gulf States, and al Qaeda. Al Qaeda stoked religious animosity, and ironically, Iran was the biggest benefactor. The Iranians pulled the strings of Shiite militia groups in Iraq. They incited retaliation whenever al Qaeda blew up a car bomb. That caused cycles of violence and mayhem throughout the integrated areas of the country. They followed a typical pattern: A car bomb exploded in a crowded Shiite marketplace. Next, militias supported by Iran conducted campaigns of intimidation in mixed neighborhoods and forced Sunni families out. Under Saddam's reign,

Sunnis and Shiites had intermarried and intermingled for decades in Baghdad, Baqubah, and other cities and towns.

Most of the Gulf States also contributed to the cascading violence. They supported Sunni insurgent groups and played into the al Qaeda narrative of Sunni-Shiite conflict, a reflection of the 1,400-year schism in Islam that split the religion into quarreling factions. Baghdad was the epicenter of the sectarian slaughter in late 2006 and early 2007. Given that both Sunni and Shiite extremists resented the American-led occupation, Iraqis who worked alongside Americans found themselves in a precarious position.

As extremist groups on both sides spread violence throughout the local populace, U.S. troops in Baghdad and their Iraqi counterparts were caught in the middle. We positioned joint security stations and combat outposts along sectarian fault lines. Our goal was to referee the fighting and mitigate it. Desperate people had lost hope in the Iraqi government, the Iraqi Security Forces, and the Coalition Forces. As we set up outposts amidst the population, those positions served as levers to force the Iraqi Army and police to coordinate with U.S. forces. For several years, Americans commuted to work from massive bases. Now we occupied small outposts in neighborhoods alongside Iraqi Security Forces, and interpreters ventured into the middle of killing fields with the soldiers.

The Iraqi people responded each time we built a new outpost. When they saw American soldiers living in the same conditions as average Iraqi citizens, they contributed to the intelligence reports that began to flow. People walked without fear to the small forward bases and provided information. They gained confidence when they saw Iraqi and American soldiers work side by side, sharing the same hardships and purpose. However, while violence near the outposts subsided, resentment of interpreters remained strong.

First Lieutenant Steve DuPerre's patrol crept along the narrow streets of Huriyah. DuPerre cared about his soldiers and drove them hard to be ready to respond to any threat. His platoon was assigned to Task

Force Justice along with his higher headquarters, Alpha Battery. He was grateful to be out on patrol but thought he and his guys could be doing more to help with the fight. As they returned from an escort mission to the Huriyah Neighborhood Council, DuPerre decided to get a first-hand sense of the atmospherics. The intel guys had mapped out the JAM bombing attacks and found that the terrorist group only conducted attacks in Shia neighborhoods where they enjoyed the support of the people. Huriyah had become an exclusively Shia neighborhood after thousands of Sunni families were forced out in late 2006. Lt. DuPerre wanted to understand the threat better. Ronnie, his interpreter, knew the area well. He'd grown up there and received regular updates from friends about the dangers.

DuPerre led from the front vehicle. Like all good platoon leaders, he would never ask his men to do something he wouldn't do.

"What's your situation?" he said over the platoon radio net.

"Normal atmospherics back here," Staff Sergeant John Garcia radioed. Garcia was a large man, hard on his men and the interpreters. Enforcing discipline exemplified the hallmark of a strong NCO, and Garcia lived the creed.

Still inside the vehicle, Ronnie said, "Sir, this is the main market area."

Cars avoided the patrol as it wound through the streets. Low hanging wires hung across the road as store owners ran lines to power their shops. We referred to it as spaghetti wiring as the disorganized cables seemed like someone had tossed a giant bowl of pasta over rooftops and across the streets. We used tiedown hooks on our vehicles to keep antennas low and prevent ripping down the improvised lines. Sometimes gunners were forced to reach out of the turret and lift wires over the cupola as their vehicles rolled by.

"What was it like to grow up here?" DuPerre asked Ronnie.

Poverty was evident everywhere in Baghdad but was especially visible in populated areas like Huriyah. "It wasn't that bad, sir," Ronnie said. He hoped no one on the street noticed him through the porthole-sized window of bulletproof glass. Even though he wore a facemask (as did most interpreters) he feared being recognized by the militia, or even friends and family. "I've got lots of friends here," he said. "Which is why I've got the long hair and beard. Sometimes when I go home, my friends and even my family don't recognize me."

"You've got to be careful doing that," the lieutenant said. "I'd put you up against any interpreter on the base. You teach us stuff we'd never know. Can't afford to lose you."

"I'm really careful. I've only done it a couple of times and only go at night. My brother checks to see if people are watching before I go. Still, I hope we don't have to stop and get out. Someone could recognize me and come after my family."

"We're on our way back to the base," DuPerre said. "But you're helping me learn a lot about JAM. Plus, seeing where they operate gives me a better feel." The patrol was bogged down as the streets narrowed. "How do we get out of here?"

"There's only one way, along the Shula road. But my friend in the Iraqi Army told me the JAM guys have been seen putting a lot of IEDs there. I don't think we should go that way," Ronnie said.

"Doesn't look like we can get the patrol turned around. Just get us out of here."

Ronnie directed the driver through the neighborhood to the main route. They edged out of the market area and left the confined district. In a minute they went from being awash in people and automobiles to a more open highway bordered by rubble and trash.

The patrol picked up speed, then a blinding flash rocked the vehicle. Dust obscured the lead. The trailing vehicles reacted, forming a herringbone formation that covered 360 degrees. They saw the flash of automatic weapons fire. Two gunners responded with fire at empty buildings on the right side of the road.

"Steel 6," SSG Garcia, the platoon sergeant, called over the radio. "What's your status?"

Silence. Garcia ordered the second vehicle to check out the situation.

Inside the lead vehicle, the driver, Specialist Kallie, shouted, "What the fuck?"

"Everybody okay?" the platoon leader said.

"Damn. Lucky I was down in the turret," his gunner yelled to the crew.

"You okay?" DuPerre asked the driver.

"Just a little rattled, sir," he responded. "Nothing bleeding."

Ronnie said nothing from the seat behind DuPerre. His side of the vehicle had been hit, but not penetrated.

"This is Steel 6," DuPerre said over the radio when he heard transmissions resume. "We're alright." Then he realized he hadn't heard from his interpreter. "Ronnie. You okay?"

"Yes, sir," came a terse, angry response.

"Got the second vehicle in overwatch of your location," Sergeant Garcia said. "They provided some suppressive fire in case anyone is still out there. No enemy in sight at this time."

"What's the damage look like on my vehicle?" DuPerre said.

"You're not driving that thing anywhere, sir," someone in the second vehicle said over the radio.

"It won't even start. Must've disabled the engine with the blast," Kallie said.

"Call Justice in case we need to get a wrecker," DuPerre said.

"Roger," said Sergeant Garcia.

Captain Stacy Bare led a squad of soldiers in pursuit of the JAM guys who had fired at the vehicles. They searched house-to-house, turning up scared civilians who claimed to know nothing along with several suspicious actors who couldn't justify their presence. Bare's men detained them for further questioning. As the situation leveled out, DuPerre's soldiers hooked the disabled vehicle to another Humvee with a tow bar and dragged it back to FOB Justice.

For about two weeks, Ronnie's hands shook when he sat alone in the mess hall to eat. He didn't want to speak with anyone. He was mad. Mad at his situation. Mad at Iraq. Mad at the world.

My patrol returned to FOB Justice the next day for a scheduled weekly task force meeting, which we held to synchronize our activities. We also did daily standup meetings of about thirty minutes long. We checked on intelligence from the prior evening, weather conditions, and any changes in the threat picture. The weekly gathering was more involved. It consisted of in-depth updates on staff projects and other matters. Sometimes the meetings would have a directed emphasis for the staff. I had designated that particular meeting to focus on the problem of how to help interpreters apply for the Special Immigrant Visa or SIV. It allowed interpreters who had served honorably for at least twelve months, and could substantiate threats on their lives, to emigrate to the U.S. following a series of background checks and other bureaucratic steps. While the meeting focused on the SIV, I was under no illusion that we would "solve" the problem in one session. It would take months to slog through the bureaucracy. More important was training the staff to be persistent and cut through the red tape.

Before the meeting, Hassan made two cups of chai in his room and brought them to my office. It became routine for us to spend quiet time together. We sipped the sweetened, hot tea and tried to keep our finger on the pulse of the troops and interpreters.

"How's your chess game with Rob going?"

"Pretty soon, I won't be able to beat him." My son was twelve years old going on twenty.

Hassan checked his watch, realized we had lost track of time and excused himself. He reappeared. "They're ready for you, boss."

"Let's hope they've started. The staff should know that meetings don't revolve around the commander. It's all about the organization. They should be rockin' on without me."

"They also know you're here, so they asked me to come get you. If you were out on patrol, the meeting would start. Plus, they know how passionate you are about fixing the interpreter problem."

Hassan always had one or two great justifications for why something happened the way it did. Like a personal Jiminy Cricket, he whispered positive thoughts and justifications in my ear.

Most of the leaders were present except for the few engaged in mission-critical activities. We never stopped our patrols or guard rotations. Those absent were updated when they returned.

"What's going on, guys?" I said.

Nick Kron, the intelligence officer said, "Sir, I'll start with a general overview of the threat in our areas of interest and operations. Then, given the nature of our special topic today, I'll dial in on threats to interpreters."

"You going to tell us that the greatest threat to our local national partners is our own bureaucracy?"

Nick laughed. "I'll let the staff responsible for tracking and getting visas talk about that one. I plan to stick to the actors pulling triggers and blowing people up.

"We have primarily al Qaeda, Sunni insurgent, and Shia militia threats. That said, many in the Iraqi government also threaten or undermine those who work closely with us. We receive reports from sources about Iraqi police, National Police, Iraqi Army, and even political figures doling out threats to Iraqi interpreters or ISF leaders who seem to be too close to U.S. Forces. Those same government officials often have relationships with Sunni insurgents or Shia militias, who end up carrying out their dirty work. For example, a Shia politician like Basem al Shammari would threaten people like Brigadier General Usaif if he appeared too chummy with his American counterparts. If he didn't heed the warning, al Shammari might have some JAM militia members leave a message at his home for his family or track his kids from school.

"JAM's calling card is an envelope with a bullet in it and possibly a letter directing someone to cease working with the infidels. And they've begun spraying graffiti on walls around Khadamiyah. Now, in BG Usaif's case, his family's been in hiding, so they're relatively protected. However, a lot of others working with us are more exposed."

Nick elaborated on the specific techniques that different groups favored to render threats. Trips to a torture house could follow the "bullet in an envelope" warning. Al Qaeda had been known to hang heads or bodies from lampposts in neighborhoods. Sunni people rejected such brutality, as did the Shia populations held hostage by various JAM street gangs, but murder and terrorist attacks continued to rise.

After other staff briefings, we came to the SIV portion. Sergeant First Class Brown, a large African American who had spent most of his career in the artillery, stood. As with most of the Task Force Justice team, he had no staff experience. "We have almost three dozen Iraqis who've either applied or expressed a desire to apply for the Special Immigrant Visa. In your folder I placed a tracker that outlines the status of each packet that's been submitted. You'll see that only nineteen have been started."

"This is a good start," I said. "Let's dig into some of the details of each case."

Brown said, "Sponsors all have the individual status of their cases. They're the ones tracking the circumstances for each interpreter."

"But you're the guy who has to call higher headquarters to get a status of the packets, right? We don't need individual sponsors trying to call them or the embassy and develop their own systems. The reason we have a staff is to take that burden off the rest of the team. Now let's look into a couple of specific cases so I can illustrate the level of fidelity expected as we develop the system."

SFC Brown frowned. My intent wasn't to reprimand him but to train him in the amount of work this would take. He looked as if he lacked confidence in his ability to do the job. I thought it would be a matter of training and repetition, but I glanced at the First Sergeant and Company Commander, Jim Egan, during this exchange.

"Let's take Ronnie, for example," I said. "Who's his sponsor?"

First Sergeant Tony Pryor said, "Lieutenant DuPerre."

"That's a good start. We need to add a column to the tracker that lists all the sponsors for the interpreters. What about Ronnie's sponsor in the United States?"

"We'll have to get back to you on that."

"Each interpreter needs to have a sponsor in the U.S. Most of them are twenty-five years old or younger and have this Hollywood vision of what things are going to be like if they make it to the States. Nobody's going to have a welcome party pick them up at JFK, and Pamela Anderson isn't gonna be their girlfriend. They'll have to work their asses off to make a living and most of them have no idea how hard it'll be."

"We're gonna need a little more time to get the details you're asking for," said Tony.

"This'll be difficult. If we're able to pierce the veil of bureaucracy and get any of these guys through, it'll take persistence and a level of attention to detail in order to work the system. Too many people are busy with other distractions on higher level staffs. I don't want to see a status like the one listed for Ronnie that says his packet is at higher headquarters. That's meaningless. Whose desk is it on?

"I want names and the last time we contacted the individual. The same goes for the other columns that describe background checks, general officer letters of recommendation, and other items. For the G.O. letters I want to see the name of the general officer in that column. That'll allow us to know whether we need to help. Maybe the transition teams don't have a G.O. in their circles. We'll need to help them with that. Remember, it's a team effort. We don't need any more memorials to dead Iraqis because they worked with us."

Tony said, "We'll make it happen, sir."

"Many of you haven't been punished by working on a staff before." Chuckles from the men. "That's okay. It just takes a little training. This is an important line of effort that'll pay off if we stay on it. Anything else?" No one spoke. "Some of us are heading out on patrol, right?"

"Yes, sir. Duty First," several of the men said. I saluted in response and turned to chat with Hassan, who'd been listening from a chair behind me. Some of the guys who were only there for the SIV portion of the meeting departed.

"What do you think, Old Dog?" I said.

Hassan smiled. "I don't know if anyone else is working on this problem in Baghdad, but I know our interpreters really appreciate that someone cares about them. There has been a buzz about the base ever since you talked about helping them."

"Let's hope it's a solvable problem and not another Gordian knot like so many crazy situations in this country." To the room I said, "What's going on in the city that we need to know about?"

Nick Kron chimed in. "As you know, one of our patrols got hit yesterday with an IED. Steve DuPerre was the patrol leader. They returned fire but didn't get any confirmation of enemy kills. They detained six suspected JAM members and took them to the detention center. The attack occurred in Ronnie's neighborhood."

DuPerre was a "take action" type of leader, the kind I preferred working with over those with personalities that needed prodding. However, DuPerre was young, without much experience. I wondered why the patrol had been in the area.

"Ronnie was on that patrol?" I said.

Cassidy Eaves said, "I spoke to DuPerre and Ronnie was pretty pissed off at JAM, and that he was patrolling through his own neighborhood and risked getting recognized."

"Why are we sending interpreters on patrols through their own neighborhoods? We could be writing their death warrants."

"I'll talk to the boys," 1SG Pryor said. "They know better. We've told them before."

"We all need to make a concerted effort to avoid areas that are risky, not only for the interpreters, but for our patrols, unless we absolutely need to be there."

Captain Jim Egan said, "We'll make sure every soldier hears it. We've had enough people killed and vehicles blown up for one deployment already."

"If we have a mission or are under extreme circumstances, then patrol leaders make the call and can go where they need to. However, for routine patrols or resupply missions, they need to stay updated on the enemy sit and avoid contact. We lose the fight when we go kinetic. The enemy wants to goad us into a firefight. Nick, what else do you have?"

"Sunni neighborhoods are dealing with al Qaeda and Sunni insurgents. Both groups use deep buried IEDs and snipers. Deep buried IEDs consist of several daisy-chained 155mm shells in a crater or sometimes covered with asphalt. If one of our tanks or Bradleys transits over it, the explosion will flip the tank and pretty much kill everyone inside. That's what happened to 1-26 Infantry in Adhamiyah. Five guys died.

"When you get to the Shia neighborhoods, the explosively formed penetrator is the most dangerous weapon. The Iranians channel the technology and training to JAM and other Shia groups. The EFP forms a molten ball of steel or copper. It pierces the armor on anything we drive. Mostly, they've been using victim activated triggers. You'll recall that they were manually detonating the bombs. They no longer take the risk of putting a trigger man in harm's way. Instead, they use passive infrared beams that automatically detonate the bomb when the vehicle crosses the beam. They still need to activate the IR beam and can do so remotely or manually.

"Bottom line, we need to adjust our tactics depending on what neighborhood we're in," said Nick. "If we're in a Sunni neighborhood, we're looking for potholes and deformities in the road. We can't do much about the snipers, but they're usually not shooting at us in the vehicles. They wait for us to dismount to take a shot. When we go into a Shia neighborhood, we look for places on the side of the road that can conceal an EFP. They've used a little of everything from trash cans to light posts or anything that can conceal a bomb until we're right on top of it. Of course, no matter what neighborhood we're in, the telltale sign of an attack is when people leave the street."

I saw concerned looks around the room. "You're just full of cheery information."

Since our arrival, Baghdad had continued to get more deadly. The enemy evolved their tactics, and there wasn't just one enemy. We had numerous threats. All of them employed different tactics, depending on the area.

"Unfortunately, that's the reality we live in, sir."

"You need to ensure every patrol does a thorough brief on every mission. All of the soldiers should understand the threat and know what to look for. That means they need to know what neighborhoods and what roles they play to keep each other safe. I've heard of organizations where guys are getting lazy and heading out the gate without a patrol brief. That's a quick way to grow complacent and get killed. We're going to make the enemy work hard to get a shot at us. Understood?"

I'd said this numerous times, but commanders had to give their stump speeches often. Good commanders recognized they needed to use multiple means of communication including repetition to ensure everyone got the word and, most importantly, understood it.

"Yes, sir," echoed around the room.

"I have a question, sir," Rodney Stanfield said. "Is every patrol we're sending out necessary? I don't get out the gate that much, but when I do, it's pretty hairy out there. I just want to make sure that when the boys are going out, it's for the right reason."

"Excellent point, which is why we keep you around. No joyriding, guys. Every patrol has a purpose. I know my patrol is on the road more than most, but every time we go out, it's to achieve an effect within the area. That could be providing access for a reporter, meeting with a sheik, or checking on soldiers at a combat outpost. However, we do not roll out the gate without a purpose."

"No need to tell me, sir," First Sergeant Pryor said. "I have no desire to go out there, unless the boys need me, or I have a mission to do."

"You're always welcome to join us, First Sergeant."

"I'll take you up on that from time to time, sir. I need to see how the MPs are doing." The MP platoon that made up the bulk of my patrol wasn't officially under the First Sergeant's jurisdiction. They were attached to his unit for logistical and administrative support. As any good NCO knew, Tony had to spend time with the soldiers under his watch to provide them with effective leadership.

"You have an extra seat today, sir?" Pryor said.

"Lt. Kronick?"

"Shouldn't be a problem."

"I'll let Staff Sergeant Gonzales know," 1SG Pryor said.

Gonzales was the Military Police platoon sergeant. Even though Pryor was senior, NCOs gave each other the courtesy of telling them when they planned to tag along. Seats on patrols were at a premium. Up-armored Humvees only had four spots plus a gunner position. Each vehicle had a designated gunner, driver, and person in charge, known as a TC, military lingo for truck commander. That left the two back seats in each vehicle for additional passengers. The normal patrol consisted of four vehicles, so that meant only eight seats for passengers. I had trained our team that they always needed to be ready to dismount, often with the MP platoon. It was routine for them to have most of the passenger seats. Our patrol also usually had additional riders like the First Sergeant, an intelligence person, or other staff member. I encouraged staff to get off the bases and experience conditions in the city as much as possible. This provided perspective and context for analyses during mission planning. The staff also knew they had to pull security and contribute to the mission, like any other soldier. There was no joyriding and no such thing as a "passenger." Everyone had to be prepared to fight.

I returned to my office and grabbed my battle rattle, soldier slang for body armor. My kit had been shaped during the previous deployment through trial and error. I preferred that my rifle hang straight down off the right shoulder from what is called a wolf sling. The muzzle pointed down, not toward others. That was important because we needed to send a signal that we did not want to point our weapons at civilians. We trained soldiers to aim their weapons at someone only when they intended to shoot.

We moved to the vehicles and adjusted our body armor. It truly increased our chances of surviving attacks, whether from bullets or bombs. We had neck protectors, groin protectors, flaps that covered the upper parts of our arms. We wore eye protection, gloves, flame retardant uniforms, and dangled weapons from our body armor. To the average Iraqi on the street, we must have looked like some form of science fiction creatures.

I kept the usual notepads, pens, pencils, water, energy snacks, and other items in my backpack during patrol. Each soldier had a pack with additional ammo, water, and other provisions to ensure we had necessary supplies in the event something happened. If we were in a firefight, we needed to be self-sufficient until help arrived. Those were rare occurrences. More often, vehicles broke down, or had an accident. Sometimes, we assisted another patrol that experienced difficulties. The NCOs checked each soldier's kit and vehicle loads to ensure we had sufficient supplies and equipment. Fire extinguishers, jacks, coolers with extra water, additional ammo and other fundamentals.

As I walked out of the building, Ronnie approached me. He'd been sitting with Barney, a stray dog the soldiers had adopted. It was strange to see him with a dog. Most Iraqis treated dogs with contempt. Iraqi Army soldiers had shot Barney twice. Each time, Americans brought him into the aid station and had the doctor patch him up. Ronnie seemed very Americanized for an interpreter. If extremist groups found out his real profession, his family would receive death threats or pressure to have Ronnie meet with insurgent or militia leaders. Other interpreters had learned that the hard way.

"Hey, sir," he said. "The soldiers call me Ronnie. You don't know me, but I wanted to ask you a question."

"What's up?" I said. I did know him because I'd heard some of the soldiers describe what a great interpreter he was, including Steve DuPerre.

"I haven't been able to get a status on my SIV packet, sir."

"Let me look into that for you."

I didn't want to promise anything because we hadn't been successful with any SIV packet. However, I liked his courage in coming straight to me. He was a civilian, but he worked with a platoon leader who had a company commander. Ronnie was "jumping the chain of command," military-speak for going over your boss's head. In this case, Ronnie went over his boss's boss, which required guts.

"I know Task Force Justice started processing packets a couple months ago. I was one of the first terps to put my packet together, and every time I ask what the status is, I get the same answer: 'It's at higher headquarters.' I did everything I was supposed to do, but the answer never changes."

"First, Ronnie, I prefer to use terms like cultural advisor rather than terp, which is derogatory and understates your significance to the mission," I said. "I know you're frustrated with the process. I am, too. I haven't received any good answers from the guys who manage the program. It'll take us a while to get it rolling, but we will. I know that's no consolation when your life is on the line. That said, I directed that patrols should not go into neighborhoods where interpreters are from. You risk being compromised when we do that."

"Yeah, that too." Ronnie looked dismayed. "That's why I grew my beard and hair really long. Nobody recognizes me when I go home, but I still don't want to be patrolling in my neighborhood. It's dangerous, and the JAM guys are everywhere. They blew us up yesterday."

"I get it. Let me look into your packet. I want answers as much as you do. Hassan will get back to you."

"Thanks, sir. That's all I was asking for. Be safe out there. There's a lot of bad guys, and you're out there all the time."

"I like to drive fast without my seatbelt on."

"Good one." He laughed. "Seriously, though. Be safe. The interpreters really appreciate what you and the guys are doing for us. We don't want to see anything happen to you."

"I'd be in big trouble with my wife if I got myself blown up." The irony of Ronnie telling me to be safe wasn't lost on me.

Chapter Five

Embeds

"The only security of all is in a free press."

~ Thomas Jefferson

IN A PRE-PATROL brief, Lt. Kronick presented the overall threat picture and what to expect in each neighborhood. He discussed the IED blast that hit a sister patrol in Huriyah, the one with DuPerre and Ronnie. He mentioned other incidents across the city. Kronick focused on northwest Baghdad, our area of responsibility, but included trends that occurred outside our area that we might expect to see in the future.

Military planners refer to the external districts as the "area of influence." Traditionally, that included zones adjacent to ours but could be expanded in time or space to incorporate other factors. As a young lieutenant, Brett Kronick did a great job leading his unit. He relied on his NCOs and soldiers to provide input, and he balanced the unenviable task of dealing with a lot of high-profile personalities who rode with us, such as journalists, general officers, dignitaries.

Today, Brett had 1SG Tony Pryor and a combat photographer as the only "VIPs." He and the soldiers considered me in that category, but I pushed back against the association.

Lieutenant Kronick rode in the lead vehicle. I was in the second, SSG Gonzales in the third, and another NCO followed up the rear. That day, Pryor rode with Gonzales to discuss soldier issues and spend time with him.

The photographer, Chris Hondros, came to us from Getty Images, the preeminent photojournalism organization in the U.S. and probably the world. They have photographers at global hot spots, major sporting, political, and other events. Toward the tail end of the patrol brief, I reiterated to the soldiers why it was so important to have members of the press with us.

"Some of you have met Chris before and gone on patrol with journalists and others trying to report on Iraq. Who can tell me why it's important that we help reporters get to the stories they're trying to cover?"

Specialist Rodin, my driver spoke up. "Because Baghdad is so fucked up that they would get killed without us."

"There is that. What other reasons?"

"Freedom of the press is part of democracy," said Lieutenant Kronick.

"Absolutely," I said. "Helping reporters get to some difficult stories is like shining a spotlight on some very dark corners of humanity. The rats and cockroaches scurry when that light comes on. It's amazing what a good disinfectant a little bit of transparency is."

They'd heard some version of this several times. Whether the soldiers believed it was another matter, but they took it all in stride. They accepted the reporters because I emphasized their importance, and because guys like Chris Hondros represented reporters well. He had no problem speaking with soldiers of all ranks. He worked to understand their stories. That day, he planned to be dropped off at Combat Outpost Casino in Ghazaliyah. From there, he would accompany dismounted patrols with American and Iraqi soldiers. Our brigade had pushed the concept of combined patrolling and emphasized dismounted patrolling. Chris wanted firsthand experience on the ground. In a world in which many VIPs would swoop in on helicopters, receive briefings in command posts, then fly away, guys like Chris were unusual. He sought experiences with line soldiers. As a result, he was welcomed and even respected by them.

"Chris has been on patrol with us before," I said. "His weapon is a camera, and that could help us win this conflict in a way that none of ours can. The images he sends back can help maintain the public's interest and demonstrate the importance of our mission. He'll be riding in my vehicle, and his nickname is Flash Dog until someone comes up with a better one."

Some of the soldiers laughed. Chris smiled but didn't say anything. The patrol brief broke up and everyone moved to their designated vehicles.

"Come on, Flash Dog," Hassan said. "I'll show you your seat."

"I can always count on you guys to keep things interesting," said Chris.

The vehicles kicked up dust as we turned out of the inner gate and halted to lock and load weapons. At the gate, each vehicle crew ensured that all weapons were in a "red" status, meaning a round chambered and ready to fire. Specialist Nate Neyer manned the machine gun in our vehicle. Other members of the MP platoon called him Nasty Nate. Given that our rule was every nickname had to have some reference to a dog, we called him Nasty Dog.

"Weapon's up," Nate said over the internal coms.

"Roger," said Rodin, as usual, the driver. "We're waiting on the trail vehicle."

"Maybe they're moving slow because Woods is back there with them," Hassan said.

"Woods is pretty good at slowing things down," said Nate.

I said, "Hey, hey. Lay off my security guy." We all chuckled.

"Yeah," said Rodin. "Not only does he get kicked out because Flash Dog is with us, but he gets roasted too."

"Nothing's changed since the last time I rode with you guys," Hondros said.

"You know the deal, Flash Dog," Hassan said. "You've gotta have tough skin to ride in this patrol."

"That's why Hassan frequently goes on sick call," said Nate. "The Old Dog don't want one of us young pups to nip his heels too many days in a row."

Hassan laughed. "You wish. I might be old, but I still hang as much as anybody else on this patrol, and when was the last time I went on sick call?"

"Whatever, old man," said Nate.

I glanced over my shoulder at Chris. "Tough crowd," I said into the microphone.

"I can imagine what they say about journalists when we're not around."

"We take it easy on you. Maybe not reporters in general, but you're cool," said Rodin. "But we ain't afraid to roast you too, even if you are one of the good ones."

"Yeah, you can come back anytime," Nate said.

Chris was a total pro. Reporters tried to maintain a neutral, unbiased relationship when they covered stories. That was a tall order considering the violence of Baghdad in early 2007. We faced death every day and relied on each other to stay alive. Part of the reason for the banter was that it reassured everyone that soldiers were alert and mentally sharp.

Given the pace of operations, a soldier could doze off from the heat and lack of sleep. If each soldier had to defend his or her honor, they had to stay alert. That meant they were more likely to be on the lookout for unusual signs that could indicate a pending attack.

Lieutenant Kronick squelched over the network. "Dismount point coming up."

"Nice day for a stroll in the city," Hassan said.

"I always like to hear from the people," I said. "Chris, you want to walk or ride?"

"You kidding? I wouldn't stay in the vehicle if we were getting shot at."

"What's wrong with our urban submarines?" Hassan said.

Rodin said, "Don't worry about it. Nasty and I'll stay here all by our lonesome. Much safer that way."

As soldiers hopped out, we moved at a quick pace in dismounted formation a block north of the main street. About half our people remained in the vehicles, a driver, a gunner and someone in charge overall. That time, SSG Tony Gonzales remained in charge of the vehicles while Lt. Kronick led the soldiers on the ground. 1SG Pryor also dismounted and walked with us. We made for a motley crew, but we'd trained for this. Every person was expected to pull his or her weight. There was no allowance for rank or position other than with Chris, who was not armed. Hassan always carried a 45mm pistol and shadowed me, ensuring that he would be within earshot should someone attempt to communicate in Arabic.

We were well known on the streets of Khadamiyah. We stopped for chai almost every day, but we were careful not to establish patterns. We varied our timing, routes and locations. Part of dismounting was to add another variable to the enemy's calculus. We knew they targeted us. They looked for patterns that provided them an opportunity for an easy shot. We worked hard not to provide it. That strategy required constant discipline and active thinking.

As conditions changed, we assessed and modified our tactics. For example, the JAM militias had employed manually detonated triggers on the EFPs. Then, they used more victim activated triggers through passive infrared (PIR) beams. We adapted. We used a lengthy metal beam that maintained a heat source in front of vehicles. Military units dubbed the contraption "the rhino." The intent behind a rhino was to hold a heat source about eight feet in front of the vehicle to replicate the heat of the engine. If the vehicle crossed the path of a PIR activated trigger, the rhino would prematurely detonate the EFP. It often destroyed the metal beam but wouldn't do much damage to the Humvee. The rhino was a low-cost technique to protect the force, even though it looked rather clumsy.

The enemy also reacted when we dismounted from our vehicles. It scared the JAM triggermen who had the mission to arm the PIR-activated bombs. A militia member had to be near the bomb to arm it. They were usually a block or two away, but often not within eyeshot. Our dismounted patrols worked the back alleys off the main roads. They tended to scare off potential triggermen and made it harder for the enemy to target our patrols. We had no way to know how successful our tactics were. We did understand that when our units became lazy, they invited attacks. That core principle had been a basic part of military discipline since the world's earliest armies took the field.

We moved on foot at a slow pace through a narrow street. We were one block north of our vehicles as they moved along the main thoroughfare. Because we were only a block away, the dismounted patrol could respond quickly to attacks against the vehicles and vice versa.

People went about their everyday business and didn't pay much attention to us. That was a good indicator. We called it "normal atmospherics."

"Hey LT," Specialist Woods radioed to Lieutenant Kronick.

"What's up?" the lieutenant said.

"We've got ten people back with the vehicles and nine on the ground. Two civilians and seven soldiers." It was a standard status report.

Kronick said, "Keep everyone spread out and stay in coms with the dismounts. I've got the net with the vehicles."

"Roger," Woods said.

We snaked our way through the narrow street. We avoided sewage puddles and made eye contact with Iraqis who glanced at us.

"*As-salāmu 'alaykum,*" Hassan said as we moved close to people. It sounded like "*Salam alaykum*" when spoken. It means "peace be upon you," the traditional Muslim greeting.

Most people responded, "*Wa'alaykum as-salām.*" "Upon you, peace also." Sometimes they indicated to Hassan that they wanted to speak further. They might complain about the U.S. military or living conditions in their neighborhood or some other issue. I often brought up the Jaysh al Mahdi, not in the hope that people would provide information, but to send a message that we were interested in JAM, to keep the pressure on.

After an exchange of pleasantries, an elderly gentleman signaled Hassan that he wanted to chat. "He is complaining about the lack of ice," Hassan told me. "Many people keep bringing up ice as an issue." Due to power shortages, ice was the only way to preserve food.

"We've definitely heard that before," I said. "Have we brought it up with Sheik Sami?"

"I don't think so. Most sheiks will probably want to hump your leg and get something for themselves, maybe a new generator or something. At least Sami isn't like that."

"I'd like to know if he's able to get ice or if he's even in touch with what the people are telling us."

"Let's go find out," Hassan said.

"We should. Hondros doesn't need to get to COP Casino right away."

Hassan made a cell-phone call to confirm if the sheik was available to chat. He nodded yes and continued to speak in Arabic.

I radioed Woods. "Tell Lt. Kronick we're gonna pay Sheik Sami a visit."

"Oh boy," he said. "Not that guy again."

We visited Sami a couple of times per month. His position as head of the Dulaymi Tribe gave him a good handle on JAM activities in the Khadamiyah district.

We hustled a block, mounted up and radioed everyone that we had changed the mission. We would still take Chris to COP Casino, but after paying the sheik a visit. Chris would enjoy hearing Sami's banter.

We arrived outside the sheik's house, left the vehicles and made our way to the front gate. Sami's young son greeted us.

"*Salam alaykum*," he said as he opened the gate.

"*Wa'alaykum as-salām*." Hassan and I responded. In Arabic, he asked the boy where his father was.

"I will take you to him."

Sheik Sami appeared and walked toward us. After we exchanged pleasantries, Hassan conversed with him and motioned to the door. Hassan was well-versed in tribal mores. I didn't understand what he said, but the tone of his exchanges was always courteous and helped our meetings begin in a hospitable manner.

In English, Hassan said, "The sheik says to come sit and have chai."

"I've never been one to turn down chai," I said.

"Yeah, we know." Hassan laughed. "The boys joke about it all the time. Woods will radio out that the sheik invited us in for chai and it'll begin."

"The guys've already started," Woods said.

"That's why I let you carry the radio," I said. "I don't want to deprive them of all the fun they're having at my expense. You know I'm just taking one for the team when I have to drink all that chai."

"If you say so, sir." Woods smiled.

Sheik Sami motioned for me to sit on the couch. Chris entered with Hassan and Woods. The young soldier checked our surroundings, didn't spot any warning signs, and slipped outside. He was our conduit to the rest of the team and closest to me whenever we moved on foot. His discretion was impeccable and allowed for intimate conversation with many of the people we met.

Sheik Sami spoke in Arabic as Hassan translated. "He asks how everything is going. He had not expected us today, otherwise he would have prepared a meal."

"Thank you," I said. "There was no need to prepare a meal. We're sorry for dropping by on short notice."

One of the first rules I learned when operating with an interpreter was to always make eye contact with the other person in the conversation, not the translator. That would allow the person, even though they didn't understand English, to read my body language. It was a way to establish rapport. Often, they would speak to Hassan and not look at me until he began the translation. Good interpreters were vital to the establishment of relationships and Hassan was one of the best. I had to trust that he accurately translated the intent of each conversation, understood important nuances in both languages, and kept track of promises made. Good relationships were fundamental to our mission. They cemented gains and helped civil society recover from the violence.

Chris Hondros sat across from us in an armchair and listened. I introduced him as a reporter.

The sheik said, "I told that CNN crew that Maliki will never get control of this country. Iraqis only understand power and force."

Hassan translated for Chris, who nodded. The discussion meandered while we sipped chai. I eventually asked the sheik about the ice shortage. He was aware of it and reiterated that the Iraqi Government was to blame for all these problems. At least under Saddam people had food, water and ice, he said. They also had more than four hours of power a day. Things had degenerated after Saddam's fall. U.S. forces and the rest of the coalition lacked the ability to control looting and the insurgency that blossomed. Now, we dealt with the mess.

We departed the sheik's home and mounted up. We made our way across Baghdad and pulled into COP Casino. We got out of the vehicles and were moving towards the command tent when a sniper took a shot at us. A round passed near the First Sergeant, who was a tall guy. Years later, I asked him about it. He said he didn't recall the incident, but it left a mark on my memory. In a similar circumstance, another commander was shot in the chest. He survived due to his body armor. The round lodged in his SAPI plate, the composite material that added protection to the armor.

We linked Chris up with a dismounted patrol that planned to head out on foot to hunt the sniper. Hondros wasn't afraid to walk the same paths as soldiers. A lot of journalists came to Iraq and interviewed leaders in the confines of their offices. Chris liked to go on patrol and see what was going on through the eyes of our troops and the Iraqi people. It was no wonder he'd been nominated for a Pulitzer Prize in photography.

The patrol tracked down the shooter, or at least a shooter. Chris returned to our base several days later and showed me a photo while we sipped chai and chatted in the rooftop lounge at Justice. His eye captured ephemeral moments in adroit fashion. The shot showed a typical Iraqi doorway to someone's home. On one side of the door two American soldiers braced against the wall, waiting to enter. On the other side two Iraqi soldiers did the same in a mirror image. The soldiers in the photo were poised to enter. They expected the shooter to fight to the death. The image showed how our new strategy worked to bring together Iraqi and American elements in integrated operations. But I almost missed the most amazing aspect of the picture until Chris pointed it out.

"See the blood trail?"

It was on the ground, leading into the doorway. Splotches of red had dripped from the shooter's wounds as he sought refuge in the house.

"Amazing picture," I said.

"Just trying to capture the moment," Chris said in a humble voice that for him was normal.

Hondros stayed a week. As he left, another reporter rolled in.

I was returning from a late-night trip to the gym when Specialist Woods saw me in the hallway. "Have a second, sir?"

"Sure, Anthony. Let's walk to my office."

"You're going back to work at this hour? You really need to get more sleep, sir."

"You didn't ambush me in the hallway at midnight to lecture me about my sleep habits," I said with a smile.

"Sir, you know how SFC Glancy, Stray Dog, has been riding with us? I'd like to go out with him on a sniper mission, or at least learn from him about sniper ops."

"Why?"

"I'm interested in going through sniper school when we get back to Schweinfurt. I think I'd learn a lot. It'll help me develop as an infantryman."

"That's a good idea. I know Sergeant Glancy wants to get back out there. He thinks it'll help our base security. We'll need to ensure the QRF is available and on alert. I'll talk to the team about it."

"I really appreciate it, sir."

"It'll be good experience for you, and it'll keep the enemy guessing. You know you'll have normal duties, even if you're up all night on a sniper mission."

"It's okay. Sergeant Glancy's got a lot to teach me."

Anthony Woods stood out as a soldier. He was trusted. Occasionally, I thought back to when we met. I had a conversation on the range in Germany with his first sergeant, who introduced us. First Sergeant Almario said the young man would never steer me wrong. He was one hundred percent correct.

I discussed the plans for Woods's sniper mission with the leaders. Everybody needed to know that a small team of "friendlies" was out in the field. The quick reaction force had to be ready to respond to any incidents.

When SFC Glancy and I first worked together in Tikrit, we operated on the fundamental assumption that the enemy knew the teams were there. We planned that our guys would be compromised in order to keep everyone's guard up. A sniper team's presence denied the enemy freedom of maneuver. If the adversary knew the team was there and was unsure about challenging them, he generally avoided the area. The strategy of placing sniper teams caused the enemy to look over their shoulders and avoid areas where the teams operated.

The Task Force Justice team planned the mission to commence a week later. We decided to insert with vehicles rather than walk out the gate. The soldiers were afraid that Barney, the stray dog, would compromise their sniper position as he routinely followed U.S. dismounted patrols out the gate. They told me the dog had become protective of Americans after the Iraqis shot him. Each time we patched him back up, he seemed to be more protective. Once, stray dogs had cornered Ronnie, and from out of nowhere, Barney came to the rescue. He attacked the other strays and gave Ronnie the distraction he needed to slip away. Maybe Barney thought Ronnie was American.

Glancy decided to monitor the sniper operation from the base since four soldiers would be on the mission. Staff Sergeant Gonzales, the Military Police platoon sergeant, would lead. We notified the brigade headquarters at Victory Base Camp and other units that operated on FOB Justice. Delta Company from the 1st of the 325th Parachute Infantry Regiment resided on the base with us. The company was active and had established a new combat outpost within Khadamiyah.

Since we lived together, it was important we collaborated. It kept everyone aware of operations, base activities, and reduced the chance of friendly fire, or fratricide. The team would be integrated into the force protection of the base, which had soldiers in towers and at the gate to our inner compound. However, the sniper team planned to operate just outside the Iraqi side of the base, a strategy that carried additional risk. The QRF was designated at high alert that night to respond to any distress signals in the event the sniper team was compromised.

The night of the mission, SSG Gonzales and Specialist Woods chambered rounds and joined the patrol vehicles that headed out to conduct "atmospherics." Beyond the gate, the patrol dismounted with a dozen people and interacted with the population. Later, only eight soldiers returned to the vehicles. The other four took up an overwatch position.

The sun had set. Two soldiers accompanied Gonzales and Woods to provide additional security. In general, we preferred at least three soldier elements so that someone could protect the team's back entrance. Sniper teams operated on a two-man principle utilizing a spotter and shooter. If the team was focused on a target, they risked not seeing an enemy approach from their rear. Another soldier or two would protect against that likelihood, but any group greater than four created too big of a signature.

They entered a building just outside the gate to the Iraqi portion of the base. The building had a second story that enabled them to observe the city. It also provided a good view of traffic that entered and exited through one of the two gates to the base. Gonzales and Woods anticipated they might witness unusual activity since Americans rarely maintained a presence near the Iraqi section of FOB Justice. Rather than climb to the roof, the team found a second-story window that offered the vantage they sought. The roof would have provided better visibility, but in urban combat, rooftops tended to draw the eye and risked soldiers silhouetting themselves. It was much harder to detect a shooter hiding in the shadows of a window. These were some of the urban warfare lessons that Glancy taught Woods.

After they searched the building for unexpected guests, SSG Gonzales placed the third and fourth soldiers at the top of the stairwell that led to the room he and Woods occupied. They were close enough to each other and the soldiers would provide early warning if someone entered.

Gonzales and Woods positioned themselves in the shadow of the window and watched streets and people below with binoculars. They set up the rifle so Gonzales could rapidly transition to shooting mode. Sound carries farther at night. Their ears might identify a vehicle or other activity before they were able to "get eyes on it." Many times, they might not see a potential target at all, given the limitations of their position. Because they selected the shadow of a window, Gonzales and Woods had a small sector to observe. That made hearing and understanding different sounds more important.

It didn't take long for their imaginations to run wild. Inspired by an endless stream of rumors and reports, Woods said, "You hear the stories about soldiers hearing screams of people being tortured all night long?"

"Yeah," said Gonzales. "They say JAM sets up torture houses and then dumps the bodies in the street the next day." TF Justice and other units had received reports for months about torture houses in the area.

Woods shivered. "That's freaky. Wonder if we'll hear screams. This place is pretty messed up."

"This is my second tour and it's worse. Tikrit was fucked up but nothing like this."

Woods said, "I heard the Sunni insurgents are doing the same things to Shia people they catch. You think they do that to our interpreters?"

"If they catch 'em, yeah. It's pretty much a civil war if you ask me. You know they changed the rules of engagement, right?"

"How so?"

"If we see a car pull up, open the trunk, and dump a body, we can take the shot. Usually, we have to judge hostile intent in order to engage. Because of all of the violence, the lawyers decided that anyone involved in torturing and killing innocent civilians is hostile, even if they're just the driver and aren't posing a threat to us."

"Brilliant deduction. I'm all for that," said Woods. "Anyone involved in this shit has some evil in them."

"Lots of evil fucks running around this city."

The snipers held their position for six hours until just before sunrise. They then made their way back to the U.S. base and cleared their weapons as they passed through the gate. At the same time a patrol headed out the gate. It was the QRF standing down, heading to Victory Base Camp for resupply.

At FOB Justice, we said farewell to Mike Glancy, who was on his way to Germany. I wanted to make sure he was recognized for his work and contributions before departure. We processed an end-of-tour award for him and held a coin ceremony. A generous friend, Juan Sabater of New York City, had paid for Task Force coins. Juan and I attended the Infantry Officer Basic Course together before he left the Army to work on Wall Street. When he heard about the coins, he offered to purchase the two hundred we needed for the task force. Juan always looked to assist with members of the military.

Coins had become ubiquitous during my almost two decades of service. Many commanders customized them to be bigger, more unique and symbolize the spirit of their unit and heraldry. SFC Stanfield designed our coins to represent our unique mission. They were in the shape of a police shield. He also designed a registry that all coin recipients signed to memorialize the service.

The ceremony was informal, but the soldiers valued the recognition. We maintained a registry book of each coin presentation that captured the story of Task Force Justice through the many characters involved. The book also provided information about the symbolism of the design and features of the unit coin. Each recipient signed his or her name, position, date and individual coin number in the book. The coins were numbered one through two hundred. Every person who received one had a unique memento to recall the crazy adventure we experienced together. SFC Stanfield and I also awarded coins to civilians assigned to us, key members of supporting units, and other stakeholders.

Rodney accompanied me for every ceremony. We made it a habit to award the coins to individuals or small units and not conduct a mass formation. This allowed us to spend time and speak with a group of soldiers or key individuals like Glancy who were instrumental to our mission. We always took photos, and recipients drew the coins at random from a bag. The random aspect was important. It indicated that no individual was more important than any other. It reinforced our leadership philosophy that everyone had a position to play on the team, and all positions were important.

Rodney held the bag for Mike Glancy. He reached in and drew out his coin. "Number three. Wow," he said and beamed.

Cassidy Eves took photos. Barney the dog sat nearby.

"I'm really proud of you," I said and shook his hand.

"Thanks, sir. It's been an honor to serve with you again. Maybe we'll get the chance again down the road."

"You never know." I laughed. "Never thought back in Tikrit we'd be here together in Iraq again. Should've known better."

"Yup," he said. "Keep driving fast without your seatbelt. I'll see you all when you make it back to Germany."

"Be safe. I hope things work out with your assignment when you make it back there."

"It will. Thanks for bringing me on to Task Force Justice. I had a bad taste in my mouth after that last transition team but hanging with you guys rekindled my spirit. Be safe." We exchanged the traditional hug.

SFC Stanfield showed Mike the proper spot to sign the registry. As he always did, Stanfield explained the history of the coin, and that we would attempt to have it displayed in a museum. That way, the task force's legacy and each person's contribution would be remembered in a special way. As one character departed the story of Task Force Justice, we prepared for a new one.

Chapter Six

The General

"There is a remedy for all things except death."

~ Don Quixote De La Mancha,
Miguel de Cervantes Saavedra

"SIR, YOU'RE GONNA love that new Iraqi commander, Mohammed." Sergeant First Class Stanfield dropped into my office for coffee. He acted as my unofficial sergeant major, providing insights into soldier and staff issues in addition to running the Five Star building operations center as the senior noncom.

"Why's that?" I said.

"That guy has his staff giving morning overview briefs at 0800 hours every day. He chews their asses when they move too slow or don't have updates. Kind of reminds me of Colonel Burton." He made the comment with a conspiratorial wink and smile. He knew Burton would give him a hard time if he heard it, but Rodney and the colonel had a special relationship that went back to Burton's days as a battalion commander at Fort Hood, Texas.

"You better watch that stuff, or JB will have your ass," I said.

"Seriously, Mohammed operates like he's going through a mission rehearsal exercise at one of the training centers, and he's up bright and early. I can't think of one Iraqi leader I've seen start the day before 10 a.m. We had to practically drag the previous guy and his staff into meetings that started before noon. This new guy has the staff hopping and popping at 0800. Pretty impressive."

"Maybe I'll come sit in sometime." It wasn't my job to shadow the Iraqi commanders, but I made it a habit to get a sense of what they were like and how they led. I had to be careful not to step on the toes of our transition team leaders. It was their job to shadow the Iraqis. Colonel Pollack, who came in after Tom Felts was killed, seemed to appreciate it anytime I was able to connect with Mohammed.

"You should," Stanfield said. "Plus, I could use the company over there. You know I don't like being out on my own FTX." He routinely commented that the staff guys were alone at the Five Star building. Rodney even adopted a cat. Of course, it was black. The guys named it Buckner.

The operations center was on the Iraqi side of the base. Our guys had to exercise caution in the event we had a green-on-blue incident, code for an Iraqi soldier attempting to kill Americans. The staff, which sometimes could be as few as two or three guys, was more exposed than usual. While in the Five Star building, their weapons had rounds in the chamber at all times. Conditions in the building made for a heightened sense of threat. However, that was balanced by the message sent to our Iraqi colleagues by the American presence and our staff working hand-in-hand with theirs every day. The transition team members also spent a lot of time there.

I first met Brigadier General Mohammed Usaif at an official meet and greet in his office. He replaced the previous commander, Abdullah, who was transferred following an investigation over JAM influence. BG Usaif and I had the standard chai and exchanged pleasantries.

"I served with the division commander in the Special Forces in Ramadi in 2004," he said. "Then I went on to be an instructor at the Special Forces school."

"My operations NCO, SFC Stanfield, has been very impressed with the new battle rhythm you instituted," I said.

"These men have grown lazy. I'm going to get this brigade functioning again." Hassan seemed impressed as he translated. "We have al Qaeda, Jaysh al Mahdi, and many others in this area. We need discipline."

"Let me know how I can assist."

"I will, Miska. Thank you, thank you."

Not long after that first meeting, we were on patrol on the outskirts of Khadamiyah in a place called Adan Square. General Mohammed was at an Iraqi-only meeting in the Green Zone, assuring leaders that the area was safe. Because of threats to the Khadamiyah Shrine from Sunni insurgents and al Qaeda, the Iraqi Army and police had closed entry into the entire neighborhood. The plan established rings of security for the shrine with checkpoints at Adan Square as the first line of defense. Tens of thousands of Shia pilgrims would journey to the shrine during religious holidays. Iraqi Security Forces needed to be efficient in how they searched for bombs and other contraband.

Our patrol pulled up to Adan Square to look around and get a feel for the atmospherics. Brigadier General John Campbell soon arrived. Campbell, the Deputy Commanding General of the First Cavalry Division, would go on to be a four-star and Commanding General of NATO Forces in Afghanistan. I had tremendous respect for him because he often circulated the battlefield to understand the challenges units faced and kept people informed. Few one-stars operated with that freedom of maneuver, so we always appreciated when he stopped by. I jumped out of the up-armored Humvee and walked toward the general as he exited his vehicle. His security team fanned out and looked outward. My patrol operated with a limited number of guys on the ground to ensure that the vehicles were manned with at least a driver and gunner. Three soldiers and Hassan dismounted. Two of our vehicles repositioned on the other side of the general's patrol to provide him with better security.

We shook hands. "You ever spend any time at the headquarters?" I said.

BG Campbell nodded. "I can't figure out what's going on out here from inside headquarters."

We had a rule that we did not salute on patrol. With salutes, snipers could easily determine the leaders and take them out. One brigade commander was shot in the groin while on patrol across the river in the former Sunni stronghold of Ahdamiyah. It was the last place that Saddam Hussein was seen in public prior to his detention and continued to be a kinetic environment.

"Out doing some battlefield circulation, sir?"

"I wanted to see what the Iraqi Security Forces are doing to protect the shrine. The threat stream has picked up a bit for this area."

"The ISF have been freaking out about it for a few days. They seem to have it pretty well under control, though."

Hassan said, "Sir, you can see that they have male and female checkpoints set up. The people must wait longer, but they understand, given the threats." He always provided context that the casual observer could miss.

"The Iraqis rally to the religious symbols fairly well," Campbell said. "How's Dagger Brigade doing? You guys need anything?"

Yet another reason why I liked this general. He didn't expect red carpet treatment when he visited units. He wanted to know what was going on and what support he could provide from higher headquarters. He was a soldier's general.

"Sir, Colonel Burton and Brynt Parmeter have the support pretty wired. The division has been very helpful." I didn't want to be involved with some of the higher headquarters' requests unless specifically asked by Brynt or Burton. That would help keep everything on the same page for our organization. Brynt, along with John Reynolds, the Brigade executive officer, did a great job articulating our needs and tracking deliverables.

"That said, my Iraqi counterpart, BG Usaif, might need some help. He's aggressively going after al Qaeda but also pushing back on Jaysh al Mahdi."

"Sounds like he's not making a lot of friends."

"I think some members of Parliament are starting to lean on him, too."

"Let us know if he needs some top cover down the road."

"Will do," I said.

BG Campbell gazed around at the ISF checkpoints. "I have to hit a couple of more stops and get on a flight to Baquba early in the morning."

"Be careful out there. We need you in this fight."

He shook my hand. "You too, Steve."

As the general drove off, Hassan said, "I like that guy."

"Me too," I said. "He has a good grasp of what's going on." I changed the subject. "Let's talk to whoever looks like they're in charge from the ISF. Might as well make the most of being here."

"That guy over there looks important."

Hassan and I joined an Iraqi Army captain and made small talk. He explained that things were going well and they didn't need our help. We stood close to the female checkpoint. The Iraqi Army had bunkers nearby. From them, two soldiers motioned people into a search area. The soldiers appeared disciplined, had sharp-looking uniforms and clean weapons. They were firm but respectful with people. An elderly woman in a burka yelled at one of the soldiers. He stood his ground but said nothing. The altercation went on for some time.

Hassan burst out laughing as he translated. "She was saying, 'You are all thieves. All the Iraqi Army is a bunch of thieves. I'm not letting you thieves search me and steal my gold.'" Iraqi women collected gold jewelry as a hedge against divorce or abandonment. In the male-dominated society, women had few legal protections against misfortune.

The soldier informed the woman that they had male and female checkpoints, and everyone would be searched. No exceptions.

"I'm not letting you thieves touch me," she said. "I'd rather be searched by the Jew." She pointed toward Saeed, one of our Iraqi interpreters. He looked professional with fatigues, body armor and dark sunglasses. As so often happened on the streets, it was hard to tell who was who.

The woman walked toward Saeed. "I'd rather be searched by the Jew," she said again.

Saeed said, "Lady, I'm not sure what you think, but I am Iraqi. I help the Americans by interpreting for them."

She became so irate, yelling at him with a good dose of Jew-bashing, that her hair came loose from under her *abaya*, the head covering worn by Muslim women. Saeed stood and took her abuse.

As the spectacle grew, the woman's husband arrived. He'd heard the commotion as he waited in the men's search line. He yelled at her. "What are you thinking, woman? Why are you showing your hair so quickly in front of the Jew?" In some conservative Muslim circles, women should not show their hair to men outside the family.

The two carried on as the husband brought her to the Iraqi soldier and convinced her to go through the search lane.

Hassan continued to laugh as he translated. He had me laughing, too. Poor Saeed didn't know what to think and whispered to Hassan how all Iraqis are crazy.

As we mounted the vehicles, Hassan informed the rest of the patrol about Saeed's bravery and heroics in the face of imminent danger.

Journalists coming and going were not unusual during that deployment. They embedded with military units to have access to stories. If they didn't, the risks were extreme. The majority used the U.S. military as their vehicle to get to the story. Dagger Brigade reached out to journalists. We believed all stories, good or bad, helped our mission and kept families back home informed.

Arwa Damon with CNN had Middle Eastern heritage. She was fluent in Arabic, French, English and Turkish, displayed a fearless attitude but acknowledged the risks in a matter-of-fact manner. Between missions, she chain-smoked on the roof patio.

She came to us to pursue a story about threats to interpreters who worked with U.S. forces. Our base was a logical destination, given our proximity to JAM, the Khadamiyah Shrine, and the number of interpreters assigned to us. After the traditional overview I gave all reporters, she interviewed Ronnie and a couple of the others. I also introduced her to BG (Brigadier General) Mohammed Usaif.

"I brought a guest today," I said in the general's office after we exchanged the traditional Arabic greeting. Even though Usaif spoke rudimentary English, Hassan would translate to ensure comprehension.

"Who is this?" Mohammed studied Arwa. She was diminutive in stature and blond, which stood out in Iraq.

"Arwa Damon with CNN," I said.

"Ahhh, CNN," the general said. "That is good. That is good." He had a tendency to repeat himself at the end of his statements, which tailed off as if buying time to contemplate.

We sat and discussed the current tactical situation. Challenges with the militia and al Qaeda, political situations in Iraq, and other subjects. The general was in a dangerous position. He lamented about his family's precarious situation.

"Miska, I can't have my family in hiding forever," he said. "The children will go crazy. I don't know who to trust." He explained that some of the politicians, Basem al-Shammari was one example, supported the militias. Mohammed thought they were encouraging efforts to kill him. His predecessor was ousted because of alleged militia collusion. Mohammed paid the price for attempting to crack down. "Miska, can you help me? I need help."

"I'm not sure what more can be done. I mentioned to General Campbell that you might need some top cover. Arwa is doing a story on interpreters. As you know, everyone working with Americans is at risk due to the militias. If you work with the Iraqi government, you're at risk for an al Qaeda reprisal. We're all taking risks."

"Yes, I know, I know," he said. "But my family, Miska, my family."

The conversation continued over chai. Mohammed was always generous and had a soldier tasked to fill our cups. Hassan spoke about the threats to the interpreters. He brought up the challenges they faced, many of which the Iraqi military knew all too well. Death threats, family intimidation, torture, and worse. We spoke for about an hour and a half. I gave Hassan a look that signaled we should move on. I had another meeting after dinner, and Arwa had planned more interviews.

"Thank you, General Mohammed," I said. "We all need to keep working together. That's the best we can do. Maybe you and I can start conducting combined patrols. That will couple our technical capabilities with your soldiers' ability to read the populace. Maybe we will both be safer that way."

"Yes, yes," the general said. "That sounds good. We should do that." After a pause he said, "I want you to meet someone before you go."

Hassan interceded since we were often ambushed with special requests at the end of meetings, but I motioned that it was okay.

"Please, come this way."

We went to an adjoining room. A young teenage boy sat on a bed playing a video game. He saw us and stood.

"This is my son," Mohammed said. "He came to visit because he misses me."

We shook the young man's hand and exchanged pleasantries. As we departed headquarters, Hassan explained that the general's other children had stayed in hiding with their mother. However, he missed his son and wanted to spend time with him.

"That makes it real, doesn't it?" I said.

"Yeah," Hassan said. "When you're able to see someone in the flesh, you hope that there will be a next time."

As we walked, Arwa absorbed our conversation then said, "It's a shame. Iraq has so much promise but is such a mess."

Hassan said, "There are many good, educated people. There's too much infighting between al Qaeda and the militias. It's very dangerous for average people."

"That's why we need to get the visas," I said. "We can't leave these interpreters here. I'll try to help the general's family too, but we've got to crack the SIV code or all of our interpreters will be dead."

We continued the discussion as we walked to the dining facility. Arwa joined us for dinner before she left to conduct another interview. Afterward, Hassan and I retired to my office and considered whether there was anything we could do to assist the general or his family.

It seemed crazy that the only people who seemed capable of a normal existence had to surround themselves with guns and soldiers. I felt guilty that I shared only some of the risks that Mohammed did. That week I saw my brother, Gene, who served in Special Operations Forces. He was able to spend a night on the base. I'm sure our mom was a wreck with both sons in a combat zone, but we rejoiced at being together for the first time in years. We'd seen each other twice in five years, both times in combat. After his visit, Gene called me to share an idea. He suggested we fly U.S. flags in both Iraq and Afghanistan that we would present to our father, a Vietnam veteran. I liked his idea, yet felt guilty that our families were safe and felt pride in our service while Mohammed's wife and children languished in hiding.

⬮

We first met Basem al-Shammari, a prominent member of Parliament, and a national-level leader, at a Neighborhood Advisory Council, or NAC, meeting. The NAC met every week, bringing key leaders together at the district level. Baghdad was divided into nine districts. Part of our challenge was to make sense of a complicated system, figure out how it was supposed to function, then find a way to operate within that paradigm. However, the situation changed so fast it became impossible to sustain relationships, a fundamental element of an effective counterinsurgency strategy. If we were focused on protecting the population and working through key interlocutors, we needed to initiate and develop relationships with those pivotal leaders.

"I'd rather stab myself in the eye with this pencil than sit through another NAC meeting," I whispered to Hassan as we sat.

"That's Basem over there," he said, and motioned toward the other side of the room.

Basem al-Shammari's brother, Haider, was the lead cleric at the Khadamiyah Shrine, so Basem took an interest in neighborhood issues because of his personal connection, as well as the fact that JAM was active there. Basem had been elected on the Sadrist ballot, which JAM supported as the military wing of the Sadrist party. Khadamiyah, while a local district within the city, had national strategic implications. Basem paid attention to the dynamics, and so did we.

We took a backseat during the NAC meetings. We listened to the discussion and tried to let the locals lead. Basem frowned during that first meeting. He sat on the other side of the room and listened to the conversation, but his face betrayed his skepticism. When the meeting broke, sheiks and other influential leaders swarmed our group and attempted to get my ear. It was the usual attempt to shake me down for money or favors. Basem al-Shammari made a beeline for the door.

Hassan nudged me with an elbow to warn that Basem was leaving. Earlier, I'd let him know I wanted to speak with him.

"Let it go," I said. "He probably feels he can't be seen in public with Americans." To many Iraqis, we were the occupiers and not to be trusted.

Disappointed, Hassan and I left the meeting. I later told General Mohammed about the incident.

"Basem al-Shammari." Mohammed said. "He is nothing. Forget about him."

Several months later, in April 2007, the security situation had deteriorated. Al Qaeda attacks created mayhem. JAM retaliated against

Sunni neighborhoods. The average Iraqi in Baghdad had at least one family member or close friend who'd been killed, kidnapped, or tortured.

We were headed back to base from a patrol on the city's west side. Lieutenant Kronick spoke over our comms system. "Dagger Six Mike, there's a firefight in Khadamiyah."

"What's the status?"

"Delta Company, 1st of the 325 has a platoon in contact. They've been engaged by JAM." Kronick responded.

"Let's monitor the situation and see if we can assist."

"Roger."

As we drove toward Khadamiyah, we learned that the battalion had sent another support element. According to radio reports, about twenty U.S. soldiers were in contact with possibly hundreds of JAM members. The paratroopers of 1-325 Parachute Infantry Regiment were highly trained, however, and JAM fighters were notoriously undisciplined.

As we pulled into Khadamiyah, Kronick said, "Should we go to the scene of the firefight?"

"Has the Iraqi Army sent reinforcements?" I said.

"The unit's been calling for them, but the Iraqis haven't responded."

"Has the unit suffered any casualties?"

"Reports indicate no casualties, but they believe they've inflicted several on the JAM guys," said Kronick.

"We should return to the base and figure out why the Iraqis aren't responding. Having a bunch of our units converging near the Shrine may only inflame the situation."

"Roger, sir. Heading to Justice."

We pulled into FOB Justice and found General Mohammed Usaif at the gate with his boss. As they spoke with each other, it was obvious to me they were nervous. I wondered why they were at the gate rather than in Usaif's office.

I dismounted.

Mohammed said, "Miska, why are the soldiers down near the shrine?"

"Why are your elements not responding to our calls for help?"

Contrary to his usual blustery nature, Mohammed demurred to his boss, a two-star general.

I said, "General, American soldiers had intelligence about a sharia court and went to investigate. Isn't that something you want to stop?"

"Miska, it's not good for Americans to be down near the shrine," Mohammed said. "It gives the JAM guys a reason to get the citizens behind them."

"I understand. But now that the shooting has started, it undermines our partnership if Iraqi soldiers are afraid to join Americans in responding to an unprovoked attack."

"Miska, the people will view this as a provocation. The Americans should not have been there. JAM will be seen as protecting the shrine. You need to call them off."

"General Usaif, I'm not sure what's going on here, but we have a unit in contact. They are greatly outnumbered. The Iraqi Army should go to their assistance. JAM is not a legitimate actor to provide security in the city. That's your responsibility."

BG Usaif looked at the ground, refusing to make eye contact with me.

Hassan gave me a pointed look that indicated it would be best to de-escalate the situation.

"If you're not going to assist my men, I'll go back out there," I said. I signaled to the team to mount up.

Both generals watched as we boarded our vehicles and headed out the gate. I was frustrated. I understood the reluctance of the Iraqi commanders. Sure, JAM was a force to be reckoned with, had a great deal of influence, and they didn't hesitate to employ violence. But those were not reasons for a fighting force to avoid engaging them when necessary.

I directed Lt. Kronick to head to the southern intersection a couple blocks from the firefight. I didn't want to interfere in the unit's situation unless they needed urgent assistance, but we could provide support and block an avenue of reinforcement that caused the enemy to look over their shoulder. It was always risky to drive to a unit in contact. We positioned vehicles at each side of the intersection two blocks south of the firefight. Rounds were fired to the north. Automatic weapons fire interspersed with a steady drumbeat of single shots.

Hassan and I walked to a local storeowner. Two soldiers dismounted to provide security while the gunners scanned from turrets. In a nearby ice cream parlor a lone soul manned the counter. I stepped inside.

"You know what's going on?" I asked him.

The man answered and Hassan translated. He'd heard the shots and remained in the building.

"We'll keep things safe while we're here," I said.

He nodded and returned to sorting his wares.

We stepped to the sidewalk and surveyed the situation. Two blocks to the north, shooting continued. People huddled inside shops and waited for the danger to subside. A thin man with a mustache approached Hassan and spoke to him.

"Hey, boss," Hassan said. "People are asking if they can cross the street."

I looked at the intersection. The street was a funnel for ricochets and possible stray rounds from the firefight. Maybe we could provide a little more cover.

"Tell Kronick to come see me," I said. What I had to tell him required a face-to-face, not a radio conversion everyone could hear.

Brett arrived. He sucked deep heavy breaths from the short dash. I suspected he hadn't been this close to a real firefight.

"I want you to position two of the vehicles in the middle of the intersection," I said. "Gunners should stay low in the turret and only come up if they have identifiable targets. Your vehicles will provide cover so civilians can cross the street and get to their homes."

"Sir?" His look conveyed a reaction he couldn't say out loud.

"We have up-armored vehicles. Small arms fire won't damage them or pose a risk to our soldiers as long as they stay buttoned up. The civilians are scared and need to get home so their families know they're okay. We're going to use our vehicles to provide cover."

The lieutenant was skeptical but saw I was serious. "Yes, sir." He relayed the orders on the radio.

Two Humvees pulled into the intersection, gunners low in the turrets. They rotated the turrets to look north toward the firefight. Our other two vehicles remained out of the ricochet zone. Their gunners faced different avenues of approach.

One by one, or in pairs, civilians made a mad dash across the intersection. For the moment, in that tiny space, we did our best to keep them safe.

When we arrived at FOB Justice, I told the patrol to drop Hassan and me at General Usaif's office. Usaif and I had unfinished business. Woods came with us. I was still frustrated that the Iraqi Army hadn't provided assistance to the paratroopers in contact. The good news: the platoon held its own without sustaining casualties. They believed JAM suffered eight deaths and possibly more wounded, but it was hard to get an accurate count. Militia members dragged the injured and dead away from the scene as reinforcements jumped into the fray.

Hassan and I walked into Usaif's building. I tried to check my emotion. Hassan was always a good presence and helped me stay calm. He cautioned me to be cognizant of how much pressure the general must be under. Mohammed's trusted lieutenant greeted us at the door. When we told him that we wanted to see the general, he grew uneasy.

"Let me see if he is available," the lieutenant said in Arabic.

"He seems a bit nervous," Hassan said.

"Probably because he knows I'm pissed off," I said.

"That's probably it. Maybe the good general won't want to see us."

"We'll see." I was exasperated.

They made us wait, which made my temper worse. The lieutenant returned and motioned us into Mohammed's office. He stood up at his desk. His boss sat in a chair next to Basem al-Shammari. Everything became clear. Mohammed would have ordered some of his troops to reinforce our soldiers in the firefight. However, that would be doubly hard to justify with a Sadrist politician breathing down his neck. The Sadrists controlled the JAM militia and had a sizable block of seats in the Iraqi parliament. Al-Shammari had traveled to FOB Justice to keep Mohammed in a bottle and let the JAM fighters have their way.

Basem al-Shammari was short with a trim, cropped beard. He carried himself with an air of arrogance and self-entitlement, as if he were exceptional being a member of Parliament, as if Parliament itself was fortunate to have his special gifts. In his circles of nationalistic fervor, the American presence was a galling irritation for the country. While none of his cohorts favored Saddam, they resisted any external influence in Iraqi politics.

"Miska, Miska, I'm glad you're here," Mohammed said.

"*Salaam alaikum*, Amid Usaif," I said.

"I believe you know Basem al-Shammari."

"Yes, we attended the Khadamiyah NAC meeting a few weeks ago." I turned toward Basem and stepped to him with my right hand outstretched. He shook it, Western style, then we both turned away as if having smelled something repugnant.

"*Salaam alaikum*." I offered a slight bow to Mohammed's boss. He responded with a nod. We sat. Mohammed's boss, the two-star, said the firefight with JAM was a setback to the good relations we had in Khadamiyah. I listened as Hassan translated, noting that Mohammed remained impassive during his boss's characterization of the events. Basem al-Shammari nodded approval.

"We haven't had good relations," I said. "JAM's been launching EFPs at my patrols. Our engineers come through and sweep the streets, but JAM reseeds right afterward or attacks the engineers. I've had to evacuate wounded soldiers off the streets, and the people of Khadamiyah don't want the violence." Wounded soldiers was an understatement. Soldiers had been killed by the EFPs, but I didn't want to give Basem al-Shammari the satisfaction of knowing his militia thugs had killed our soldiers.

"You are right," Basem al-Shammari said. "The people don't want the violence. If the Americans weren't here, there would be no violence."

"Most of the Americans don't want to be here. We are here because your government can't provide the security your people expect. If you'd eliminate the sectarian nonsense and treat the people fairly, they'd probably judge you better."

Mohammed interrupted and addressed Basem. "The Americans are trying to help us. Why are we not trying to work with them to solve the problems?"

Mohammed's boss gave him an apprehensive look, as if to remind him who Basem was.

Basem al Shammari responded. Hassan whispered the translation in my ear. "The Americans occupied our country illegally and do not belong here. The sooner we retake control of our country, the sooner we will be able to stabilize the situation."

The conversation continued but did not progress beyond that unproductive impasse. I would explain why the current government had no legitimacy in the people's eyes, and Basem would continue to blame the occupation for all of the country's problems.

After an hour of fruitless stalemate, we agreed to adjourn. Hassan remained nonpartisan and objective throughout the entire episode. How had he been able to pull that off?

Basem remained indignant and obstinate. He considered Mohammed a traitor for implying that a partnership with the Americans could be an option. Mohammed's boss fell in the noncommittal camp. He kept his cards close to his chest and attempted not to alienate a powerful member of Parliament while not losing the trust of a close friend.

This marked my first real engagement with a Sadrist member of Parliament. Basem proved to be a worthy adversary on many fronts. He prevented the Iraqi Army from reinforcing an American unit in contact with militia elements. He held his own in an argument about how to proceed. In subsequent days, to my frustration, he got the better of us. He successfully lobbied members of Parliament to prevent U.S. forces from being within one thousand meters of the Khadamiyah Shrine. We stated that we would not allow JAM to dictate the terms of our access anywhere. However, we kept our patrols away from the shrine. Although we won the firefight from a body count perspective, we had lost the strategic narrative. We no longer had freedom of maneuver in Khadamiyah and had to work hard to regain the trust of the people.

It was routine for Brigade patrols to find bodies in northwest Baghdad. Numbers had climbed for several months. Headquarters tracked the statistics. Brynt Parmeter told me units in our sector discovered on average 275 bodies a week. Iraqi Police, Army units, and citizens also reported hundreds of bodies. The morgues piled up with bodies as family members attempted the often impossible task of identification. Even that process became perilous in JAM infested areas. Rumors abounded that the militia had spies watch the morgues to identify other family members for purposes of extortion or worse. People sent proxies to identify bodies to prevent the disappearance of more relatives. CNN had characterized January 2007 as the "Month of Mayhem." In the months to follow, it grew worse.

One day Hassan slipped into my office. As usual, he waited for me to finish typing an email. My ten-year-old daughter Heather and I played a game of *Guess Who* via email. Each player eliminated choices in order to guess their opponent's character. I typed an email telling her how proud I was of her.

"Hey boss," Hassan said. "Some of the interpreters are coming back with pretty bad stories. Their families are finding bodies with drill holes in the knees and elbows and temples. They're speaking with people who hear screams all night long."

"What do they think is going on?" I said, although I suspected the answer.

"More JAM torture houses in some of the neighborhoods where our patrols don't go. They capture Sunnis and torture them with power drills and chains and other gruesome things. Then they dump the bodies in the street before dawn, so the families find them." Hassan was close to our local interpreters. In many cases he acted as their confidant. They told him things about their families, friends, and struggles. His duties as the godfather of the interpreters tested his emotional stamina.

"How are you doing?"

"Ohhh, I'm okay, boss. I'm trying to keep the boys and our interpreters focused on the importance of their mission, you know? When I pay attention to others, it helps me not worry about myself so much. How are you doing?" Hassan always looked out for me, too, as part of his fatherly orbit.

"You know me. I like to drive fast without my seatbelt on."

He laughed. "That's what I'm worried about. You concentrate on the mission and everyone else and forget about yourself. You need to get more sleep. You're no good to the team if you're exhausted."

"Okay, Dad," I said. "But will you check on the TAC and make sure they're ready to head out tomorrow? We're supposed to go to a meeting at COP Casino."

"Gather at 1330, right?" Hassan always double-checked details. Redundant communications were critical during complex military operations. They helped avoid simple misunderstandings that could get people killed, especially when soldiers and leaders were fatigued.

"Correct. 1330 internal patrol brief."

"Roger. I'll see what the boys are up to and let you know."

About an hour later Hassan returned. "The patrol is almost ready to go. It's got the latest intel on torture houses, IEDs, and other threats. And we got another bit of information you might want to know. Nalah is back from Syria. She attended her dad's funeral. She's hoping to speak with you."

Nalah was one of the older interpreters. She was fiftyish, heavyset, with dark long hair. Female interpreters were rare. Nalah had been with us for some time and had taken a couple of weeks to travel to Syria after her father's death.

Hassan motioned into the hallway. Nalah entered my office.

"Hello, sir," she said. "Thank you for being willing to speak with me."

"Anytime." I wanted to put her at ease. Many of our interpreters expressed nervousness when they came to speak with me. "I was very sorry to hear about your father. Please accept my condolences."

"Thank you. Our family had been expecting it for quite some time. He was sick and wasn't exactly getting the best medical care."

"Did your children or other family members attend the funeral?"

"A couple of the kids did. They live there now, so it was easy for them. Many who are here in Baghdad were not able to be there. We thought about bringing him back here, but he told me he did not want to return. He couldn't believe what was occurring, so he decided to be buried in Syria. Plus, he didn't want to put the family at risk. I flew in and out of BIAP. When I got back, I had to take two different taxis to get to FOB Justice." Even our interpreters used military acronyms like BIAP, which stood for Baghdad International Airport.

"It's good to have you back safe with us, Nalah."

She paused, looking at the floor. I was still puzzled about why she wanted to speak with me. As soon as she left, Hassan adopted a patient, fatherlike air. It was routine for him to interpret meanings that were culturally elusive.

"What she didn't say, boss, is that she got out of the first taxi, walked through a building and immediately jumped in a different taxi heading in a different direction. It's like a James Bond movie. People have to take multiple taxis to cross the city without being killed. It's crazy."

Hassan laughed at the absurdity of it. Then he railed against the brutality of the militias and insurgents, and the general preposterousness of the situation we confronted. How could our politicians and leaders make the case that we were attempting to create a normal environment? The situation that confronted the average Iraqi on the street was anything but normal. The months of mayhem continued to play out during the first half of 2007. Later, in the summer, fundamental changes began.

Chapter Seven

Celebratory Gunfire

*"Some people think that football is a matter of
life and death. I don't like that attitude. I can
assure them it is much more serious than that."*

~ Bill Shankly, Scottish Football (Soccer) Player

My PATROL PICKED up a CNN crew in late July 2007. We met them at their guarded bureau in downtown Baghdad. Arwa Damon joined us for another embed for a couple of days. It was her second time with Task Force Justice and the third CNN crew to cover us. She planned to broadcast our celebration of the Iraqi national soccer team's improbable appearance in the Asia Cup championship game. Damon's coverage was projected to be a good news story. So we hoped.

The years 2006 and 2007 would be the bloodiest of the Iraq conflict. They exceeded even the levels of violence achieved by ISIS when they shocked the world with the overthrow of Mosul in 2014. According to the Iraq Body Count database, more than 29,000 civilians died in 2006 and about 26,000 in 2007. To put that in context, during those two years the same number of Iraqi noncombatants died as American soldiers who were lost during the entire Vietnam conflict. During that carnage, a small band of soccer players began an amazing journey that galvanized their country, if just for a moment.

The Iraqi soccer team, composed of Sunnis, Shias, and Kurds, had progressed through the Asia Cup championship to the final round. They were a Cinderella story, heavy underdogs not expected to make the playoffs. The fact that players from the country's rival factions played on the same side ignited the ire of al Qaeda in Iraq. Practices were held outside of the country due to violence and death threats. The team lost their physician, killed by a suicide bomber while he attempted to pick up his airline tickets. Every player knew someone who had been killed or kidnapped. The team experienced a hard time just obtaining passports. On top of that, they were poorly funded. As the team departed for the tournament, each player had just one jersey.

The semi-final game against the South Koreans was a nail biter: Nil–nil at the end of regulation play. The game went into penalty kicks to determine the winner. Fans everywhere sat on the edge of their seats, but in Iraq, a country devastated by violence, people pinned their hopes on the unified team. The Iraqis defeated a heavily favored South Korean team. They won, four to three in penalty shots, and advanced to the finals. At the game's conclusion, joyful Iraqi fans took to the streets.

Al Qaeda struck quickly. A suicide bomber attacked a party of celebrating Iraqis, killing more than fifty people. As the team watched the reprisal on international television, many of the players were devastated. Their improbable wins only seemed to create more violence. People were killed because they represented a unified Iraq.

British sports commentator James Montague summed it up this way: "When they won a game, crowds would celebrate on the streets in Baghdad; suicide bombers would target them leaving hundreds dead. Players wanted to stop playing and the semi-final versus South Korea was worse. They watched the aftermath and the celebrations in the dressing room after the game. There were fifty dead. But the grieving mother of a young boy who was killed pleaded with the cameraman that they should win it for her son."

Led by Brazilian manager Jorvan Vieira, who'd been in charge for only two months, the team held a meeting to decide whether or not to withdraw before the final match. Every player expressed remorse that

Iraqis were killed each time they won. In the end, they decided to play. The grieving mother carried the day. Some players said she refused to bury her dead son until the team brought home the trophy. The inspirational play of a united team ignited waves of hope throughout the country.

Task Force Justice had several contingencies for the big game. We would broadcast over all command networks when the Iraqi team scored a goal. That had become a standard operating procedure as the team progressed through the tournament. With each goal, Iraqis took to the streets and fired their weapons into the air to celebrate. While the "big sky, little bullet" idea sounds okay in theory, what goes up must come down. All those bullets had to land. Some reports cited civilian casualties from falling bullets. Coalition forces directed all soldiers to take cover each time the team scored, and at the game's final moment. Worse than falling bullets, we expected suicide strikes and other atrocities during or after the final match. Intelligence indicated that al Qaeda planned to conduct an attack to coincide with expected celebrations, regardless of the outcome of the game.

Heavy underdogs, the Iraqis prepared for the final match against Saudi Arabia, which had been to the Asia Cup finals five of the last six times. The Saudis won three of the contests. In the 2007 tournament, they scored twelve goals on their way to the final game, more than any other team.

Arwa Damon set up her crew on our rooftop café. We had upgraded the facility in anticipation of more events. We added restaurant-style tables and chairs and a couch near a big screen television. The TV would be the center of attention while Arwa interviewed Iraqis about the excitement.

The ambience on the rooftop was electric. Iraqis wore team jerseys. They painted their faces with the colors of the flag. They gave some of the Americans jerseys to wear. Chai, Rip It, an energy drink common in the military, and smoothies flowed. All eyes were glued to the TV. Each time Iraq took a shot on goal, people screamed and jumped or winced. They clenched their fists as if grasping an elusive victory.

The Iraqi players outshot the Saudis but couldn't get the ball between the goalposts. The first half ended 0-0. Everyone celebrated at halftime. A tied game left hope that the team could perform a miracle. Then, with less than twenty minutes remaining in official play, our world erupted when a corner kick found the team captain, Younis Mahmoud, open for a header that whizzed past the Saudi goalkeeper. Iraqis and Americans launched from their seats, danced for joy and jumped up and down. If someone had held a lightbulb in the air, it would have lit from the energy.

Arwa was broadcasting live when one of our interpreters draped an Iraqi flag over her shoulders. She continued to broadcast interviews with ecstatic fans and didn't remove the flag. Later, her bosses in the U.S. reprimanded her for leaving it in place, citing it as a show of partiality improper for a journalist.

The celebration had just begun. As the final minutes wound down, every Saudi shot and near miss found the crowd on the edge of their seats. They held their breath and bit their nails. When the game ended, Baghdad erupted with celebratory gunfire. Iraqis kissed each other. They kissed Americans. They jumped and danced and took photos. The exhilaration lasted almost an hour. As the excitement on the rooftop wound down, we decided to patrol downtown and check on conditions in Khadamiyah. The intelligence reports deemed attacks probable. A presence on the streets gave us a faster reaction time should anything happen. CNN went with us. The streets were so crowded that our up-armored vehicles couldn't move. We dismounted and waded into the enthusiastic throngs of people. Everywhere, Iraqis celebrated.

We were on high alert. Insurgents had targeted the celebrations during previous victories however, it was difficult not to get swept up in the enthusiasm and symbolism of the win. Football fervor infected everyone. The people of Iraq had suffered so much, everyone needed the triumph. It was a glimmer of hope they could clutch in a very dark time. One observer, Hassanin Mubarak, later wrote, "Eleven footballers, just ordinary individuals had done what the whole Iraqi parliament could not do, unite a nation and bring smiles on people's faces instead of tears and suffering. The Iraq national team has succeeded where politics has failed."

We waded through the hordes of people. Many sprayed aerosol cans of silly string over the revelers. Every so often, the crowd parted to allow parades of small cars through. Horns honked. People waved Iraqi flags out of windows. Eyes were filled with happiness. For a moment, thoughts of sectarian violence subsided. The players who represented the major sects of Iraqi society inspired the nation to look beyond the messages of despair that insurgents and militias broadcast every hour of every day.

Later, Arwa joined us after finishing a cigarette on the back patio where we were drinking chai. "You think it was all an illusion?" she said.

"Feels that way," I said. "We still haven't figured out how to get an interpreter a visa. Maybe the soccer match was a good omen."

"What about the general and his family?"

"Haven't made any progress. Our brigade ran it all the way up to General Petraeus and Ambassador Crocker. Nobody has a legal solution." Crocker had championed expansion of the SIV legislation that allowed interpreters to immigrate to the U.S. If he didn't have a solution for Mohammed, nobody did.

"Looks like we might be screwed," Hassan said. "I feel bad for the general's kids. No school. Staying cooped up all day long."

I thought about my own kids back in Germany, the idyllic life they lived. How could Iraqi leaders not see the damage they inflicted on everybody because they were unwilling to find ways to bring different parties to the table? Where was the common ground? It seemed so obvious yet elusive. I would leave for R&R the next day to spend a much-needed two weeks with the family back in Germany.

I inhaled Amy's scent as sweat beaded on my forehead. Her hand rested on my shoulder. It gently imparted her spirit, her energy. I opened my eyes.

Dog tags hung from a rifle stuck muzzle down in the ground. A helmet rested on the stock. On one knee, I bowed my head and reached for the steel tag. The name Palermo was engraved on it. I felt the letters press against my thumb. Two other tags dangled from rifles: Specialist Ryan S. Dallam and Private Damien Lopez Rodriguez. Sobs echoed throughout the chapel. My knees turned to rubber, as if I were back at West Point in plebe boxing in the ring against a mauler. Could I stand up?

Somewhere deep down, I reached for the mask of command, the mask that allowed a human to perform in public, on stage, as a commander in the community. I rose and reached for Amy's hand. I avoided the tears in her eyes as we departed the chapel. Soldiers in fatigues lined the walls. Military family members packed the pews. Emotion spilled out of the building. Amy peeled off and sat with the widow, Captain Kristy Palermo, eight-and-a-half months pregnant. The same rank as her deceased husband, a status that didn't shield her from gut-wrenching grief. Kristy's mother, in town for the birth, held her daughter. My wife embraced the expectant mother and new widow.

I stepped into the cool spring air of Schweinfurt, Germany. I thanked the soldiers in the firing squad and the first sergeant who had the unenviable task of calling the final roll call. After the eulogies and final chaplain remarks, the first sergeant stood in the back of the chapel.

"Captain Palermo." He shouted, then paused.

"Captain Anthony Palermo." The second pause filled the chapel with muffled sobbing. One more time, "Captain Anthony Palermo, Jr."

Three rifle volleys fired. A bugler performed the lonely strain of "Taps," a tune engraved in the psyches of all servicemembers. Tears flowed.

These soldiers had a tougher mission than I. Many of them were injured from combat or unable to deploy due to other medical reasons. The rear detachment, as the Army called it, provided invaluable service to our families, the wounded, and local authorities. They performed casualty notification when soldiers fell, wounded or dead. They provided as much information as they could to anxious family members. They interfaced with local agencies, schools, and the German authorities. They honored the fallen during memorial services. No, they didn't face the dangers that soldiers in Baghdad confronted, but I wouldn't trade positions with them. In combat I checked my emotions at the gate as we headed on patrol, no matter how many memorials we attended. In combat, we packed our emotions in a footlocker and threw them in the trunks of our armored vehicles. We rarely let those demons surface. In Schweinfurt, with widows and wounded, people wore anxiety, dread, and fear like everyday clothing. The uncertainty created an astounding tension.

In the garrison, there was time to ask questions such as, "Why him?" In Baghdad, leaders had no time for that. Too many soldiers depended on solid leadership and sound minds focused on the problems that stared back at us, right then and there. Problems that could not be avoided. If I let my mind wander, more soldiers would have ended up in body bags. I had to get back to FOB Justice.

Chapter Eight

Next Stop on the Underground Railroad, Amman

"Yossarian was moved very deeply by the absolute simplicity of this clause of Catch-22 and let out a respectful whistle. 'That's some catch, that Catch-22,' he observed. 'It's the best there is,' Doc Daneeka agreed."

~ Joseph Heller, *Catch-22*

RETURNING FROM PATROL, Hassan and I walked on FOB Justice. It was our habit to discuss city dynamics, major personalities, and sometimes family matters when we caught time together.

"Iraqis can't stop talking about the soccer match a couple weeks ago," he said.

"I think it was the most exciting athletic event I've ever seen. And I've been to a bunch of Army-Navy games."

"I've never been to one of those, but that game against the Saudis was sure something else. And the Iraqis were ecstatic that we held the party so they could watch the game."

"It was fun." I saw Captain Eddie Vargas near the entrance to a building, waiting for us.

"You have a minute, sir?" He said with a thick Hispanic accent.

"Shoot."

"George's visa got approved for his final interview at the Embassy," Eddie said.

"Hey, that's great." I responded uncharacteristically optimistic. Maybe the R&R had rejuvenated me."

"Except now there's another issue. Embassy Baghdad has closed its doors to Iraqis. He has to go to Amman for the final interview in the process."

"What?" Hassan said. "How are they gonna get there? The Jordanians have sealed the border because of the refugee crisis. And the road through Anbar Province is a deathtrap. Even Sunnis wouldn't try to drive through."

"Exactly," Eddie said. "We'll figure this out for George, sir. I want to help him, even though I don't want to lose him. He's great, but I know that going to the States is his best option. Now, we need an excuse to get him into Jordan."

"Our bureaucracy is amazing." Hassan's tone was sardonic. "Just when we think we have it figured out, they throw a catch-22 in the system."

"Call brigade," I said. "This is fucking ridiculous. We need answers."

George was the contractor who led the remodeling effort on the Five Star building. He'd been working on FOB Justice for the past twenty-six months when he received word of his visa interview.

Initially, when George's military sponsor told him the team had secured a general officer letter of recommendation on his behalf, he was elated. That part of the process had seemed elusive to local nationals who rarely met senior officers. George's excitement about the letter soon dissolved into disillusionment when he heard gossip that only fifty interpreters would gain acceptance through the SIV program. He knew the Americans had hired hundreds and probably thousands to support the war effort. When George received an email that stated he was approved for an interview, he felt he'd won the lottery. Then, skepticism crept back.

He still had to travel to Amman, but the Task Force Justice staff had so far kept all their promises. Major McCormick sought out and secured the general officer letter. Captain Eddie Vargas took up George's cause when McCormick's team transitioned out. Sergeant First Class Brown had finally guided a successful SIV packet through the byzantine process. It took three months and many painful phone calls, but George had been approved for the final interview. He also went through more background checks, something each contractor did every six months anyway. Given the sensitivity of our mission and what the interpreters were asked to do, it made good sense to have our counterintelligence teams keep close tabs. Adversaries were numerous, patient and innovative. They waited for any opportunity, probed perceived weaknesses, and worked the asymmetric seams where they could gain advantage.

George also had a sponsor in the United States who would help him adjust were he lucky enough to get to Amman and pass the interview. Other interpreters wondered when they would find out their status. Some questioned whether they should have applied for the SIV at all. Most expressed excitement that George's case proved the program was real. Rumors ran rampant in Baghdad. It was often difficult for interpreters to parse authentic information. Sometimes the militia, which always worked to undermine U.S. legitimacy, insinuated that promises of visas was yet another way for Americans to string along Iraqi partners. George's approval made the interpreter dream a hopeful reality. He was, however, far from out of the woods.

First, George needed to navigate Baghdad International Airport. Credible rumors of JAM infiltration persisted. He might not even make it to the airport if the wrong ears heard about his pending departure. And if he got on the plane, would the Jordanians let him enter? Many risks and uncertainties remained, but Task Force Justice was closer than ever to saving one person.

George decided to call his younger brother. "When is the family getting together again?" This was code indicating he wanted to meet. They set a date without discussion of a location.

After dark two days later, Ronnie drove George out of FOB Justice. "I'm really excited for you."

George was anxious. "I'm gonna miss you and everyone."

"Tell me where to go."

"Straight through Khadamiyah." They trusted each other with their lives but knew not to ask questions that could get them killed if separated. If Ronnie didn't know where George was, he couldn't confess the fact to the militia if kidnapped.

"We're only going a little more than a klick," George said. "I'll jump out near Adan Square." Klick was military slang for kilometer.

"Roger," Ronnie said. They were a couple of minutes out. He was on high alert.

George scanned the streets for known militia members or other trouble. "Pull over there." He pointed at an intersection near a dark alley.

Ronnie stopped. "Be careful." He checked the rearview mirror. "Seems clear."

"I'll be back in a couple of days for the ceremony," George said. "I'll text for pickup."

Ronnie hugged him. George jumped out, glancing at three men smoking a hookah and drinking chai in a nearby café, and ducked into the alley. He stopped in the shadows and allowed his eyes to adjust then passed through to the next street. He saw a familiar car whose headlights suddenly switched on. He walked to the sedan, opened the passenger door and slid in. "Good to see you, brother."

"Time to surprise the family," his brother said. George smiled.

His brother navigated twisty backroads toward their sister's house. George's brother lived at home with his parents, wife, and young son. Their sister had moved and lived with her husband's family in another neighborhood.

They stopped in front of a walled house. George stepped out and opened the gate. He walked to the house and entered. He caused a sensation since the family hadn't expected him. They believed he was on a business trip. The celebration lasted forty-eight hours. He never ventured outside the entire time. George gifted his car to his brother and gave his parents a sum of money that would pay for the haj to Mecca, something they'd always dreamed about. He felt as if he'd unmoored a boat and was ready to cast off into unfamiliar, dangerous waters.

After months of cutting through endless bureaucratic red tape, the Task Force Justice staff experienced its first SIV success. We made a big deal out of it. We knew how to throw a party. We decided to host a ceremony the following week to honor our Iraqi associates. As we neared the date for the "Underground Railroad" ceremony, interpreter excitement built. as did the staff's. Many were junior officers or NCOs with little staff experience. George's SIV approval was a big win for them, as well as for our Iraqi colleagues.

Hassan came by my office with a cup of chai. "Hey boss, I thought you could use this." As he set the cup on my desk, he said, "Interpreter morale has gone way up. You can see hope in their eyes."

"Yeah, it's pretty cool," I said. "After the losses we took earlier in the year, this is a nice win. But we aren't there yet. George has to get to Amman and pass the final interview."

"Our guys are surprised you're hosting a ceremony in their honor. Nobody's done stuff like that for them before."

"We couldn't perform our mission without them. They're our cultural eyes, ears, and mouthpieces."

On the day of the ceremony, anticipation was palpable. Eddie Vargas was excited but regretted that his most trusted partner would soon depart. He had a plan for a backup contractor. George had worked it out, of course. However, Eddie and George had to keep the plan secret until after he departed for Amman. If the militia found out, they would certainly target George and his family.

We held the ceremony in the Task Force Justice conference room. Some of the team had remodeled it early in the deployment. It served as our central meeting location. We hosted the ceremony inside, rather than the traditional outdoor military ceremony, to keep it hidden from prying eyes. It allowed us to invite some of the transition teams, the dozens of interpreters, and Task Force Justice staff.

At one point in the ceremony, I looked at George. He was beaming. His normal demeanor was subdued and professional, but the occasion awakened something deep and vibrant in him. He was close to realizing his dream of a new life. I wondered how many threats he had survived and how his outlook might have become jaded as the security situation degenerated. On that day he could hope again. He still had to make it through Baghdad Airport, fly to Jordan, clear passport control and pass the embassy interview, but he was closer to escaping the violence than any other Justice interpreter.

First Sergeant Tony Pryor and I exchanged looks and a thumbs up.

"Listen up," the First Sergeant said over the rumble of the crowd, standing around in groups. Soldiers not on duty or who worked with George attended, as did transition team members and interpreters who were chattering and smiling.

Eddie Vargas spoke first. "It means a lot to us that you would take time to be here and wish George farewell." Eddie displayed a certificate and choked up.

I joined him and said, "Before we do this, I want to let everyone know that Major Stetson just came out on the lieutenant colonel's list. Everybody give him a round of applause." People clapped and hollered congratulations. Some of the staff shook his hand.

Teasing, I said, "Lord knows we need more senior ranking people around here. And he's already starting to act like a lieutenant colonel since we had to wait on him to get here before we could start." The soldiers chuckled. "This is an important time. I'd like to take a moment to talk about, not just George, but all of our Iraqi partners." I walked to George and placed a hand on his shoulder. "You represent them, and you are a pioneer for many who hope to follow in your footsteps." George bowed his head, humbled, then returned his gaze to mine.

"The United States was created by a group of people who fled Europe because they were being persecuted. Many of the Iraqis allied with us find themselves in a similar situation. They are sought by militias, Shia extremists as well as Sunni takfiri or terrorist outsiders. You can't say enough about their patriotism because in many cases their work also exposes their families to danger. Unlike us. We're somewhat insulated here. Our families are in Germany or the States. But our Iraqi allies end up living in shadows to protect their families and help us. They don't tell people where they live. Sometimes they don't even tell their families what they do. They can only share that information with the most trusted people in their lives, and even then, it's dangerous as hell because somebody might slip up and endanger themselves and others. So, what they do requires the highest form of courage."

I looked at George. "And our whole task force appreciates that. It's only right that we should help you in your quest to lead a safe, secure life. You are a pioneer for us from Task Force Justice, so I'm going to ask you to do a little bit more. You've got to stay in touch with us and let us know what kind of frictions and frustrations you run into. How you get into Jordan and get to the embassy and what kind of challenges arise. Because if we're not working to help our policymakers, this will fail.

"That's why CNN was here the other day. Of course, they wanted to be here for the soccer game because that was a hell of a lot of fun. But they also came here to tell a compelling story of immigration. They're going to come back and keep reporting about it. It's not about making a big deal out of George or anybody else. It's to expose policy shortcomings to force those who make policy to do the right thing and keep the energy and attention on this issue. I stay connected with a whole lot of folks who are interested in this in the U.S., Europe, wherever, and they want to know how we can help you. So, we need to know how things go and where you run into problems."

I motioned to George. "We might not be able to fix the new problems you encounter, but we can shed light on them in a way that gets other people to fix 'em. That's the way you get policy shaped in this world. Now is it my job to do that? Probably not. I mean Miska, he's some lieutenant colonel who got sent out here to try to take care of transition teams and stuff. But it is my responsibility as a leader, and I refuse to underestimate my ability to impact those around me. That's why I found the guys who built that lounge upstairs. You can make a difference. Everybody in this room can make a difference. A lot of people sell themselves short in this world. If you sell yourself short, you underestimate the impact you have on others. So, I would ask you to look around, and look at the things that you can help change. I believe that George and I can help change U.S. policy.

"He and I can do it together, with some help from you guys. It just takes putting your mind to it and having the will and the courage to go through with it. So that's what we're going to try and do. George is going to be our pioneer. Do you know who Davey Crockett was or Daniel Boone?"

George smiled and shook his head. "No, sir."

"They were pioneers way back when, walking through the woods in harsh country. They ran into pitfalls. And when you do, you figure out how to get around obstacles and bypass the naysayers. A lot of pitfalls are just the bureaucrats stuck in their own small-minded world. They don't want people to rock the boat because it might make more work for them. They don't want to be forced out of their comfort zone. Don't be a bureaucrat and don't let the bureaucrats stop you. I tell my guys don't accept the first 'no' and after you get seven 'no's,' elevate it to the next level. Continue to bypass and then everyone will make up stories about how we got on the phone with Condoleezza Rice and got your problem solved.

"I'm very proud of you," I said to George. "I'm proud of all of the work you've done here. I know all of your colleagues are proud of you as well. We want to recognize you with this certificate for everything you've done, not just for this task force, but for your country."

Captain Vargas displayed the certificate. "From Task Force Justice, a certificate of appreciation."

George held the other side of the framed document as I read the text. "Presented to George from Task Force Justice, Second Brigade Combat Team, Dagger. The soldiers of Task Force Justice would like to thank you for your service as a linguist for the Combined Operations and Intelligence Center and the time and effort you expend to make our lives more comfortable every day. We appreciate all the hard work you have done in support of the global war on terrorism and for your part in making Iraq a safer place for future generations. Best of luck in all you do in your future endeavors. Congratulations."

We shook hands and smiled. George and I each held a side of the picture frame and faced the cameras for photos. Applause and cheers exploded. Many interpreters huddled together and yelled. Some stood shoulder-to-shoulder with their American counterparts bolstered in the confidence that their foreign friends would stand by them.

"The floor is yours." I nodded to George and stepped away.

George cleared his throat and wiped his eyes with a knuckle. "First, I want to thank everybody here. It is nice to know that you are here to support me. It's very hard to leave Iraq. You know that you are not coming back, and you have to start somewhere else. It is as the colonel suggests. All the difficulties, my colleagues here—" He pointed at the crowd. "They might take advantage of that. I want to tell you guys, that as one of the Iraqi people who had a chance to prove that we want an opportunity to make a better country, I've been working for the U.S. forces for four years. There are a lot of fellow Iraqis who didn't have a chance like that, to work and to actually apply themselves. So, I want to say that a lot of good people outside the wire, they really appreciate what you guys do for them. They appreciate your sacrifices, dedication and hard work." More loud applause and cheers.

An NCO from the Viper team, a military transition team partnered with the Iraqi Army brigade on FOB Justice, presented George with a gift. After that, several officers awarded George gag gifts that included a pack of cigarettes, a box of condoms and a SpongeBob doll. One officer, who hadn't heard about the ceremony, took off his rank and Velcroed it on George's uniform. The officer re-claimed the insignia when the celebration finished, but George laughed about the photos with him wearing U.S. Army captain's rank.

"This is a big deal," I said to the new Lieutenant Colonel Eric Stetson.

"We've finally cracked the code on the red tape," he said.

"We're not done. We've got dozens of others in the pipeline, and George still has to make it to Jordan. If he survives the trip and gets to the embassy, he still needs to pass the final interview and then make it to the States. He's got a sponsor waiting for him in Phoenix, so the final step is taken care of if he makes it."

Eric noted that a female soldier with a previous transition team based at Justice had agreed to sponsor George. She had rotated back to the States and was back home at her normal job but was ready to receive George when he arrived. Army Staff Sergeant Laurie Miller would start a trend, the first of many courageous women who stepped up at the last station of the Underground Railroad. That last stop, in the United States of America, proved to be more daunting than most Iraqis could imagine. There were numerous and onerous assimilation challenges, even for people with command of the language. Most Iraqis had no credit history, few resources, and a Hollywood image of life in the U.S.

The day after George's ceremony, another interpreter, Gary, was approved for his final interview. George and Gary decided to travel to Amman together. Ronnie drove them to a rendezvous point a mile away from FOB Justice early in the morning to avoid prying eyes. They still scanned the streets for possible threats, notably from JAM, as they drove.

George indicated a spot in the middle of a block, and Ronnie stopped. The three said discreet goodbyes. George and Gary exited the car, met George's younger brother and drove to the airport. Escaping the capital was no easy feat. JAM had infiltrated many agencies, including the airport. However, risking discovery at BIAP was a better alternative than driving the highway of death from Baghdad to Jordan through Anbar Province. The road was controlled by insurgents and al Qaeda. The chances of reaching the border unscathed were slim.

George and Gary drove along Route Irish, the main artery from the Green Zone to the airport. Heavy security along the highway was a slight comfort. They thought it was unlikely they'd be stopped at an illicit checkpoint although the National Police were infiltrated and subverted by JAM.

George gazed out the window at the Baghdad cityscape. At regular intervals armored vehicles, manned by National Police, sometimes accompanied by Americans, punctuated the scene. He was anxious. His heart fluttered with the realization he might never return. The three men stopped at a security checkpoint outside the airport and exited the vehicle.

"Please tell Mom not to worry about me," George said to his brother. "Now, you be safe and get out of here. This needs to look like a normal goodbye for a routine business trip."

Signs in English and Arabic dotted the exterior of the large passenger screening building. The three exchanged heartfelt hugs and thanks.

George and Gary approached the Iraqi guards stationed at an entrance. The interpreters hid nerves as they looked for any indicators that the guards had JAM affiliation. They presented identification and tickets and watched as their bags were searched.

After the final farewell, Ronnie drove back to FOB Justice, his home for many months. Conflicting emotions roiled his mind. He was excited George and Gary had been selected, but the notion that he would ever make it out of Baghdad seemed fanciful. He didn't want to allow himself to believe he could escape.

A couple blocks ahead, a police officer walked into the street. A police vehicle was parked nearby. Several other policemen with automatic weapons stood on the corners. Twenty minutes earlier no cops had been there. Most Iraqis considered the police corrupt or in bed with JAM.

The officer signaled Ronnie to pull over. He angled the car toward the side of the road. The thought of making a run for it to FOB Justice flashed through his mind. He was less than a couple minutes from the base gate. But he knew that would be a foolish move.

Ronnie stopped the vehicle and suppressed his anxiety. He watched as the policeman sauntered toward him. Everyone knew they accepted bribes and could be bought by the highest bidder. Ronnie noticed two men in civilian clothes who spoke with a couple cops on the side of the road. They glanced his way.

The officer approached. "Morning," Ronnie said through the open window.

"You are up very early," the officer said. "What are you doing here at this hour?"

"Just dropped my friends off at their parent's house, officer." Ronnie didn't want to speak directly about George and Gary but knew they may have been spotted on the way to the drop off point. Ronnie had to acknowledge their presence in his car without divulging the truth.

"Very nice of you. Can you get out of the car?"

Ronnie stepped out. He tried to discern in the officer's eyes his intentions. Civilian men smoked cigarettes and watched from the sidewalk with the other cops.

The officer ordered, "Open your trunk."

Ronnie walked to the rear and obeyed. The policeman pointed, indicating that Ronnie should return to the driver's open door. He poked his rifle barrel in the trunk, then reached in and rummaged through the contents. After what seemed like an hour but was only a minute, he shut the lid. "You are free to go."

Ronnie drove several blocks, turned a corner and found a place to pull over. He opened the trunk and looked for anything suspicious. Iraqi police were known to place contraband in cars then search and extort drivers at the next checkpoint. The last thing Ronnie needed was to reach the base gate, be searched by the Iraqi Army, and be detained for possession of a weapon or drugs.

George and Gary were cleared and entered the terminal building. They scanned faces for people looking for collaborators or easy prey for extortion. Many Iraqis were masters at acting nonchalant although their lives spun in violent turns.

George was dressed in what Americans called business casual. It was his attempt to present an impression of a man of ambition who had yet to attain wealth. Gary wore sporty clothing. They passed ticket counters: Royal Jordanian, Turkish Airlines, and Iraqi Airways. They didn't check any luggage. They carried SIV paperwork, airline tickets, and minimal changes of clothing, which indicated a short business trip.

The previous evening, Gary and George had discussed the many ways things could go wrong.

"I heard the Jordanians are turning Iraqis away at the border. Some who fly get turned around and sent back to Baghdad," said Gary.

"I heard that, too," George said. "We have business at the American embassy. I don't think the Jordanians will do something to anger the Americans."

"That's if we make it to Amman. I heard the Iraqi Ministry of Interior extorts people if they're trying to leave the country, in addition to the JAM kidnappers."

"We've got money if we need to pay off people. The most important thing is to get on that plane."

Gary said, "With our luck, we'll be on the random aircraft shot down like the one four months ago." The conversation seesawed between hope and the macabre.

"We'll make it."

"This is way better than risking the *Highway of Death* through Anbar Province. We'd be killed by insurgents or al Qaeda before we ever made it to Jordan."

"Four months feels like four years in this crazy place. So many ways to die," said George.

"What if we get there and the Americans deny our visas?"

At the airport, neither man spoke with any animation. Except for occasional short bursts under their breath, they attempted to appear determined and professional to anyone watching.

They arrived at the control point for departure gates and shuffled into line. Passengers ahead of them were searched. Gary and George showed their identification and tickets, then stepped forward. Bomb-sniffing dogs checked everything and everyone at the security checkpoint. Some people were pulled aside and hand-scanned. Despite the cooler temperature inside the terminal, both men broke out in a sweat.

Cleared to proceed, George and Gary searched for seats near their departure gate. Popular retail stores packed the terminal, a jarring contrast to what was available to average Baghdad residents.

"Almost there," George said under his breath. They found a couple molded plastic chairs and sat.

Antsy, Gary said, "I'm going to check on the flight." He walked toward the check-in desk and looked at a display of departure times. An hour to wait and they'd be on a flight out of the most dangerous city in the world, their home, where everyone they knew had lost a cousin, child, or close friend.

George struggled to bottle his anxiety. He experienced a complex mix of difficult emotions. The sense of impending loss at the thought of abandoning his family. The longing to escape the eventual torture and death that awaited if he stayed. He'd seen the drill holes in mangled bodies dumped in gutters. The militia dropped corpses in high-traffic areas for maximum visibility. He was convinced that same fate awaited him if he remained in Baghdad. Nearby, two men in business suits smoked cigarettes and eyed him.

Gary returned. "Our plane's been delayed for an hour and half."

"What? Why?"

"They didn't give a reason. *Inshallah*, we'll get out of here." *If God wills it.* The word was said in many ways, similar to the American use of "okay." "Okaaay" could be a threat, a terse acknowledgement, or happy acceptance. As an expression, *inshallah* had a variety of meanings, but Americans often inferred a negative connotation.

George said, "The Americans call Iraq Airways 'Inshallah Airways.'" The joke had taken on new meaning for the two men.

Demoralized, George checked his email. "I have an email from the consulate. My appointment's on August fifteenth." That generated excitement. "Now the Jordanians have to let us in."

"We have to get on that plane," Gary said. He doubted he would because he had no email confirmation.

And they did, only ninety minutes late.

An hour and twenty minutes later, the flight touched down at Queen Alia International Airport. George and Gary lurched forward in their seats as the pilots decelerated the plane. Applause accompanied a muffled announcement, "Welcome to Amman, ladies and gentlemen." George and Gary tried, but failed, to hold back tears.

"Still have to make it through customs," said George. "I don't want to get my hopes up. They could still refuse us entry and put us on a plane back to Baghdad."

"But we're closer now than ever." Gary was still nervous. "It's going to take time to get over the fear of being shot or kidnapped or tortured at any moment."

George scanned the cabin. Iraqis had learned the hard way to be hyper-vigilant and searched for signs of trouble by instinct. He watched the flight attendants run through their final duties. Passengers unbuckled seatbelts and stood. Others smiled, chatted, and gathered carry-on luggage, happy to reach their destination.

Gary and George retrieved their backpacks from the overhead compartment. They fidgeted as they waited, then shuffled off the plane and onto the jetway with the others. Signs in three languages directed them to customs and passport control. Barriers and armed police kept them on track.

They reached the end of a long line. It inched forward as officials examined passports. They were held under a light, then stamped. George hoped they had a lenient customs official. The uniformed officer looked up and cocked his head but said nothing. George and Gary moved forward together.

"What is your business in Jordan?" the agent said.

George said, "We have an appointment at the U.S. embassy." He had an air of confidence, convinced no lowly customs official would dare deny the Americans.

The dour officer looked them up and down then stamped both passports.

They hid their elation as passed through the airport, exited the terminal, and looked for transportation to deliver them into an alluring new city. "I don't even have an appointment yet," Gary said.

"He didn't know that. If he'd asked, I'd have shown him the email and said we were both attending the meeting."

They stepped into warm, late afternoon air. George phoned a friend, an Iraqi who lived with her children in Amman. He had reached out to her weeks ago on the chance that he'd make it to Jordan. She had agreed to help.

"I know a Jordanian who just returned from the U.S." she said. "He was deported and needs the money. He has an apartment in a nice part of town."

George didn't ask why the man had been deported, as if the question might jinx his own chances. He hung up. "We have a place to stay tonight."

The next two weeks, George and Gary enjoyed the freedom of a westernized Arab culture without the threat of violence at every corner. Amman was a city of seven mountains draped with buildings. It teemed with people, more immigrants than Jordanians. The capital thrilled them: the freedom, energy, and Westernized women sometimes unescorted by men. But many Jordanians resented the Iraqis who flooded their country. A major migration of Iraqis in 2004 drove up rental prices. Even taxis cost more. 2006 brought another wave. Prices again rose as fast as a high tide. George and Gary were aware of the looks some Jordanians cast toward them and couldn't set aside their Baghdad baggage of paranoia. They remained alert.

Sitting in a café, sipping tea, Gary said, "I'm still nervous about getting to America. What if they don't give us a visa?"

"Even our landlord got sent home," George said. "Plus, I heard rumors that Jordanian police patrol the refugee parts of the city, asking for papers and harassing people. Some people have been sent back to their countries."

"I saw them the other day when we were out. Even though we don't have to sleep with a gun or worry about illegal checkpoints here, I'm still nervous about getting sent back."

"Me, too. Let's lay low 'til the embassy visit."

A couple days later, Gary received the all-important notice of an embassy appointment.

They wanted to look sharp for their interviews. They had their suits dry cleaned. A day later as they returned to the dry cleaners from their rental, they witnessed two police officers approach a couple on the street. The man was dressed in the dark, tired, wrinkled clothes of someone without money. Baggy slacks, a jacket that had lost its shape, and a shirt that needed to be washed and ironed. The woman wore a burka. George's survival instincts kicked in. He stopped and did his best to hide in a nearby alley. He couldn't suppress habits developed from years of living under false pretenses.

They watched the Jordanian police officer extend his hand to the couple. The man reached into his breast pocket and produced what appeared to be a passport and other papers. The policeman studied the documents. His colleague surveyed the crowd.

George elbowed Gary. "Look like you belong here." They walked past the police and overheard snippets of conversation. The man tried to explain their purpose in Amman. The woman looked at the ground.

Gary and George collected their clean, pressed suits. They paid and checked outside to see if the officers were still there. They breathed a sigh of relief. The police had moved on. They hurried back to the apartment, suits hanging over their shoulders.

The next day, George rose early, showered, and dressed in his fresh suit. He'd tossed and turned all night. He sipped coffee but wasn't hungry. Butterflies fluttered in his stomach, stifling his appetite. Gary wished him luck as George stepped out the door.

In the heart of Amman, he approached the U.S. Embassy, a boxy, three-story, cement block fortress. The exterior perimeter was barricaded and guarded by Jordanian riot police in ballistic vests and visored helmets. Some were on foot, others manned up-armored vehicles.

George arrived forty-five minutes early for his appointment. He wanted to give himself ample time because the Americans maintained extreme security protocols. He showed his paperwork and documents to the Jordanians and was admitted to the compound. He presented everything again to armed U.S. Marine guards. They examined his credentials, frisked him, and then he was permitted to enter the massive building. Though the temperature in Amman was mild, relative to Baghdad, sweat seeped into his shirt under the suit jacket.

In the consular section, George entered an office and smoothed his jacket. "Thank you for seeing me today." He attempted to be casual and matter of fact but felt as if he'd failed.

The unsmiling U.S. Consular Officer said, "Sit," and held out her right hand. "Papers."

"Yes, I have them right here." George removed his paperwork from a folder. His hands trembled. He hoped she didn't notice. Indifferent to or unaware of his nervousness, the woman reviewed his papers. They included recommendations, his base access badge, proof of employment, the letter from the general, and other indications of good conduct. For some of the papers, she asked questions as if attempting to punch holes in a cover story.

After what seemed like an eternity but was probably about three minutes, she said, "You have any other badges to prove you worked for us?"

George was dumbfounded. He stared at her. What did that mean? "No, I only have this one."

She looked him over. "Okay. You can go. We'll send you an email after we make a determination."

"Thank you." George was unsure how to assess the interview. He felt stuck halfway between hope and dejection. "Is there anything else I can provide?"

"We have everything we need," she said and picked up a piece of paper. "Have a nice day."

He left the embassy and replayed every second of the experience in his head. Could he have done something different? Were false allegations made about him to the Americans? That often happened to Iraqis. The "can do" culture of the U.S. military, in particular, made it vulnerable to being used by neighbors to settle old scores.

Gary later shared with George that his embassy visit was similar. Neither man knew if he'd been accepted.

Three weeks passed, an intoxicating time of newfound liberation peppered with bouts of anxiety. They dodged police and never shook the fear of potential rejection. Both George and Gary felt as if they would be killed if they were sent back to Baghdad. After nearly a month of anxious waiting, George's cell phone rang.

"Please visit the embassy to pick up your visa," he was told.

"Gary." He rushed into the kitchen. "They told me to go get my visa."

They yelled and embraced. After the initial elation, George felt a pang of guilt. What if Gary, his friend with whom he had shared tremendous hardship, didn't receive his visa? He knew Gary would tell him to go on to the U.S. He could imagine his friend's words of encouragement, even as he masked disappointment, "Like Miska said, you are a pioneer." George could justify moving on if it was to help the others learn the trials of the underground railroad.

He knew the dangers continued to mount in Baghdad. Other interpreters were in dire straits. They had missions that put them in the crosshairs of the militia and other bad actors.

Chapter Nine

Many Flavors of JAM

"Anyone supported by the United States is cursed by us."

~ Iraqi Cleric Muqtada al Sadr,
leader of the Jaysh al Mahdi (JAM)

MAJOR GREGG HALEY arrived in Baghdad as a team leader for a military transition team, or MTT (pronounced "mitt" in mil-speak), as the Army referred to the training teams. Gregg and his people had gone through a preparation regimen at Fort Riley, Kansas, but no training could have prepared him for the challenge that awaited. His team, nicknamed the "Dingos," was partnered with the 3rd Battalion of the 1st Brigade, 6th Iraqi Army Division.

The entire Iraqi brigade had a reputation for unsavory JAM affiliation and the 3rd Battalion was the most notorious. The previous battalion commander and his intelligence officer had been sacked as part of an investigation into militia influence following the brigade commander's removal.

Brigadier General Mohammed Usaif had been assigned to replace the previous commander and clean house. Yet rumors of JAM influence persisted within the 3rd Battalion. It suffered mass defections after the removal of senior commanders. Most defectors were assumed to be JAM members involved in previous bad acts. One of the acts was rumored to be a conspiracy to kidnap one of its company commanders, a Sunni, who attempted to push back on JAM influence. The disappearance of the Sunni officer triggered an investigation into militia influence.

After the removal of senior members of the chain of command, soldiers refused to appear for work. Some outside the unit accused the commanders of running ghost rolls, meaning they padded the books with names to pocket the extra payroll money. Gregg and his team were brought in to assist the Iraqi battalion and get it into some semblance of a military organization. The task was daunting.

The Dingo Team oversaw the battalion's recruiting efforts and other sensitive operations. Throughout 2006 and into early 2007, the Iraqi Army struggled with recruiting. The pay was substantial, relative to other job possibilities in the local economy, but al Qaeda and other Sunni insurgent groups targeted recruiting sites. Their goal was to delegitimize the government and scare people from enlisting. Suicide bombers struck locations where new recruits were lined up. The terrorists targeted buses that transported new soldiers from recruiting depots to training bases. They blew up the buses or stopped them and assassinated the passengers. For people in the Iraqi military, the danger was constant. To survive, soldiers changed into civilian clothes when off duty, much like the interpreters who worked with the Americans. The environment established ripe conditions for sectarian-based enlistment.

Day one at FOB Justice, Gregg met "Dave," his team's lead interpreter. Dave was tall and thin. His brother and father also worked on the base. Gregg and Dave quickly formed a bond based on shared hardship. Neither realized how important they would become to each other in the months ahead.

Gregg sat with Dave in the team office and said, "What'd you learn today?"

"I went with your intel guy to 3rd Battalion headquarters at the edge of base. Things are bad. The rolls for the battalion are down to about sixty percent. Nobody knows for sure. And Charlie Company is worse. They have maybe twenty percent. And nobody knows where all the weapons are. These guys are thieves."

"This is really dangerous. We're essentially partnered with Jaysh al Mahdi. You sure you're okay to stay with us?" said Gregg. "Don't get me wrong. You're amazing, not just translating but also for the information you provide. But I don't want to see anything happen to you or your family."

"Not to worry. I am doing this for my country. If things get too bad, I'll let you know."

"Deal."

It was routine for Gregg's team to enter situations and not know who they could trust in the Iraqi unit they were assigned to train. JAM had targeted U.S. forces for some time. They used lethal technologies that penetrated up-armored Humvees and one Iranian-backed militia kidnapped two U.S. soldiers. The Dingos were at high risk for those types of attacks.

"Big day tomorrow," Gregg said to Dave. "We're headed to the JAM headquarters. I mean, 3rd Battalion." He smiled. "We'll see if we can't turn this ship around."

Next day, the Dingos assembled in their office and discussed last minute preparations for an operation they had developed over the previous few weeks. In consultation with Dagger Brigade, Gregg planned to implement an inventory and regain accountability of the people and weapons in the Iraqi battalion. Dave joined to hear the details of the mission.

Gregg said, *"Allah Bukhayr."* He'd worked on his Arabic and was eager to show the team that he valued learning the language. He motioned towards an empty chair for Dave to sit. The interpreter gave him a puzzled look but sat and said nothing.

"Alright guys," Gregg said. "We're heading out to regain some control over this situation. The battalion rolls are down and lots of weapons are missing. We need to help the Iraqi Army Brigade rein in this battalion. They've been soft on cracking down because everybody fears reprisal from JAM. We're going to provide some plausible deniability to help the IA brigade."

Some of his people asked questions about how to spot and understand the facts of the situation. Another interpreter, nicknamed Zorro, was also at the meeting.

Dave said, "Zorro and I will keep our ears open and look around, too. We know JAM has guys in this battalion. *Inshallah*, we will figure them out and help you to get the unit back to good."

To Dave, Gregg said, "*Inshallah*." Then addressed the group. "We're gonna give it our best shot. I know we didn't train for anything like this back at Riley, but we're playing the cards we've been dealt. It'll be dangerous, so nobody operates alone. Be disciplined about the buddy system; all of our lives depend on it. And I don't want to have to go to anyone's wife about why you got yourself kidnapped or killed. Don't do that to our team or your families. Now let's kit up and get on over to the vehicles and head to the enemy. I mean, 3rd Battalion headquarters."

"Yes, sir." The guys laughed, but Dave only smiled. He knew it was a joke but couldn't bring himself to laugh with the others.

Gregg and his team drove their vehicles to IA headquarters. Half the team stayed with the Humvees, the rest entered the building with Dave and Zorro. MTT teams were small. They had ten men, the bare minimum needed to man a patrol of four vehicles.

Gregg addressed the new Iraqi battalion commander. "*Salaam alaykum, Sayidi*." He added *Sayidi* to the traditional Islamic greeting. It meant "sir" in Iraqi military jargon. Most of the MTT teams addressed their Iraqi counterparts with the Arabic term of deference.

"Welcome, my friend," the commander said in English.

Gregg explained the purpose of their visit and ended with, "We're here to help." Dave translated. The mission was no surprise. The units had previously coordinated with each other.

"Please, why don't we have some chai," the Iraqi commander said. "It is early in the day. We can start the work soon."

"Maybe a quick cup," Gregg said. He didn't trust this traditional offer of hospitality. Previous visits had been more confrontational. He sensed something wasn't quite right. Dave picked up on Gregg's mood. He was curious.

"Please, please," the Iraqi commander said. "This way. My staff has some chai prepared. We were expecting you."

Gregg and Dave entered the commander's office. Zorro and the intel officer looked around the building.

"Please, everybody is welcome for chai." The commander was insistent.

"That's okay, *Sayidi*," Gregg said. "My guys came ready to work. They know we have a long day ahead of us."

The commander frowned. The group engaged in small talk during the short chai session. Gregg asked operational questions, like requests for new recruits from higher headquarters. The commander gestured fatalistically and said that much of this was out of his control.

"You're in charge, now." Gregg was exasperated with the *inshallah* approach to command, which seemed to him an excuse to shirk responsibility.

"Yes, but these problems began before I arrived at this battalion. You know that I have a very sensitive job."

"We all do. We have to work together to achieve security. If we just throw up our hands, nothing will happen."

"*Inshallah*," the commander said. Dave looked at Gregg. He didn't need to translate that.

As they drank the ritual chai, Gregg's S2, the intel officer, and S4, logistics, examined the battalion arms room with Zorro and the Iraqi armorer. Most of the weapons racks were bare. The armorer claimed that all the soldiers were on duty and had checked out weapons. The intel officer asked to see the sign out logs. He asked basic questions about when soldiers had signed out the weapons, what their missions were, and other inquiries. The armorer hemmed and hawed as if deciding whether to lie or say nothing.

The team personnel officer, commonly referred to as the S1, had a similar experience with his Iraqi counterpart. A check of the rolls revealed that a majority of soldiers received pay, but other indicators demonstrated that the battalion manpower shortage was critical. At the end of the day, the U.S. team returned to base and compared notes.

Gregg was perplexed. "These guys are cooking the books and can't account for more than half of their weapons. What do you think?"

The S2, the intel officer said, "No surprise. We've received consistent reports that the former chain of command sold weapons to JAM for profit. We also know they lost a lot of people when the former leadership was sacked. When those JAM guys got the boot, lower-level guys ran, thinking they were next. We've got a long road ahead with them, and they can't be trusted. We need to take it slow."

A senior NCO said, "And we've got to maintain rigorous discipline to ensure that we don't drop our guard. If we do, these guys could be all over us."

"This keeps getting worse," Gregg said. "We can't trust them, and they're going to read that in our body language every time we're over there."

The senior NCO said, "I'm on my second tour, sir. In my experience, most Iraqis realize, or at least think, that we don't trust them. We carry our weapons with us loaded everywhere. I know some teams drop their guard with units that can be trusted a little more, but that's pretty stupid. Most American units keep their guard up all the time."

"Then we have to keep the pressure on these guys and hope we can turn that unit around. I have some ideas for how we crack that code. Let's meet this evening after I've had a chance to run this stuff by the colonel. Go grab chow."

After most of the team left, Dave approached Gregg and said, "Sir, you said something to me at the start of the meeting last night that confused me. You pointed to a chair and said something."

"Yeah, I said *Allah bukhayr*. That means pull up a chair, right?"

"No, sir." Dave laughed. "It means by the goodness of God."

The senior NCO laughed too. Gregg was a bit confused. "Whenever I greet a sheik or police chief or Iraqi Army leader, they always say that and then welcome me to sit down. I thought it was the equivalent of our saying, pull up a chair."

The three of them laughed about his language skills all the way to dinner. At the table, they sat with other members of the Dingo team and shared the story. *Allah Bukhayr* would become a running joke amongst the Dingos for the remainder of their deployment.

Hassan looked in my office and didn't see me. "Hey boss," he said. "You in here? Somebody wants to chat."

I was on my cot, propped up on a pillow reading Georgina Howell's account of Gertrude Bell called *Queen of the Desert*. My cot was on the side of the room concealed by the door. I closed the book. "What's up, Hassan?"

"Major Haley is here."

I sat up as Gregg entered. "How are you guys doing?" I said.

"Thanks for taking the time, sir."

"My job is to be available, even to you guys from Riley." I smiled.

"But other units don't exactly treat their MTTs that way. Some of them don't give their teams the time of day. Dagger Brigade's been great though, especially Task Force Justice."

"No thanks necessary. What can I do for you?"

Hassan, hovering in the doorway, interrupted. "Boss, can I make you guys some chai?"

"He makes the best," I said.

Gregg said, "Love some. It'll be good to sip chai and not have to wonder if someone's gonna shoot me or try to hit my vehicle with an IED when I leave."

Hassan left the room.

"What's your situation?" The Dingo Team had inherited a tough scenario. The previous team struggled to gain clarity on the infiltrated Iraqi battalion.

"The boys and I went down to the 3rd Battalion headquarters today. We tried to get a handle on it, but it's a lot worse than we thought.

He filled me in on the stats and elaborated for the next ten minutes on the challenges and complete lack of trust his men faced. His team was in a barely tenable situation where the Iraqi soldiers knew the Americans didn't trust them. The charade occurred each day during meetings and attempts to "train" the IA unit.

Hassan returned with chai. He placed a cup in front of me and one in front of Gregg.

"Let's have Hassan sit in. He might have some insight. I always appreciate Old Dog's input," I said.

Gregg said, "We're going to conduct monthly personnel and weapons inventories. I plan to use our biometric equipment to ensure that the IA isn't padding the rolls. At a minimum we'll get the entire battalion added into our dataset to track in case they're JAM."

"Sounds like a good plan," Hassan said. "In order for them to collect pay, they'll need to go through your system."

"It's not foolproof, but it'll make it a lot harder for them to embezzle. The weapons are a whole other deal."

"You mentioned you're a good poker player, right?"

"Yeah, and the boys and I are good at bluffing, but this is a delicate situation. We've got a plan for the weapons if they get more. I heard they might be fielding M-16s soon."

"That's the plan," I said. "I'm not sure I agree with it. I know it's good for defense contracting, but Iraqi Army culture has the AK-47 so ingrained, it seems stupid to push M-16s on them. Plus, they're a lot harder to maintain."

"Whether they get them or not, my guys are working through a scheme to hold the leadership accountable. I'll give you another update when the plans develop."

"Good."

"Can I speak to you about one more subject?"

"Shoot."

"Dave has been an absolute lifesaver for the team."

Hassan said, "I've heard good things about him."

"We all trust him. But I'm worried that he's in a really difficult situation being assigned to us. The IA guys have a lot of JAM in their ranks. The JAM militias have been going after interpreters. I've heard Task Force Justice has been helping them apply for a U.S. visa."

"That's right," I said. "We haven't cracked the code yet, but the staff has had some success. You want to help Dave apply?"

"Yes, sir. That's the least we can do for someone who's really sticking his neck out. His family could be in grave danger. His dad and brother have been working on FOB Justice too."

"Ask SFC Brown about it. You or someone on your team will have to sponsor him and help get a general officer letter of rec and a sponsor in the States, but it's worth a shot. Don't make any promises. Fucking JAM could get him before we cut through the bureaucracy."

"Thanks, sir. Nobody on our team wants to leave here without making sure Dave's taken care of."

"It's all about looking yourself in the mirror. But I guess we could leave Hassan here to fix all the problems when we're gone."

"Hah." Hassan laughed. "Good one. Always I have to clean up the mess you make."

"We can start by cleaning up these cups," I said. They chuckled as Hassan grabbed the chai set and headed for the door.

"Duty first," Gregg said on the way out.

"Keep doing a great job looking out for that team of yours."

"Wilco, sir. That's why they pay me the big bucks."

I returned to my cot and Gertrude Bell's escapades with the hope I'd glean a better insight into Iraqi culture.

◼

When Task Force Justice started processing SIVs, the floodgates opened for interpreters who qualified and expressed a desire to immigrate to the U.S. As a rule, an interpreter could not apply unless they substantiated threats received because of their employment. Given the levels of violence in Baghdad, most Justice interpreters catalogued multiple threats against themselves or their families. Gregg was surprised by the speed Dave's packet moved through the system. It took months to process the mounds of paperwork generated by George's and Gary's applications. By the time Dave applied, the team at FOB Justice received new approval notifications almost every week.

Gregg was faced with the prospect of losing his most trusted interpreter. He had others who worked with his team, including Dave's brother, but Dave had been an invaluable addition and had a strong grasp of English.

One evening as he Skyped with his wife, Lia, Gregg gave her a heads up. "You remember I mentioned that Dave the interpreter might be able to come to the U.S.?"

"Is he?" Lia said. She was Brazilian and her English was lightly accented.

"Yeah. Looks like he might get approved pretty soon."

"Where will he go?"

"Most of the interpreters don't really have a plan. I was thinking. Let's get Dave an apartment somewhere near our place so I can help him get used to the States when I get back."

Lia thought about that. Their move to Manhattan, Kansas, was a culture shock for her, and she was already living in the U.S. She'd had the benefit of a nearby Brazilian community where she found many new friends who also relocated from her native country. There were few people from the Middle East in the area. The transition for an Iraqi could be traumatic. She said, "Can I help you?"

"I know how much you're already doing to raise the boys with me gone. I'll take care of it."

"Okay. But you know I had a hard time coming to the U.S. from Brazil. I'm happy to help if I can. The boys are a handful, but I can do some little things and advise him on culture stuff."

"It's okay, honey. I'll take care of everything when I get home."

Several months afterward, Gregg called the team together to celebrate. Dave's SIV packet was approved. They'd received a general officer letter of recommendation. He'd passed all background checks and been instructed to travel to the U.S. Embassy in Amman for the final interview. Other interpreters had left FOB Justice for Amman in previous months. Many had developed a cover story because the Jordanian government had closed its border with Iraq. For decades, Jordan had been safe haven for waves of refugees in the Arab world. In 2007 it was bursting at the seams with Iraqis.

As Dave and Gregg walked into the team office, one of the NCOs grabbed a couple of chairs, waved his arms and said, *"Allah bukhayr."* Everyone laughed.

Dave and the team swapped stories. A lot had happened in the months it took to approve Dave's packet. In that time, the Iraqi battalion they'd trained had gone from bad to worse. One day, when the MTT team arrived, the battalion announced they had filled all their personnel shortages. Gregg later learned they had recruited from the militias in Khadamiyah. After some digging, Dave and the S2 informed him that almost all of Charlie Company were JAM members. Dave had been critical to the team's understanding of what transpired inside "the JAM battalion." He helped identify JAM leaders and kept sharp ears and eyes during engagements.

"We're gonna miss you, brother," Gregg said. The rest of the team sat around the office with the other interpreters. A few new interpreters had joined the team after they heard Americans took care of Iraqis by protecting them and sending them to the U.S.

"Yeah, who's gonna make us chai?" the S2 said. Laughter filled the room.

"I will miss you guys," Dave said. "I love this team."

A senior NCO teased him. "Whatever, dude. But let's toast him anyway. Roll out the near beer."

Bottles were distributed and caps removed. "To Dave," said the NCO. Near beers, chai, and a few Rip It cans were raised and clinked. Then the team feasted on traditional Iraqi falafel and kabobs that another interpreter brought for the farewell.

Dave stood. "Thanks." He looked at the floor and wiped a tear. "I still need to get to Jordan. I hear some Iraqis have been sent back, and the Jordanians blame us for rent prices going up. But if I make it to the States, I'll drink a real beer for you."

"That's what I'm talking about," the S4 said from his chair. "Can't wait to toast you with a real beer."

"We're gonna do our best to make that a reality," Gregg said.

As another interpreter began the Underground Railroad journey to Amman, the risks for Americans and our allies in Baghdad became more perilous.

Chapter Ten

Wartime Allies

*"When we are no longer able to change a situation,
we are challenged to change ourselves."*

~ Viktor E. Frankl, *Man's Search for Meaning*

"Miska, Miska, you need to tell me what I should do," Brigadier General Mohammed Usaif said, sipping chai in his office on FOB Justice.

This request popped up with more frequency as we edged closer to the end of our deployment. He wanted to get his family out of Iraq. Usaif started asking me for help after he heard about the first interpreter who made it through the Underground Railroad. His family had been in hiding since he took command months ago. Hassan gave me a knowing look.

"I can't tell you what to do." I tried to imagine myself in his position. I had no idea what I would do. He was in a difficult spot. His family needed a father, but his country needed good leaders. If he stayed, odds were he'd be killed. His loss would place his family members in more jeopardy. If he fled with them, the guilt of leaving his position would gnaw at him. Another consideration was that the

Iraqi Army was the most trusted institution in the nation. Would he ever receive that level of esteem in another country?

My professional relationship with General Mohammed had evolved. We often combined patrols. If I had American business, like visiting Dagger Brigade headquarters on FOB Liberty, I'd launch alone. If we had business somewhere in the city, Mohammed and I joined forces. We'd circulate the city, check on positions and roll into bases with our eight to ten vehicles. Americans led the patrols since we had the technological capabilities to defeat IEDs. Lieutenant Kronick's vehicle was in the lead, mine was right behind. The Iraqis took middle and end positions, which allowed their soldiers to read the population.

All U.S. personnel and interpreters wore headsets to communicate in our vehicles. Few Iraqis had that technology. They used hand signals to alert each other. As commander, General Mohammed alternated between his vehicle radio and several cell phones. Because he and I valued our ability to communicate, Hassan rode in Mohammed's vehicle. He listened to the Iraqis and passed the info to us via portable radio. We scheduled several combined patrols each week as pressure on the general increased.

In early August, Mohammed left the base for an Iraqi-only meeting near the Khadamiyah Shrine. He and local community leaders were asked to attend by Basem al-Shammari, our old nemesis from the firefight in Khadamiyah. No Americans were invited, nor were we expected near the sensitive religious site. Mohammed could contribute a perspective about the IA's role in defending the shrine and pilgrims against possible vehicle bombs and suicide attacks from al Qaeda.

By all accounts, the general provided a routine update. Journalist Greg Jaffe was embedded with us at the time. He wrote a front-page story about the encounter for the online edition of the *Wall Street Journal*. As Mohammed later described the events, what happened after the meeting was more critical.

One of Mohammed's lieutenants approached him at the conclusion. *"Sayidi."*

"Yes?" Mohammed said, watching the meeting break into small clusters of sheiks, police and politicians.

The lieutenant said, "Sayid Hatem asked if you would have chai with him."

"Hatem al-Shammari? No. Absolutely not."

"He said it would just be for a short period of time."

"Why would Hatem want to meet with me?"

"You should talk to him."

Mohammed glared at the lieutenant. Did he have a tribal or familial relationship with al-Shammari? Why else would he persist?

"I will let his secretary know." The lieutenant departed to deliver the general's response.

Mohammed prepared to depart, irritated that the senior cleric of the Khadamiyah Shrine and brother to Basem al-Shammari attempted to manipulate him. He couldn't figure out their scheme. The brothers were suspected of coordinating efforts through JAM militia, pressuring Iraqi military leaders and attacking U.S. forces. The militia used intimidation. In many areas it held the population hostage. While JAM had a reputation as nationalists, which many people supported, the various factions of the militia had devolved into common street thugs. They extorted entire neighborhoods for protection. If he accepted the invitation, Mohammed knew it would provide the impression that he was somehow in the militia's back pocket.

As he was about to exit the conference room, a member of his security detachment hurried up to him. "*Sayidi*, we have JAM members surrounding our patrol with vehicles and weapons."

Mohammed looked into the room and noticed a glance from Basem al-Shammari. "Let's go." The general moved out of the compound. As he reached the vehicles, approximately one hundred JAM fighters surrounded his patrol. Mohammed's men had been alert at their posts, but the militia members had surreptitiously occupied nearby areas out of view of the soldiers. Many also arrived in BMW sedans, which blended into traffic. Some showed up in confiscated Iraqi Army vehicles. Dozens of fighters jumped out of trucks.

Mohammed's personal security detachment numbered about twenty men. They were hemmed in by vehicles and armed militia. Only a dozen of his people were in the area of the vehicles. He assumed the others were at posts throughout the complex.

"What is the meaning of this?" Mohammed shouted. "We are soldiers of the Iraqi Army."

"You are under arrest, general," said a masked militia member. The circle of weapons aimed at Mohammed and his soldiers tightened.

Mohammed moved to the center of his men and tried to defuse the situation. "That is ridiculous," he said. "You have no authority here. I am in command of security for all of Northwest Baghdad." A firefight this close to the holy pilgrimage site would be a disaster for all.

"We have the supreme authority within the area of the shrine," the militia leader said. "You have to come with me."

Mohammed understood the extreme peril of his situation. He noticed that some Iraqi Army vehicles had been commandeered by militia who manned the turrets at nearby intersections.

The militia leader issued an order. "Tell your soldiers to drop their weapons, general." He moved to a position where he spoke directly to Mohammed from two meters. He said everything in a voice loud enough for all soldiers and JAM fighters to hear.

"Your men know this is the right thing to do," the JAM leader said. "Some of them have taken off their uniforms and joined our holy effort."

That caught Mohammed's attention. He realized his missing men were not pulling security. They'd either fled or known in advance and joined the kidnapping or assassination attempt.

The noose tightened. Groups of militia, weapons ready and aimed, inched closer. Other fighters held positions on rooftops and aimed their AKs at the street.

"General, tell your soldiers to put their weapons down."

They were outgunned. Mohammed decided it was possible he could negotiate a political solution without loss of life. He glanced at his detachment leader who was near several soldiers. Their backs were against a vehicle. Mohammed nodded at him to comply. The security detachment leader barked a command. Most of his soldiers lowered their weapons to the ground.

As eyes shifted from the detachment leader, another soldier near Mohammed grabbed the general from behind and threw him into an open Humvee. The gunner in the vehicle swiveled his weapon toward the militia leader. He was shocked but stood his ground. The soldier who threw Mohammed into the vehicle jumped in the driver's seat and floored the gas.

Soldiers raced to their vehicles as militia members closed in. Gangs of fighters grabbed several of the general's men before they reached their vehicles. They were dragged to the ground and restrained.

Seven soldiers made it to Humvees and jumped in. Engines roared. The vehicles careened through the crowd that had formed. Militia members dove for cover. They feared being run over more than being shot.

Mohammed's vehicle raced through the conference center's access point. It sped down the street. Three other Humvees trailed. He'd taken only four vehicles on this patrol because it was close to the base in an area thought to be safe from al Qaeda. Plus, the streets of Khadamiyah adjacent to the shrine were too narrow for a Humvee.

"Who betrayed us?" he yelled to the driver.

"Let's get back to base, then we can worry about what happened," the driver said.

"I'm going to kill Basem al-Shammari and his brother. They can't get away with this." He looked out the windows. "Anyone following us?"

"No, *Sayidi*," his lieutenant said from the backseat. "There were no shots fired, and we have all of our vehicles." He had communicated with soldiers in the other vehicles and summed up the situation. "I'm trying to get accountability. I don't know how many deserted or how many didn't escape."

The small convoy barreled up to the main gate of FOB Justice manned by Iraqi soldiers. The patrol weaved through jersey barriers that prevented vehicle-borne IEDs from penetrating the outer base perimeter. The patrol vehicles cleared the gate and headed towards headquarters.

"Give me a report as soon as you know anything," Mohammed said. "Take me to Miska, and thank you for saving my life."

I sat in my office typing an email to my wife. In addition to personal news, we coordinated on Family Readiness Group (FRG) issues and other things going on in the Schweinfurt community. The FRG provided a volunteer organization that empowered families to thrive during deployments. It was an information conduit to keep people informed and deal with serious wartime notifications. Amy had her finger on the pulse of many issues within the community as both a full-time schoolteacher and an advocate for the hundreds of families within our command. Much of our correspondence revolved around those issues since we both believed that tamping down potential drama back home helped the soldiers stay focused on their mission in combat.

First Sergeant Pryor interrupted. "Sir, we have an issue at the gate."

Hassan rushed in. "Brigadier General Usaif is calling for you. I just spoke to one of his guys. There was some sort of incident at the shrine."

Pryor said, "General Usaif's entire patrol just raced through the inner gate to our side of the FOB without clearing any weapons." The First Sergeant was agitated. I had changed policy for Mohammed. Routine procedure on all U.S. bases was that Iraqis had to be escorted. I trained my team that if we were going to trust our Iraqi Army counterparts, we had to demonstrate trust. Thus, I allowed Mohammed to enter our base without an American escort as long as his soldiers cleared their weapons, as the American soldiers did. Mohammed had agreed.

Mohammed's dash through the gate without stopping to clear weapons could have caused a fratricide incident. It was a clear violation of policy. Guards might have assumed the vehicles had been stolen by insurgents or militia, which occasionally happened. That had the potential to lead to a firefight.

"Hold on a second," I said. "Is Mohammed here?"

"Yes, boss," Hassan said. "I think he's coming into the building now."

"Those soldiers and weapons need to be cleared," the First Sergeant said. "The Iraqis have had ADs before. We don't need anyone killed or injured because of stupidity." ADs stood for accidental discharges.

"I'll take care of it," I said.

Tony didn't answer. He was annoyed. I'd seen that look from him and other NCOs when they thought an officer took too much risk.

Mohammed marched down the hallway, distressed. "Miska, we need to talk."

"First, I need your soldiers to go back to the gate and clear their weapons. We don't need any incidents."

Mohammed was frazzled but recognized he was safe with us. "Okay, okay, I'll tell them," he said. He issued orders to a soldier in Arabic. Turning to me he said, "Some of my soldiers betrayed me. I need to find out who."

We stepped into the conference room and conferred. Mohammed decided to return to his headquarters and assess the fallout with his people. I would accompany him. Greg Jaffe, the *Wall Street Journal* reporter, heard all the commotion and tagged along.

BG Usaif made a couple calls on his cell phone while his lieutenant used another line. They evaluated what happened to the general's soldiers and who abandoned their posts. We walked toward the Iraqi side of the base as they fielded calls. Mohammed tried to reach his immediate superiors but couldn't get through. "I don't know who to trust, Miska," he said. "Six, maybe eight of my soldiers stripped off their uniforms and joined the militia during the standoff and my boss isn't answering."

"Does he usually pick up?"

"Yes. He's my friend. Like an older brother. We served together in Ramadi and elsewhere."

We passed through the U.S. gate. I thanked the soldiers for their discipline in spotting BG Mohammed and not overreacting to the situation when his patrol screamed through the gate. One of the soldiers said that he almost opened fire but recognized the general.

I caught up with the group as they entered Usaif's office. His lieutenant provided an update, as he fielded phone calls.

Hassan interpreted. "He says he received a call from soldiers at a checkpoint near the shrine. The loudspeakers are blaring that if the general returns to the area, he will be killed. They are trying to intimidate him even more."

Mohammed summoned the officer who had brought the message about the meeting with Hatem al-Shammari. The junior officer arrived and stood at attention.

The general paced back and forth behind his desk, yelling, "There is no law in Iraq. Only power. Power creates the law." He pointed at the officer. "You were involved in the kidnapping. You kept telling me to go see him."

"I didn't know." The officer shifted his feet. "I am sorry."

Disgusted, General Usaif dismissed him and took a seat near Hassan.

I said, "You and I should return to the shrine. We can go together and retrieve your vehicles and weapons. We can't allow the militia to get away with this." I had no idea if going to the shrine would solve the problem or cause an even bigger fight. It was the only thing that came to mind.

Mohammed slumped in his chair and said nothing. He was exhausted from the experience. He knew it would place him in jeopardy with powerful men if he challenged a member of Parliament and the senior cleric at the Khadamiyah Shrine. Plus, the militia was its own wild-card factor. They were influenced by the likes of the al-Shammari brothers but operated their own independent raids and attacks. Iraqis passed us rumors that at least two militia factions had assassination squads targeting Mohammed.

Frustrated, I said, "Right now the Mahdi Army is the only Iraqi security force with any legitimacy in Khadamiyah." The Mahdi Army was a nickname for JAM.

Mohammed told his lieutenant to call the Prime Minister's Office. He would seek approval to return to the shrine. Then he called to his sleeping quarters. Most Iraqi commanders had a private bed and bath near their office. They could refresh themselves after work and be available should the need occur. Out of the bedroom area emerged his son and oldest daughter, who were visiting when the kidnapping attempt occurred. Mohammed asked them to greet us. They did, with deferential body language, eyes lowered and shy, then returned to the bedroom.

The general, his aide, Hassan, and I sipped chai. We discussed more of the details of the attempted kidnapping. A short while later the call came from the Prime Minister's Office. Request to return to the shrine denied. The official response stated that the Iraqi Army should not challenge the militia because a pilgrimage was imminent. The Prime Minister's Office did not want to upset the balance of power near the shrine and risk giving al Qaeda or Sunni insurgents an opportunity to create havoc during a massive influx of pilgrims.

Hassan and I returned to the U.S. side of the base. I needed to update my boss on the situation. Intimidation and undermining of Iraqi Security Forces had perplexed us throughout our deployment. We attempted to provide reassurance and guidance in ways that allowed leaders and their forces to stand on their own without American handholding. Incidents like the attempted kidnapping of the general undercut our efforts. I recommended that Colonel Burton notify Brigadier General Campbell. I had previously tipped off Campbell that Mohammed might need high level support.

Then I thought about Mohammed's children. I recalled an incident in Tikrit in 2004. We partnered with very capable Iraqi officers who worked in the Joint Security Station. A trusted officer, Lieutenant

Colonel Khalid, had gone home across the Tigris River. One evening, he was asleep on his rooftop with his family. Many Iraqis slept on the roof in the summertime because their houses, stuffy with the heat of the day, lacked ventilation. Given the dangerous times, many people also slept with weapons. Khalid awakened to hear his wife pleading. On her knees, she begged an intruder not to kill her husband. A masked man held a pistol to her head. He had climbed onto the roof to assassinate Khalid.

Khalid's son also woke up. He grabbed an AK-47 and shot the intruder. There was an exchange of gunfire. The son and wife were killed.

Khalid came to work the next day and told me the story. I couldn't find the right words. All I could say was, "I'm sorry." I could not imagine waking up as my wife begged an intruder for my life. I couldn't begin to comprehend what it would be like to watch her and my son shot to death. And what possessed him to return to work the day after?

I thought about that incident when I saw Mohammed's children. I decided if something could be done to help the family, I would do it. There were too many stories like Khalid's. Too many incidences of brave Iraqi leaders who took a stand and made incredible sacrifices. We needed to take home good stories, also.

The next day, it was 9 p.m. in Baghdad when BG Usaif visited me. We met in the Task Force Justice dining facility, which remained open after hours so soldiers could grab snacks or drinks. Mohammed selected an ice cream bar, and I made a cup of coffee. I had a bad habit of drinking coffee after dinner to stay up late and work. Greg Jaffe and Hassan joined us. Greg was working on his story about the general, and Hassan provided everybody comfort when he was in the room. "Greg is joining us because listening in allows him to better understand the complexity of the fight, so he can write better stories," I said.

Mohammed nodded at the reporter.

"General, how are your children?" Hassan asked.

"Fine, fine, they are fine," Mohammed said. "The situation scared them, but they see that I am okay now." He bit into an ice cream bar. "I didn't tell them everything that happened." He dabbed his mouth with a paper napkin. "Miska, I haven't heard from any of my bosses. I'm worried that they have not called to check on me or return my calls."

"That's not good," I said. "Colonel Burton called General Campbell to inform him of the situation. He said he'd speak to General Aboud." Lieutenant General Aboud was the senior Iraqi Army commander in charge of all Baghdad security. A heavyset officer with a serious demeanor, Aboud commanded the respect of Iraqis and most American leaders.

"Thank you, thank you, Miska." Mohammed took another bite of the ice cream bar. "I'm worried that they plan to replace me. There are rumors that I cause too much trouble."

Trying to lighten the mood a bit, I said, "Then you shouldn't hang around with *abu Mashakel*."

"Hah, hah, yes, yes. I know this. You are a very dangerous man, Miska. Maybe that is why we are partners."

I turned serious. "We'll challenge any attempts to transfer you. Colonel Burton and General Campbell will help, too." I said this with as much confidence as possible, but I knew we had no real authority if the Iraqis decided to relieve him.

"Thank you, thank you," Mohammed said. "My soldiers were released, but we did not get back the weapons or radios. I also have not heard from the soldiers who deserted."

"What do you think about doing more combined patrols together?"

"That is good, that is good. We should do that more." He finished the ice cream bar. "Miska, if I get transferred, I will lose my security. I'm worried that someone will kidnap my family."

"You need to keep them in hiding. We're trying to figure out a solution. We asked General Petraeus, and he said there was no legal option. We also asked Ambassador Crocker. Colonel Burton and I are working on this." I didn't have the courage to mention that we had exhausted all legal options, according to U.S. leadership.

Mohammed nodded, but his shoulders sagged. He was under immense pressure. "I am in a very tight place," he said. "Things are happening too fast. My mind is going 500 miles per hour. I don't sleep at night. It is beyond my control."

Anthony Woods stopped by the office to remind me about our patrol brief. "Hey, sir, you ready?"

We'd been together since Grafenwoehr when First Sergeant Almario transferred him up to brigade headquarters in exchange for Specialist James. Woods was a driver for several months in Baghdad before he expressed a desire to try a new position and learn more. He later confessed that he'd been terrified of driving. He feared that an explosive would rip his legs off, or worse. We rotated him to the M240 machine gun in the turret for several months before we brought him into the more complex role of dismounting and providing security anytime we stopped or entered a building. I was a proponent of rotating soldiers through different positions. It allowed for a broader experience base and kept their edge. When faced with a new opportunity, most people rose to the challenge and approached the new task with higher levels of intensity. Complacency killed in combat.

"I'm right behind you," I said. "Where's Hassan?" Old Dog was usually the guy who poked his head in my office to remind me about upcoming events.

"He's headed over to the Iraqi side to ensure the general and his patrol are on time."

Vehicles and soldiers waited. Our plan was a short pre-brief with American crews before we united with our Iraqi brothers. With them we'd conduct a combined patrol brief. It included a comprehensive assessment of the threat, the environment, and what actions we would take should certain contingencies arise.

The mission was to drive to Combat Outpost Casino. We needed to check in with Iraqi forces and coalition leaders about the security situation in Ghazaliyah. That neighborhood was one of the epicenters of sectarian strife. We rolled out of the American gate with locked and loaded weapons. *Clicks* and *schwacks* sounded in every vehicle as weapon bolts rode rounds into chambers. Headsets squawked with curt communications to signal readiness.

Nate keyed his microphone. "I'm up," his machine gun prepped should we make contact.

"Red," Woods and Rodin both said over the intercom. That meant their weapons had a round in the chamber and were ready to shoot.

"Roger. Me, too," I said. Soldiers in the other vehicles radioed they were all set.

We dismounted on the Iraqi side of the base and greeted our counterparts. General Usaif had arrived with Hassan and the lieutenant who had saved his life the previous week.

Iraqi and American troops gathered around Lieutenant Kronick for the patrol brief. It would take a little longer than usual since our Iraqi interpreter, Frank, would translate for the Iraqi soldiers. Frank had replaced Jack when he was killed by insurgents in Balad.

When we got to the question-and-answer part, Mohammed whispered, "I took away the soldiers' cell phones."

"Me too," I said. "I've never allowed soldiers to carry them on patrol. I don't want them to accidentally call their wives during a firefight."

"I am worried that someone may have tipped off the militia. This way, they cannot call and discuss what routes we take, where we go."

We mounted up and checked radios one last time. Hassan called from BG Usaif's vehicle. They were ready.

Brett Kronick keyed the radio. "Moving." His vehicle led. Mine was second, followed by an Iraqi vehicle, then BG Usaif's, two more American Humvees and the remainder of the Iraqi patrol. Ten up-armored vehicles. Dust kicked up and blanketed all of us in a coat of brown.

"How ya doin up there, Weather Dog?" I asked Nate, the gunner. We had nicknamed him Weather Dog because he experienced all the elements in the turret. Conditions could be horrendous with the dust. Lucky for Nate, as the second vehicle, we didn't get as much. The Iraqi vehicles at the back, however, would eat grit until we were in the city on asphalt pavement.

"Good as can be, sir," Nate's response was muffled by a handkerchief over his mouth to filter the dust.

"Don't be so cheery," Rodin said. "Ain't like we live in Iraq and have to suffer 120-degree weather every day."

"Plus, the food is exactly like Mom serves back home," Nate said.

Woods said, "I kinda like the food. Cooks are pretty good. Could be a lot worse."

"Yeah, but you're weird like that," said Rodin.

"We got a lot to be thankful for." Woods, always the optimist.

As the banter continued, we noted normal atmospherics in Khadamiyah. People were outside on the streets. Vendors hawked their wares. Traffic flowed, but as usual, cars pulled over or turned off the main road when they saw our patrol.

Kronick's lead vehicle cleared an intersection. I saw an ice chest on the corner, the kind a vendor would use for sodas. At that moment, a flash erupted on the vehicle's right side. Everything went dark. Time slowed to a crawl. The Humvee lurched to a stop. The windshield looked as if a spider had spun its web over the bulletproof glass. A second or two later, I heard a grunt from the gunner in my headset.

"Nate!" I yelled. I grabbed for his knee. Missed. The gunner's knee was within easy reach of the driver and passenger unless he stood in the turret to look out or sight the weapon. He sat on a suspended seat formed by a hanging belt. Had Nate been hit? We'd seen presentations from engineers and forensic experts about the technical sophistication of bomb- making. The Iranian militias trained JAM and others to build the weapons and employ them for maximum damage. They knew how to angle the aim of the blast from the side of the road so it would hit the person in the front passenger seat and the gunner with the same shot. Miraculously, I didn't feel pain anywhere and concluded that the blast must have missed me.

I got hold of Nate's knee.

"I'm okay," Nate said. "A little rattled."

I was relieved. "Everyone else okay?" One by one they reported back. Everyone was fine. "Let's get out and find the trigger man."

Woods said, "Dismounting," to ensure everyone knew he was leaving the vehicle with me.

"Six Mike is out," Lieutenant Kronick radioed over the platoon net.

I grabbed my rifle, exited the vehicle and walked to where I thought the bomb had exploded. The vehicle had drifted past the area, carried by its momentum before it halted. It was difficult to judge how far the Humvee had rolled. Woods stood by my side. We didn't hear any weapons fire. Complex attacks sometimes began with a bomb and were sustained by automatic and precision-weapon fire that picked off anyone who exited the vehicles. JAM tended not to be that brave in Khadamiyah.

I said, "Check that building."

Woods moved toward an open doorway. I surveyed the intersection. Shards of glass framed storefront windows in the immediate vicinity. About a dozen wounded or dying people lay on the road and sidewalks or against buildings. Everyone not injured by the blast stayed hunkered down out of sight.

Ambulances showed up within a minute of the explosion. Paramedics loaded bodies and wounded into the ambulances. I was so focused on finding the asshole who had triggered the bomb I didn't think to wonder how the ambulances had been so responsive. Later, we assessed that JAM had staged them in advance of the attack. They were known to commandeer emergency vehicles to transport arms and ammunition throughout the city.

Woods returned from the adjacent building. "All clear, sir. Just a family inside, scared out of their minds." What I didn't know at the time but found out years later was that Woods had almost shot the family hunkered inside the building. He went in with his M-4 rifle switched to three-round burst. He found them cowering behind counters, fragments of glass from the blown-out front window scattered all over the floor.

Adrenaline raced from the bomb attack. Woods combat instincts kicked in. He almost sprayed the room with bullets, but his mind flashed to the oft-discussed notion that we lost the fight the days we shot. Plus, we had to live with the consequences of our actions for the rest of our lives. Woods said in a postwar interview, "I was twenty-one years old with an automatic weapon. Who would have questioned it?" In retrospect, I should have never ordered him in there. I violated the principle of staying in buddy teams.

Hassan approached. "You okay, boss?"

"Yeah. Let's start chatting with people to see if anyone saw something."

"A lot of Iraqi wounded," Hassan said.

"Or killed. Son of a bitch. Woods," I yelled as we walked towards the vehicle. "Check the truck with Rodin and see what kind of damage we have." He ran to make the check.

Hassan and I looked for people to interview, but everyone had vanished, frightened by the attack. It was a behavior that occurred with more frequency in Khadamiyah. It had been a safe neighborhood, by Baghdad standards. However, in the six previous months, attacks had gained in frequency. They were always directed against U.S. patrols and only when no Iraqi civilians were present. If streets were empty of people, we went into defensive mode and attempted to preempt an attack. That day was different. JAM killed or wounded a dozen innocent civilians to get a clean shot at us. They raised the stakes.

Brett Kronick radioed the base and provided an update. The Quick Reaction Force geared up to reinforce our position should we need assistance. Brett asked them to send a wrecker in the event my vehicle was inoperable.

It didn't take long to realize the Humvee wasn't headed anywhere. Both front tires were flat, the rubber shredded like grated cheese, the windshield shattered.

Hassan noted that the presumed EFP had hit an adjacent building on the other side of the road. It must have gone over the hood or been prematurely detonated by our rhino, the eight-foot-long heat device used to trigger a passive infrared EFP. We counted our blessings. Had it hit the hood, it would have at least destroyed the engine. Had it struck the passenger door, some of us might not have walked away.

The QRF arrived about twenty minutes later. We had not identified a trigger point, but the men spotted wires that may have been used to manually detonate the bomb. That seemed unlikely. An actively laid wire would have alerted people that an attack was imminent. The more plausible scenario was that the bomb was placed in a container and detonated remotely. It would have required perfect timing and enough space between our vehicles; otherwise, our jammers would have prevented the signal from activating the bomb. Or, it had been detonated using a hard wire. We never figured it out.

Lieutenant Stephen DuPerre dismounted and coordinated with Lieutenant Kronick. I decided we would swap out my vehicle and continue the mission. We did not want to cede an inch to the enemy. If we turned around, that would be spun as stopping the Americans. Instead, we replaced the vehicle and continued the mission. While working through the switch, the junior leaders also decided to swap out Nate Neyer on the gun. The doctors at the base radioed and asked for anyone shaken up by the blast to return and be checked for traumatic brain injury (TBI). The intensity of recent conflicts made the Army much better at diagnosing potential medical challenges.

They kept TBI and post-traumatic stress disorder (PTSD) front and center in everyone's awareness.

We left the scene of the attack with DuPerre's Humvee. Brett Kronick still led, and my vehicle followed second. We often shuffled the deck or mixed up the order of our vehicles to make it harder to target leaders. However, I made the calculation that JAM wasn't good enough to have two attacks planned for the same day. We also varied our route and split the patrol for a time, which called for me to jump up front. The QRF remained on site to conduct a thorough investigation with the Explosive Ordnance Disposal (EOD) team.

Fucking JAM. The rest of the mission was a blur. We arrived at COP Casino. A few hours later, we safely navigated a different route back to Khadamiyah through northwestern Baghdad. Upon our return to base, the new doctor cornered me, demanding I have a medical examination. Officers and senior NCOs were sometimes known for ensuring their men and women adhered to the standards for medical checks but disregarded the same criterion for themselves. Historic stories heralded those brave enough to fight through injuries. Doc Hanes would not allow me to skirt the rules. I felt fine but followed her to the aid station.

Jim Egan stopped by to check on me. "I provided an update to brigade and the FRG. Rumor has it the FRG was already tracking."

"Why does that not surprise me?" I said. The spouses in Schweinfurt stayed on top of the rumor mill. They were hungry for any information about the unit and soldiers. Proper protocol was for the unit in combat to call to the rear detachment, managed by uniformed soldiers, and notify them of any casualties. The next call would come from me or someone in the chain of command to my wife to let her know about the situation. In that way, we could ensure that the uniformed chain of command and Family Readiness Group leaders were alerted in advance. The rear detachment and FRG would then initiate a formal set of calls to ensure every spouse and others who needed to know were informed of the official message. By using that protocol, we preempted the rumor mill and kept information from being distorted and spinning out of control.

I went to the office and dialed my wife. I knew it would be good for her to hear my voice. "Hey, babe."

"So, you haven't been staying on the base like you told my mom," she said. At least she joked about it. Her mom, Carol, had emailed me about a photo she saw in *The New York Times* in which I wasn't wearing a helmet. Carol gave me a hard time about that. I told her the photo had been taken on a military base, a lie, which was why I had no helmet. I also told her I didn't need to leave the base anymore. I had completed my twenty-five-patrol quota, an allusion to the Joseph Heller novel *Catch-22*. Carol believed me and mentioned it to Amy the next time they spoke. Amy called and gave me a hard time for fooling her mom. She worried about me, and so did our children. I tried to mitigate the uncertainty with as much information as I was allowed to share. If Amy was comfortable, she could project confidence when she spoke with the other spouses. That helped keep the atmosphere in Schweinfurt calm.

Time to get rid of the rumors. "We had a little mishap," I said. "No worries, though. The enemy's not that good. A couple of flat tires. Nate, the gunner, is okay. Just a little shook up."

"I spoke to Bob Whittle, and he gave me the details, at least what he was told," she said. Bob, a West Point classmate, served as Rear Detachment Commander. He would go on to be a general officer.

"Seriously, I'm okay. The doc already took a look at me and everyone else in the vehicle. The militia guys are street thugs, so we usually outsmart them. Today, they made an error. They wounded or killed a lot of innocent people by not warning them in advance. People were all over the streets when it went off. We'll see how it plays out."

"Please be careful. Your children and I need you to come home. I'm not going to tell them about this, so let me know if it's going to come out in some magazine or newspaper. I don't want this incident to be like the last time when your son read a magazine some reporter mailed to the house. Remember? He asked me who JAM was and why do they want to kill Daddy?"

"Got it. I'm sorry." She was right, as usual.

"Be careful. I love you."

"I love you too, babe." I heard the click on her end and hung up.

Humor tends to take a dark turn when the psyche endures long periods surrounded by extreme cruelty and violence. It's understandable that I would write in my notebook that evening:

Famous sayings modified for Iraq:

- Good fences with sniper screens make good neighbors.
- A penny saved each day turns into a hell of an explosively formed penetrator [EFP] over time. (Many EFPs were made of copper. Steel was the other variant.)

The pressure on BG Mohammed and me continued to mount. I escorted him to the Prime Minister's Office to be questioned after he was almost kidnapped or assassinated. Think how insane that was. It would be like me being called to the White House to backbrief the President's Chief of Staff or National Security Advisor. At this point in my deployment only two things kept me moving forward: my commitment to my soldiers and my family. One mistake could result in radical changes to our lives forever.

Chapter Eleven

Goodbyes

*"No one can travel here and come back the same.
It sets its seal upon you, for good or ill."*

~ Gertrude Bell in *Queen of the Desert*
by Georgina Howell

IT BECAME ROUTINE to form our combined patrol on the Iraqi side of the base. Mohammed and I decided to have one of his officers give the patrol brief. The Iraqi lieutenant and Brett Kronick coordinated in advance and ensured each tracked the other's information. They covered places to avoid, threat attacks, and other trends. Frank, our Iraqi translator, interpreted for the Americans.

The atmospherics in Khadamiyah had changed since the attack two weeks previous. We received overtures from people in the neighborhood who were fed up with JAM. It appeared several groups had competed for turf and chose to attack the American patrols. The people had not complained if they were given fair warning and ample time to clear the attack zone. So many civilians were killed and wounded in the attack against my patrol, citizens lodged complaints. The militia's stated reason for existing was to protect the people from the occupiers. JAM had violated that agreement and lost civilian support.

The IED attack on me had the exact opposite effect of our previous firefight at the shrine. In both instances, the side that experienced tactical success lost a strategic advantage because acceptance rested with the populace. The militia detonated a bomb against my vehicle but lost popular support. The same happened when our paratroopers engaged the militia near the shrine. They killed and wounded many militia members without suffering any casualties. However, American forces lost legitimacy in the eyes of residents.

As a result, some Iraqi power brokers negotiated with us to bring back other JAM leaders who had gone into hiding in Iran. They proposed that if U.S. patrols would not target these men, they would drive the "bad" JAM out of Khadamiyah and prevent future attacks. The battalion from the 82nd Airborne operating in the area conducted the negotiations. Leaders worked out an agreement most parties could stomach. The attacks in Khadamiyah stopped after months of escalation. The new agreement forged a benign environment, at least until we left the neighborhood. Once we rolled into a Sunni-dominated area, all bets were off. Al Qaeda and Sunni insurgents recognized no such armistice.

The mission that day was to head to FOB Honor, a sub-base within the broader Green Zone. We were scheduled to meet with Arwa Damon, the CNN journalist who had broadcast the Iraqi soccer victory from the roof of our building. Since General Mohammed and I had struck out on viable options to help his family in official channels, we pursued a nonstandard option and enlisted the assistance of a journalist.

It was common for media organizations to operate with local stringers, or fixers, in journalistic parlance. These brave locals covered areas where Western reporters couldn't gain access. Given the threat to news people, host-nation nationals operated then and now with extreme secrecy in conflict zones. If their identities are compromised, many correspondents and news organizations took immediate action to move the locals out of harm's way, even relocating them to another country. I hoped that Arwa's experience might help us move Mohammed's family out of Iraq to a place his children could live normal lives.

We drove through Khadamiyah. People were on the streets and in the markets as they were two weeks earlier during the attack. Some watched our patrol drive down the road. Others ignored the noise. They either hoped to not draw attention or were numb to the sight of military vehicles. The agreement seemed to be working. There had been no bombs in Khadamiyah since the attack on my vehicle.

We had a bargain but took no chances. Our patrol walked out of both gates on FOB Justice. We did this a couple times per week. It gave the impression we were conducting a dismounted patrol within Khadamiyah. Dismounted patrols tended to scare potential triggermen away. Even if a bomb awaited us, the triggerman may not be able to detonate it after fleeing from soldiers on foot. Our vehicles followed out of the gates and picked us up at a designated point. We proceeded on patrol after we linked up with the Humvees. Varying our routine helped prevent attacks.

Dismounting and walking out of the gate added about thirty minutes to the patrol. We factored in the extra time to ensure that we didn't rush to meetings or other events. If we hurried, the tendency was to cut corners, increasing risk. That day, we met the vehicles a couple blocks from the gates on the outer side of the neighborhood. We wound the patrols on two different routes and headed south toward the Green Zone. We entered the base through an Iraqi checkpoint with Americans on overwatch.

As we drove into the small inner base, I was reminded of an investigation I was tasked with two months before. At the time, the Dagger Brigade lawyer called to ask if I had received the tasking letter informing me that I would be the investigating officer for a military 15-6 investigation. Before I read the details, I thought Colonel Burton had made a mistake assigning me as the investigator. Did he not think I had enough to do? We ran a hard pace in support of Iraqi Army operations and synchronized a variety of transition teams and other coalition efforts in the area. That was in addition to dozens of other activities that were my responsibility.

Then, I read the details of the report. They alleged possible war crimes by a U.S. company commander. Widespread drug use in the unit. Possible prostitution of female interpreters. I realized the investigation called for someone with mobility around Baghdad, a trusted interpreter who could review sensitive details, and someone senior enough who would not be intimidated by the possibility of officer and NCO misconduct. In short, the investigation looked like a potential mess and a setback in relations with Iraqi Security Forces in the area. The 1st Calvary Division, our current higher headquarters in Baghdad, assigned the investigation to our brigade. The alleged perpetrators belonged to a sister brigade with responsibility for Green Zone security.

Over the month of July, Hassan and I made about a dozen trips to FOB Honor. We combined our routine tasks of synchronizing ISF activities within our brigade sector and investigative visits. We conducted dozens of U.S. and Iraqi interviews. They revealed that female interpreters had been pimped out by the senior noncommissioned officer in the company. The company commander may have been aware, and he either looked the other way or was inundated with his own problems. Also, many NCOs had worked with Iraqi interpreters to find over-the-counter drugs for soldiers in the unit. Given proximity to civilian establishments within the Green Zone, the unit procured alcohol and drugs in clear violation of General Order Number One, which mandated no alcohol while on deployment. Most critically, the company commander's patrol had been struck by an IED and responded by ordering an attack against a JAM-affiliated gas station. They burned it to the ground. Later, he abused Facilities Protection Service (FPS) members at a nearby government building. The company commander also had a history of abuse with his other Iraqi colleagues.

The company clearly suffered from a crisis of unethical leadership. The investigation, which began when a senior NCO blew the whistle, took a couple intense weeks. Afterward, I prepared a report and sent it to higher headquarters. The overall affair had dampened my morale with respect to the resiliency of our forces in such a chaotic environment.

Back on FOB Honor, we attempted what seemed to be impossible through official channels, help an endangered Iraqi family relocate to a safe environment. We met Arwa at a small coffee shop for chai, a discrete place to chat with BG Usaif and Hassan. She spoke fluent Arabic, but Hassan translated to keep me in the loop.

Arwa arrived before the general.

I said, "Brigadier General Usaif keeps asking me what he should do, meaning whether he should go with his family or stay in Iraq to fight."

"It's gonna be tough," she said as she lit a cigarette. "If he stays, there's a good chance he'll be killed. Then, what will his family do? If he leaves, he risks losing everything he's worked for."

"All the more reason that I don't want to be responsible for helping influence him. He'll have to live with the consequences, regardless," I said.

She nodded toward the doorway, blowing smoke from the side of her mouth. The general walked in with his trusted lieutenant in tow.

"Arwa." Mohammed gave her a warm hug. "How is my favorite CNN reporter?"

"He said that in English," Hassan said.

"I know. I speak English," I said.

"Fooled me."

Arwa smiled at our banter.

"Arwa, please," Mohammed said. "You need to help me. Miska won't tell me what to do."

"Let's focus on your family. We'll come up with a plan flexible enough to give you options."

"Yes, yes, that's good. Options are good."

Hassan and I listened to their discussion for a while, then left so they could hammer out details in private. The gist of the plan involved scheduling Mohammed for R&R in the Kurdish region. However, the family would go on to Turkey. From there, we would work to relocate them to the United States. Before the war, Mohammed had conducted training in Germany, but had always wanted to visit the U.S. Those two countries were his primary options. I lived in Germany at the time, and it could have worked out well. However, the Germans had revoked seven thousand provisional visas for Iraqis already in the country. The atmosphere was not conducive to moving an Iraqi family there, especially if the sponsor was American.

As Hassan and I left the meeting, I was more hopeful about human nature. People like Arwa, willing to go to extremes to shed a spotlight on an important story or help a desperate family, always reaffirmed my faith in humanity. I was worried about the general, however. He was more frantic than usual. He had justifiable levels of paranoia, compounded by worries about his family.

The end of my time in Baghdad approached. Our unit would return to Germany in about two months, ending my sixteen-month deployment. BG Usaif would remain. He faced the prospect of a new American partner, perhaps one who wouldn't have the same commitment to work with Iraqis. What would I do in his position? I couldn't answer the question.

—

I feigned annoyance and rolled my eyes when I looked up and saw Hassan in the doorway to my office. I'd almost finished a silly poem that Amy, the kids, and I were composing. I wrote a stanza about a mouse named Cheese and emailed it. In my letter, I suggested the kids and Amy include our pets, two cats and a dog, in the next verse. We zapped emails back and forth, laughing at the absurdity of each successive stanza.

"You busy?" said Hassan.

"What's up?" Sometimes Hassan's ambushes were a quick check and other times they could be a serious issue.

"General Usaif. He plans to marry a second wife."

That took me a second to digest. "Is he crazy? He knows it's illegal in the States, right?"

"I tried to tell him that it would complicate getting his family out."

"Complicate things? It could derail the whole fucking plan. He's jeopardizing his entire family because he wants a second wife?"

"It's not even a younger woman. She's ten years older than his first wife. It's supposed to be good in the eyes of Allah if a husband takes in a widow. I think he wants to rescue her from the violence."

I was exasperated. "We've been working on this plan to get his family out of the country for months, and at the eleventh hour, he throws in a serious monkey wrench that risks his kids? Let's go see him."

"I told him that you might want to speak to him about it."

I shook my head, grabbed my notebook and patrol cap. We walked to the Iraqi side of the base. Hassan carried his 45-caliber pistol that had been confiscated. I carried my 9-millimeter on a leg holster.

At Mohammed's office we exchanged greetings with his lieutenant and were welcomed by the general.

"Miska, Miska, how are you?" he said in English.

"*Eamid* Usaif." I used the Arabic word for brigadier general.

"I missed you. Where have you been? I have good news."

"So I hear."

"Did Hassan tell you?"

"Oh, yeah. He told me alright."

"Miska, this is a good thing for me to do," Mohammed said.

"You know that it's illegal in the United States, right?"

"Yes, yes, but I have to do this. I cannot leave this woman here in Iraq."

"You could be placing the entire plan at risk. What about your children?"

"They know her," he said, as if that made his intentions sensible. "The older children, they agree it is the right thing for me to do."

"What about your wife?".

"She will learn to appreciate it."

Hassan gave me a look that implied he would explain the nuances of all this to me later.

The lieutenant brought chai. We sipped the sweet tea and discussed the security situation for a few minutes. Manners observed, I told the general I wished him luck and had to return to work.

As we walked back, Hassan explained that the general's first wife was not happy. He had spoken to Hassan in confidence. People tended to trust him with private information and opened up to him. Usaif's wife was upset about her husband's new arrangement for a variety of factors. The most important was her family's safety.

"I don't understand Iraqis." I shook my head. "What the fuck. I've lived in this country for over two years now and still don't understand the people, the smoke and mirrors behind the politics, none of it."

"You and me both, boss," Hassan said. "Arabic is my native language, but I'm still a foreigner here." His Libyan roots and decades spent in the U.S. set him apart.

A couple days later the Iraqi interpreters approached Hassan with a proposal. They wanted to throw a party in my honor with Iraqi food. By that time, several interpreters had departed for Jordan. A few had made it to the States and were in the early phases of assimilating or enlisting in the U.S. military. Other translators waited on paperwork, and some chose not to apply for the SIV. Despite the levels of violence, they couldn't break from their culture and way of life. They had families and social mores they understood. The concept of America seemed too distant.

Whether they were staying or going, Hassan said all of them wanted to celebrate. I told him that I didn't like parties in my honor. I believed it cut against the grain of my training and education. The Iraqis persisted. They attempted to shame me by saying that in their culture it was impolite to refuse a gift. We finally agreed the party would be billed as a celebration of Task Force Justice and the Underground Railroad and would be a salute to all of us. We had prevailed against the bureaucracy and the forces of violence and helped a small group escape. We would celebrate each other.

Planning for the party began with the understanding it wouldn't interrupt the daily operations tempo. Soldiers patrolled, went to meetings and checked on other teams. On top of that, all of us had duties and preparations for our redeployment back to Germany. It was up to Iraqi interpreters and storeowners to figure out where to buy the food and other gifts they wanted to give their American friends.

During that time, the State Department approved more Task Force interpreters to be interviewed in Amman. Ronnie was one of them. He was surprised.

"I decided not to leave for Amman yet," Ronnie said. "I don't want to arrive in the States and have to rely on anyone, so I plan to save up some money for a while."

"You sure? That sounds crazy," I said.

"I know it's dangerous, but I need to be independent when I get there. Having to rely on other people to support me would be a fate worse than death."

"If I can assist, I will. I'm already on the deployment timeline to return to Iraq in another year." My hope was that it would all be over by then, but experience told me it wouldn't.

We held the party the following week at our favorite gathering place, Corporal Huffman's creation on the roof. The chai shop had become a staple of the base, a place where interpreters met and consulted with each other. Soldiers and civilian contractors smoked cigarettes, played cards, or watched the big screen television. It was a social spot where patrons could unwind from the stresses of Baghdad and forget the threats and uncertainty for a brief while.

Loud, Arabic music pumped from the stereo system as if in a night club. Most of the interpreters were young and could remember clubs in Baghdad. Those places no longer existed unless fabricated in American enclaves in the Green Zone or on bases. JAM had driven the modern, pre-war, urbanized culture from most of the city. In public, women were covered from head to toe and usually accompanied by a male. Here, on a tiny base within an Iraqi FOB, interpreters experienced a sense of what a free life could be.

Food overflowed on tables in the chai shop. Interpreters didn't allow an American plate to be empty. The Iraqis had gone all out with selections of lamb, chicken, and fish on heaps of rice with fresh vegetables. They served falafel and kabobs, in addition to sweets like dates and Lebanese pastries. Iraqis piled additional helpings on the plates of any American about to finish. For some of the soldiers who didn't often leave the base, this was a novelty. Those of us who routinely patrolled ate Iraqi food three or four times per week.

The music never stopped. Some people danced as a group and enjoyed the sense of release and spirit that filled the rooftop.

Hassan stood next to me and said, "Mark would like to present you with a gift."

I shot him an exasperated look. "Thought we agreed the party would not be about me but a celebration of Task Force Justice and the whole team."

"Yes, but you need to accept these gifts on behalf of the Task Force. Plus, they're giving gifts to all the Americans. Some are getting different presents. They want to thank all of you."

"Got it." I smiled. "Don't want to cause a cultural faux pas."

Mark stood with a couple interpreters and watched us until Hassan waved him over. Well-respected, thin, fit, and sporting dark, curly hair, Mark worked with one of the Iraqi Army transition teams. He said, "All the interpreters, we wanted to give you something to remember us. We are very thankful for everything you and the soldiers have done. You've saved lives, and we will never forget."

"It's been an honor serving with you and the many who have come here and have left us already," I said.

"We want you to have this." He presented me with an Iraqi flag, about two feet by three feet. "All of the Iraqis left, we signed this flag. We know that you probably have lots of things in your office…"

"You haven't seen my office."

"We hope you will put it in a spot to remember us when you get back to your family," he said.

"Thank you." I was deeply touched and made eye contact with the four or five interpreters who had participated in the unofficial gift giving. Some wiped away tears which caused me to choke me up.

"We couldn't do it without our cultural advisors," I said. "You keep us safe and help us understand what's going on."

"None of us ever believed that we could make it to America," Mark said. "It was always a dream, but you and Task Force Justice made it real. We are very thankful."

"I will hang this in a place of honor."

The interpreters nodded and smiled. "Come," one of them said. "We can't keep the colonel from eating all of this food."

Another said, "Sir, you going to dance?"

"I don't think anyone wants to see that. You've already suffered from me singing karaoke."

"No, no. We want you to dance." They clapped and yelled.

I looked to Hassan for help. He took pity on me, as he so often did, and intervened. He diverted their attention elsewhere. One or two made fresh attempts to get me on the dance floor, but I couldn't bring myself to do it until the mission was complete. We were so close to returning home to our loved ones. We were even closer to turning the mission over to another unit rotating in from the States. That caused stress because there was no guarantee the next unit would embrace our Iraqi associates the way Task Force Justice did. I worried about that unknown as we approached the transition, as well as the many stories about soldiers killed only days from redeployment. Those thoughts kept me from dancing.

Hassan and I made our last trip to BG Usaif's office, but we didn't know it at the time. I made the decision to not know the actual details of the Usaif Family escape. Arwa Damon handled the plan directly with Mohammed. Discretion was a part of her profession, and she told only those who needed to know. When we met for chai, we spoke in hushed tones. The general had not made up his mind whether to accompany his family. They would receive round-trip tickets for a vacation in the Kurdistan Region. The general's boss had offered to procure a house where he could leave his family in safety. Following two weeks' leave, BG Usaif would fly to Baghdad and resume duty. The house was part of the deception plan. From Erbil, the family would then fly to Turkey and declare refugee status in Istanbul.

"Miska, tell me what to do," he said.

"I am not going to do that, and you know it. You have to live with the consequences of your decision. If you stay and get killed, I'm not gonna look your wife and kids in the eyes and tell them I advised you to stay. If you go, it'll be tough."

"I don't know what to do." He looked at Hassan.

"We're sorry we can't help more but knowing that your family is safe will be very important, regardless of the call you make."

"I know, I know, Miska. You're a good man even if you are *abu Mashakel.*"

Hassan laughed at the mention of my nickname. It was a running joke with many of the Iraqis, and even some Americans.

Task Force Justice prepared to redeploy from Baghdad to Germany in early November 2007. As soldiers say, we were short timers, only several days from departure. I was mentally, physically, and emotionally exhausted. For the last couple of months, I had trouble putting on my body armor. Most of the soldiers had deployed for fourteen or fifteen months. As Deputy Brigade Commander, I had arrived early. The bonus package, my tour stretched sixteen months, during which I missed both my kids' birthdays, twice.

There was no time to rest. We had to hand over the mission, say goodbye to our Iraqi colleagues, and ensure a safe exit from theater. The unit would have the next couple of months in Germany to reset the formation and enjoy the Christmas holidays. I was soon to take command of 1-18 Infantry, the Vanguards, and get them ready to redeploy to combat. We had an additional complication. As part of base consolidation, two-thirds of the brigade, our higher headquarters, and sister units, were relocating to Grafenwoehr, several hours from Schweinfurt.

Hassan planned to stay on. He wasn't sure whether he would remain at FOB Justice or relocate. He said it depended on how the next unit behaved. If he liked the command climate, he'd stick around. If not, he'd head to the Green Zone or Taji, where we had attended the COIN Academy early in the deployment. Taji doubled as an Iraqi training base and logistics hub. I suspected I would see Old Dog again, maybe even in Iraq.

Several days before I left, Hassan and I sipped chai and compared notes. We received a call from BG Usaif's boss asking if we had heard from him. Hassan responded that we thought Usaif was on vacation. That didn't satisfy the general.

Hassan held the phone away and whispered, "He's saying that *Emiad* Usaif is not answering his phone."

"Tell him we saw Usaif a couple days ago before he left on vacation." I had the cynical thought that perhaps he should have answered Usaif's calls when he was almost kidnapped by JAM.

"I did. But he's saying Usaif didn't arrive at the house in the Kurdistan Region, neither did the family. He even paid the first couple months' rent." He spoke a little more Arabic and ended the call. In English he said, "Usaif's boss is mad because he paid the rent, but he's not sure if something had happened to them. He thinks we know where they are."

"Our official response is that they went on vacation," I said.

"That's what I told him. I don't think he's buying it. I guess we got our answer on whether Usaif was staying or going."

"You never know. He could get his family in place and decide to come back."

"And risk getting killed? He has two JAM groups and al Qaeda after him, and a few politicians, too. You know it's only a matter of time. Plus, who's going to take care of his family if they're refugees on their own? They're going to have a long road."

"I know."

"Gonna miss you, boss."

"Me too, Old Dog. But it seems like you'll probably be here when I get back."

"I'll be here," he said. "Maybe not on Justice, but you probably won't be coming back here, either."

"What's Louise say about you staying on? At least I've got an excuse with Amy. The Army's making me come back."

"She's okay with it. She knows that I can help pay for the kids' education. All three are in college now."

"Good luck. And stay safe. Don't go running around getting in trouble."

"Hah. Look who's talking. What's going to happen when you come back and don't have me to look after you?"

We hugged and promised to keep in touch.

We marched through the open doorway to the base gymnasium and emerged from dry ice fog like a football team taking the field. Any thought of keeping in step to the cadence was obliterated by screams and cheers, most from women and young children. Conflicting thoughts ricocheted through my mind. Guilt and pride, excitement and anxiety. Like drinking a Red Bull and vodka, a popular drink amongst soldiers, my thoughts had a simultaneous effect of stimulation and depression.

Guilt gnawed that I hadn't done enough for Iraqis left behind, for Americans dead, for others with hidden wounds. Maybe I had some of those same wounds yet to be confronted? I was addicted to the rollercoaster ride of the human experience in combat. Maybe I wouldn't care about the mundane details of life with my wife and kids. But my pride snuck through. I had worked hard to maintain an individual relationship with both of our kids, and Amy and I had communicated almost daily, even if it was 90% work-related.

Task Force Justice was proud that we'd saved almost three dozen Iraqis with the Underground Railroad. Our soldiers became adept at navigating the complexities of an urban counterinsurgency environment and attempted to integrate every tool at our disposal. We valued all team members and made a point to create the most inclusive climate possible. We could take satisfaction in all those things which heightened both my excitement at being home and anxiety about things to come.

I was thrilled to hug Amy and the kids. We all cried when we embraced. I held them close. It seemed almost too unreal to believe. The honor and excitement of command loomed in the future. Command of a unit that had multiple combat deployments and much trauma to plumb. I was proud the Army selected me to lead the Vanguards (later reflagged as 1-2 Infantry, the Black Scarves).

Amy and I had intimate knowledge of the soldiers and families. We would be able to lead them through a challenging preparation for combat. Anxiety of my own making intruded. Would I measure up to the task? Would I make the transition from virtual parent and husband to in-person? Would I cope with a dizzying array of tasks? Planning a catch-up birthday experience for both kids. Having my car inspected, registered, and winterized. Fixing lights and other things around the house. The next deployment was twelve months away. Much of that time would be consumed by preparation for combat, and a potential relocation for the unit. Experience of two deployments also bred in me anxieties about the unknown. They would later manifest as war crimes trials and other tragedies. I worried that the soldiers would be unleashed on Schweinfurt after spending a year cooped up and boxed into armored vehicles and outposts in Baghdad. They might even release the demons in their emotional footlockers. Free from the war, they could speed on the autobahn at two hundred kilometers per hour or drink until they passed out in the downtown bars. It was critical that we maintain good relationships with the local *polizei*, the German police.

The third consecutive deployment for many of these soldiers and families awaited. Our ranks had been reduced by the deaths of one hundred and nine soldiers, fifty-nine from Schweinfurt, and many others wounded. U.S. Army Garrison Schweinfurt slowly shed its widows and fatherless children and made room for new arrivals.

Meanwhile, Muhammad's family languished in Turkey, but they were alive. I had so many blessings that empowered me to focus on leading, serving our soldiers and families and powered me to move towards the challenge of command. Who would step up if I didn't? My family was safe, not sheltered as refugees in Turkey or surviving threats from insurgents in Iraq. Why shouldn't we have to sacrifice too?

Hassan (Center) and the author conducting "atmospherics" on the street. Sipping chai with the old men helped keep us informed about issues of concern for the populace.

Meeting with Sheik "Sami" to understand dynamics within Baghdad. Hassan was on leave to the United States, so a soldier and linguist accompanied the author during that time.

Memorial display for Colonel Tom Felts. Commanders and Sergeants Majors would leave tribute coins or patches during memorial ceremonies.

MAJ David Mikkelson, Dagger Brigade Chaplain, escorts "Sheik Miska" to visit some of the soldiers during a holiday celebration.

Ronnie after EFP strike, mad at the world.

The author poses with Chris Hondros (left) from Getty Images and Regis LeSommier (right) from Paris Match. Chris was later killed covering the Libyan uprising in Misrata in 2011.

Iraqis and Americans celebrate the Cinderella story, Iraqi soccer victory against powerhouse, Saudi Arabia in the 2007 Asia Cup championship.

Arwa Damon broadcasts live for CNN at the Task Force Justice lounge during the improbable Iraqi soccer victory in the 2007 Asia Cup championship. Someone draped an Iraqi flag over her shoulders while live, which got her in trouble with producers.

Farewelling "George" when he got approved for his Special Immigrant VISA.

Garry and George enjoy their first beer in the US at the airport in Phoenix, Arizona.

Colonel J.B. Burton (left) meets with the author on FOB Justice. Frequent coordination became critical, with commanders checking on soldier conditions and each other during the lengthy deployment.

Colonel J.B. Burton (left) gives SFC Rodney Stanfield his end of tour award at FOB Justice. The author and Burton tease the grizzled Master Gunner.

Task Force Justice produced a yearbook for every soldier to take home good memories, as well as remember the fallen. We were grateful to King Publishing Company, Inc. for donating the yearbooks after learning of the purpose.

Sergeant First Class Stanfield designed the Task Force Justice coin and the Registry, that captured each soldier's signature and unique coin number, and told the history of Task Force Justice.

Miska Family reunion in November, 2007.

*Madame Betty (right front) celebrates "Baby Amy's" arrival in the world.
Amy (left), "Najla" with baby, and the baby's Iraqi grandmother.*

Task Force Justice interpreters signed the Iraqi Flag and presented it as a gift to the author in gratitude for the Baghdad Underground Railroad. The flag hung in my office as a symbol of motivation to write the book. (Flag intentionally blurred to mask signatures.)

Part Two

America

IN BOUND FOR *Canaan*, author Fergus Bordewich makes the case that "the Underground Railroad—offered the chance to live out prayer in action, to put faith to *practical* effect," sowing the seeds for African American emancipation. He also states that "women were, for the first time, participants in a political movement on an equal plane with men, sheltering and clothing fugitive slaves." Women also played a prominent role in the Baghdad Underground Railroad, specifically as sponsors for Iraqis arriving in the United States. Staff Sergeant Laurie Miller, who sponsored George as the first passenger on the Baghdad Underground Railroad, was the first of many women who helped the Task Force Justice interpreters adapt to a new life.

Three women in particular, my mother, Betty Eble, Madonna Felix (Captain Felix's mother) and Lia Haley (Gregg Haley's wife) ensured that Iraqis felt welcome and helped them assimilate to their new country. Many men also played a part in the harrowing escapes from sectarian chaos; women, however, played a dominant role at the end of the journey, where nurturing and support were vital to the integration of Iraqis into American culture. These women were certainly not the only ones to engage in helping Iraqis find refuge and adapt to American life, but they are the best cases known to me.

As Betty, Madonna, and Lia struggled to help Iraqis assimilate, I prepared to redeploy to Iraq from Germany. Amy and I were transferred back to 1-18 Infantry, The Vanguards, our old battalion, a subordinate unit within the Dagger Brigade. This would be the fifth consecutive deployment for the Dagger Brigade in less than a decade and our third, which would bring me to forty months in combat by the end. We were tired but felt fortunate to stay with the men and women we had come to know and love.

Preparations for another combat deployment were intense. Three soldiers died due to noncombat-related incidents. Stress permeated the community, as units and families readied for the next separation. In the course of that year, I lost track of the interpreters as they settled in the United States. For them, other forms of stress and pressure played out as they attempted to adapt to American norms.

Chapter Twelve

Lia

"When I found I had crossed the line,
I looked at my hands to see if I was the same person."

~ Harriet Tubman

KANSAS CITY INTERNATIONAL Airport sits fifteen miles northwest of Kansas City in Platte County, Missouri. In 2007, eleven million passengers passed through its gates. The interpreter we called Dave was one of them. In the fall of that year, he arrived from Amman, Jordan. Major Gregg Haley had assumed that Dave would be in Jordan for months, however, the process was smoother than expected. Three weeks into his stay, he showed up at the U.S. Embassy on the appointed day. Less than twenty-four hours later he was on an Air France flight en route to Atlanta via Charles de Gaulle Airport in Paris.

At Hartsfield-Jackson Airport in Atlanta, the world's busiest with over 89 million passengers passing through its gates that year, Dave waited four hours to process through customs. First, he retrieved his luggage then waited in line to turn in his customs declaration. Next, he was escorted to an office where he filled out reams of paperwork.

Ironically, part of the bureaucratic in-processing required him to register for the Selective Service. Dave was a military-aged male entering the United States for residency. He was eligible for the draft, should it ever be reinstated. As he filled out the forms, he recalled telling Gregg Haley that his goal was to become an officer in the U.S. Army. Maybe he would enlist first, but the idea of attending college appealed to him. Dave could master English and earn a commission. He didn't have the resources to pay for college, so the military route was attractive.

On board a Boeing 737, preparations were made for arrival into Kansas City. As the plane descended, Dave thought, "I'll always remember this day." Tuesday, October 2, 2007. He glanced out the window at the litup night landscape below. His first-ever flight was Baghdad to Amman, three weeks earlier. Now he had flown halfway around the world.

The pilot announced, "Weather in Kansas City is 54 degrees and cloudy. We hope you've enjoyed your flight."

Dave converted the Fahrenheit temperature to Celsius. It was cold for him, which added to his anxiety. Lia Haley would pick him up at the airport. Dave had seen photos of her in Iraq and was excited to meet the major's family.

The aircraft touched down. Dave removed his carry-on luggage from the overhead bin and waited for the line of passengers to exit the plane. As he walked into the terminal to baggage claim, he took note of the signs on doors, "No turning back after passing." That brought the point home. While he was excited about the prospect of a new life, he couldn't help but feel that he'd left his homeland and culture behind forever.

Lia Haley was a bit nervous as she waited in baggage claim. She knew it was childish. Gregg trusted Dave, but she was the mother of two little boys and her protective instincts overruled logic. She had asked her friend Maria to accompany her to the airport. "I skyped with Gregg last night," she said to Maria, then switched to their native Portuguese. "I'm a little nervous about picking Dave up at the airport."

Maria was also nervous. She'd never met someone from the Middle East. The news in the U.S. often reported on terrorism in that part of the world. While most of the attacks occurred in Iraq or Afghanistan, post-9/11 hypersensitivity remained high. The United States and much of the world remained engaged in a global war on terror, and the news media heightened the sense of the threat. Maria didn't know what to expect from an actual Iraqi.

Open. Close. Open. Close. The doors into baggage claim coughed up travelers. None resembled a Middle Easterner. Then Lia spotted a tall, thin, olive-skinned man who carried a small backpack over his shoulder and was anxiously glancing at the unfamiliar faces. She walked toward him. "Dave?"

"Hi," he said.

"I'm so glad you made it." Lia noted how much he reminded her of her brother who had died when she was nineteen.

"Thank you very much for picking me up," Dave said. He bowed. "I told Major Haley that you didn't have to get me."

"I know what it's like to come to a strange place where everything is different. I'm from Brazil. Even though Gregg helped me the entire time, it was hard. People here do not understand how different things are. I told Gregg I didn't want you to worry about transportation. We'll take you to your apartment."

Maria balanced Lia's youngest child on her hip and tried to wrangle the four-year-old, who was excited about meeting someone who worked with his daddy. Maria gripped his collar and joined his mom.

"This is my friend, Maria," Lia said. "And this is my son, Lucas. The little one is mine, too."

"Nice to meet you," Dave offered Maria an awkward smile. "And very nice to meet you, Lucas."

"I'm four," Lucas said.

"You are a big boy."

After picking up Dave's luggage, which consisted of one bag, Maria slid into the back with both boys. Dave rode in the front passenger seat.

"You hungry?" Lia said. "We could get some dinner."

"I had pretzels on the flight."

"We can pick something up on the way back. What would you like?"

"They have McDonalds here?" He'd eaten Burger King in Iraq. Some of the bigger bases had Burger King, which had a military contract. Dave had seen TV commercials for McDonalds all his life but had never tasted it.

In the backseat, Maria chuckled, and Lucas said, "Yay, McDonalds."

Lia laughed. "That settles it. We'll stop before we get on the highway. We have a two-hour ride."

Ten minutes later they pulled into a McDonalds drive-through. Lia rolled down her window and motioned toward the menu.

"What is this?" Dave said. "Some special kind of door to the restaurant?"

"This is the drive-through. No need to go inside. Order what you want."

Dave was amazed. He'd seen drive-throughs in a few Hollywood movies. Now he really knew he was in America.

"See anything you like?"

"Everything," Dave said.

Lia laughed and said, "I'll get you what Gregg usually orders. And I know Lucas wants a Happy Meal. Maria?"

"Just a decaf, please."

Order placed, Lia paid. Dave offered money, but she refused, "You are our guest. Plus, you're gonna need to save until you get a job. I know Gregg is working on that for you."

"Thank you. You are very kind."

They pulled forward. At the next window a teenager in a McDonald's uniform wore a headset that reminded Dave of what he and the soldiers used when on patrol in Iraq.

Lia handed him a bag and a drink. She motioned towards the cup holder. "Place your drink there. That way it won't spill."

Maria took the Happy Meal and Lucas gnawed on chicken nuggets and French fries.

Dave opened his sack and found French fries and a double cheeseburger. He dug into the food. "Fries are different from Camp Liberty, but really good." He took a bite of his burger. "Different, too, but very good. Thank you so much."

They entered Interstate 70 and headed to Manhattan, Kansas. Even at seventy miles per hour, which he converted to about 110 kph, Dave was struck by the similarities between the open spaces in Kansas and those in Iraq, but also the many differences. Lia's vehicle seemed almost from science fiction, with electronics and features Dave had never seen. He was also struck by the lack of people on the streets.

"Where is everybody? In Iraq, even at night, there's always lots of people. There were only a few people back by the airport."

"It's very different here," Lia said. "In Brazil, there would be many people out at night, too. Kansas City is sleepy."

"Is everywhere in America like this?"

Lia laughed. "Wait 'til we get to Manhattan. There will be nobody out."

Dave shook his head and recalled the signs at the airport. No turning back.

Lia had programmed the address for Dave's new apartment in the car's GPS. Gregg had found the place online and sent her the address. She'd never been to this neighborhood and didn't like it. Her mom instincts kicked in as they made several turns and arrived at the building. Cars parked on the street were old and in various states of disrepair. Three young men stood at the back of one with a wide-open trunk. A lone woman sat and smoked a cigarette outside a building entrance.

Lia said, "Okay, we're here."

Dave said, "Thank you so much. I am grateful you picked me up."

"Need help with your bag?"

"No, I'll be alright." He opened the door. "It's late. Thank you."

As Dave moved to the trunk, Lia turned to Maria. "I can't leave him here."

"What are you going to do? We don't have a lot of options."

"Take him home and put him in our basement."

"Are you crazy?"

"Look at this place. I bet it's drug infested and not safe. He's brand new to this country. I can't dump him here."

Maria knew her friend well enough to know when she'd made up her mind. "You want me to spend the night?" said Maria. "I have to work tomorrow but I might be able to swing it."

"I'll be alright. There's plenty of room in the basement. You've already been so helpful."

Lia hopped out and hurried to the rear of her car. Dave was ready to haul his luggage into the building.

"Stop. Put your luggage back in the car. I can't let you stay here."

"What?"

"It's obvious Gregg never saw this place and that he's never been in this area before."

"Yes. He found it online," said Dave.

"I don't like it. I can't let you stay here. We have room in our basement. You'll stay with us."

Dave slid his suitcase and backpack into the luggage compartment. They drove another twenty minutes and arrived at the Haley residence. Dave yawned. His long trip from Amman had taken a toll. Everyone was exhausted: Maria because she'd entertained Lucas and looked after his baby brother; and Lia, due to the drive, her kids and the fact she hadn't slept well the night before. To top it off, she was allowing a strange man from Iraq to sleep in her basement. She thought again how Dave looked like her deceased brother. He'd been the only boy in a family of girls. She missed him.

The next day, Lia awoke early as usual. She changed and fed the baby then enjoyed a cup of strong, dark coffee as she collected her thoughts. She was impressed by how respectful Dave was and by his excellent English.

Lucas ran into the kitchen. She gave him a cup of juice and watched him. This would be his last year before kindergarten.

Pepped by the juice, Lucas said, "Is Daddy's friend here?"

"Yes, honey. Daddy's friend is named Dave. He'll stay in our basement for a while."

"Can I go see him?"

"We have to let him sleep. He had a very long flight yesterday and came a long way."

"Please, Mommy. I wanna play with him."

Lia changed the subject. "How about *Thomas the Tank Engine*?"

Lucas ran to the family room and plopped down on the couch near the television. Lia sat, grabbed the remote and adjusted the volume. Lucas snuggled with her, enthralled by the exploits of the blue train.

In the kitchen, Lia poured more coffee. She sipped and opened her laptop. It was her habit to check the internet each morning for overnight news from Iraq. Baghdad was nine hours ahead of Central Time in the U.S. Sometimes, she would read about events in Iraq and ask Gregg about them when they Skyped or emailed. As she absorbed the morning's news, she heard the stairs creak and Lucas say, "Hi."

A moment later Dave said, "Good morning." He stood in the kitchen doorway.

"I'm so sorry," Lia said. "Lucas was supposed to watch TV."

"He wanted to tell me about someone called Thomas. Maybe he drives a train?"

Lia smiled. "He wants to tell you about his favorite TV show. It's a cartoon."

"I love cartoons. Is it okay if I watch it with him?"

"Of course. I hope you didn't want to sleep more. Hungry? Want some coffee?"

"Coffee would be great."

"Milk or sugar?"

Lucas pulled Dave toward the television while Lia fixed him a cup of coffee.

"Black, please."

"You don't have to watch TV with him."

"It's okay. I love kids. I helped with brothers and sisters when I was growing up." Dave sat on the couch next to Lucas. Lia handed him the coffee. Soon, they were engrossed with Thomas attempting to overcome a challenge along the tracks of life.

As they adjusted to the new lifestyle, Dave offered to help around the house and watch the boys. Even the baby crawled around and looked for him to play. Dave would lay a blanket on the floor. The boys took turns lying on it as he pulled it around the basement. They'd laugh as Dave twisted and turned and made Thomas sounds as the boys hung on. He demonstrated a real knack for kids and was happy to pitch in with the cooking and cleaning. Lia appreciated an extra hand around the house. Time passed faster for her. Gregg's deployment had dragged for months, but Dave's arrival helped speed the clock and made her husband's return seem imminent.

From Iraq, Gregg found Dave a job. A retired Air Force colonel had a business in Manhattan that crafted parts for small aircraft. Lia took Dave to the interview with the colonel, who agreed to hire and train him.

They fell into a routine. Lia drove Dave to and from work each day and he helped with the house and kids in the evening. Given that Lucas missed Daddy, Dave helped fill a void during the final weeks of a year-long deployment. As Gregg prepared to come home, his dad, John Haley, made a trip to check on Lia and the boys and to see if he could assist Dave.

Chapter Thirteen

Dave

"There is no easy walk to freedom anywhere."

~ Nelson Mandela

A COUPLE OF weeks after Dave arrived, John Haley drove his Ford Ranger the six hours from St. Louis to Manhattan, Kansas, on I-70. He knew from Gregg that Dave had taken up residence in the basement. John thought it was a little crazy to have a strange Arab man in the house. He didn't know too many immigrants. In fact, Lia was the first foreigner he knew well. She was a great wife to Gregg and mother to the boys. If she made the call to bring Dave into the house, John figured she must've known what she was doing. He rang the bell. Lia opened the door and Lucas shouted, "Grandpa."

"You little rascal," John said.

"Hungry? Can I get you something to drink?" Lia said.

"Glass of water? I could really use a beer but maybe I ought to meet your house guest first."

"Dave's downstairs with the baby. They play all the time."

They trooped to the basement and found Dave and the toddler on the floor. He stood and approached John with an outstretched hand.

"Hello, sir." He treated John with deference.

"How ya doin?" They shook. "My son tells me a lot about you."

Dave said, "Major Haley is a great leader."

"I'm sure he is." John never heard much about what happened downrange. He figured Gregg would tell him if he wanted him to know. "I hear you're gonna take a driving test tomorrow."

"Yes, sir. I'm a little nervous because it's in English. I think it would be easy if it was in Arabic. I took a sample test a couple of days ago. It didn't go well."

"I'm sure you'll do fine."

"*Inshallah*. I could drive okay in Baghdad, but Iraqis are crazy drivers. We don't follow rules like here."

The next day, as John drove Dave to the Kansas Driver's License Office, they discussed how different life was in the States. "Lia has been like a sister to me," said Dave. "Gregg is like a brother. We were always together in Baghdad. He helped me get the job, too."

"How's work been going?" John said.

"My boss is very nice. I don't see much of him after he hired me. I went to the training. I work, get lunch break, and work until it's time to go home."

"My son told me that you saved his ass many times. We're all thankful for whatever you boys did together over there. It must've been hard."

"We were always in danger. Our mission was very sensitive."

"I'm sure it was." John changed the subject. "Lia says he'll be home by the New Year. Maybe we can get the family all together." He checked a street sign and pulled into a strip mall with a liquor store, a beauty salon, and other businesses. Among them was the driver's testing location.

"Hope it's not too crowded. You ready?"

"I think so," said Dave. "I studied the book. I don't want to keep coming back to this place."

They walked into the office. It was small and packed with people from all walks of life.

"What a zoo," John said.

Dave got in line behind ten people. He had his visa and other paperwork that proved he was authorized to be in the U.S. A driver's license would be another big step towards assimilation. Not only would it allow him to drive, but the license would also give him the identification he needed to do anything for himself, from buying a beer to cashing a check. In Dave's mind, he had to pass. He'd be so much closer to becoming a real American.

He reached the desk. A heavy-set, middle-aged woman asked his purpose for being there without looking up.

"I would like to take a driving test," Dave said.

She reacted to his accent. "Let me see a valid form of ID and residency documents."

Dave handed her the paperwork. Lia had gone over the requirements to ensure he had everything. It took time to figure out whether his documents would pass. During his previous trip, when he had failed the written test, Dave made it past the monotone lady who screened paperwork. Second time was no exception.

"Papers are good. I'm putting your name in the system. There are ten test stations over there. Take a seat and wait for your name to be called."

Dave thanked her. He stood in the waiting area as John sat. The discomfort of the crowded office was coupled with Dave's cultural anxiety. He feared embarrassing himself and his gracious hosts. He didn't want Lia to continue being his taxi driver.

A half-hour later, an older man in the testing area called Dave's name. Dave took his time on the twenty-question test. He read each question slowly. Admittedly, he hadn't studied much for his first test. He'd been hung up on phrases like "parallel parking" and other driving terms he'd never come across. The second time, he was prepared. He'd studied for several days and reviewed all the material the night before. Even so, he had a lump in his throat when he finished his final answer. When he saw on the computer screen that he'd passed, he shot his hand in the air with triumph. "Yes," he said.

John chuckled. "Gregg had the same reaction when he got his." Dave, a twenty-two-year-old Iraqi who had spent years on the front lines of war, was as excited as a high schooler. "Congratulations," said John. "This is one huge deal."

"Thank you." Then it reality hit. "Oh boy. Now I gotta take the driving test."

"Have you practiced?"

Dave didn't want to sound too confident. "Lia let me drive a little bit until she saw that I'd done it before. I'll try not to drive like an Iraqi."

John watched as Dave and the examiner drove away from the test station. Twenty minutes later they returned. Dave gripped the steering wheel, an anxious look on his face. Then he beamed at John. It had gone well.

The Kansas Driver's License Office issued a temporary license. He'd receive his permanent one with a photo in the mail in about two weeks.

Lia waited at the front door when they pulled into the driveway. She raised an eyebrow. "Well?"

Dave hung his head. "Not so good. They said I couldn't come back for another six months."

"What? I have to drive you around for another six months?"

John couldn't hold it. He laughed. "Fooled you. He passed with flying colors."

"You're just like my brother," Lia said. "Always teasing me."

Dave was, as his soldier friends said, pumped. He had a job, driver's license, and an apartment lined up. Lia and Gregg had looked near Kansas State University. When they found a place they liked, Gregg co-signed the lease. It was a small studio, so it saved on funds. It would be similar to student housing. He'd have his own bedroom but with shared common space with all of the college-type activity available to him.

A couple of days later, they purchased a bike Dave would ride until he could afford a car. His new apartment was about a mile from his job with the colonel, and a grocery store was close.

Several days later, John returned to St. Louis after a week's stay. That was enough time to give Lia a break and help Dave get on his feet.

Dave biked to work every day, but the weather was turning colder. He added more layers of clothing and borrowed gloves from work to shield himself against the icy wind. Despite the cold, pride kept him on the bike. Lia had done too much. He wouldn't ask for more.

One evening, he telephoned her. "Good news, Lia. I received my first paycheck."

"Wonderful. I am so proud of you."

"I'd like to take you out to dinner to celebrate."

"That's sweet, but it's expensive."

"That's not important. You and Major Haley have done so much for me. It's the least I can do."

"I understand." Lia was gracious in her acceptance. "When do you want to go?"

"Tomorrow night? And the boys should come with us."

"Lucas might have a hard time sitting still, and the baby sometimes gets cranky."

"They will be fine. I can help, plus they really like McDonald's."

"Hah. I can bribe Lucas with a Happy Meal."

"You can bribe me too. I miss playing with the boys."

Gregg returned home from his year-long deployment several weeks later. He and his team had spent Christmas in Kuwait. They joked that Army planners worked out the troop flow to ensure both the incoming and outgoing teams missed spending the holiday with family.

Fort Riley hosted a welcome home ceremony. Many soldiers were not local to the area and would have to wait to see loved ones. Gregg's had the good fortune to be within driving distance. His brother and family lived in Colorado, his parents and others in St. Louis. Gregg and Lia's house in Manhattan was in the middle.

The military had an established process of family notification when soldiers returned from deployment. They assembled families into the right place at the right time, based on air schedules. But everything was fluid and timetables could change at the last minute. Bad weather at both ends. Troops delayed departing Iraq or Kuwait. Flights rerouted based upon military necessity. So much could bump a soldier or an entire airplane load of soldiers to a later date. As a result, many didn't plan for family to attend the welcome-home ceremony. Gregg decided to celebrate at his house and not drag everyone through the process. He'd given Lia a heads up several days in advance of his scheduled arrival when his flight plan was locked in. He asked her to alert his parents, Dave, and the rest of the family that they needed to be flexible. If the schedule changed, he'd send word.

Lia was excited. She'd missed Gregg much more than anticipated. She looked forward to him being around the house. And other things. The year had been a challenge, but helping Dave assimilate had helped. It gave her a task and a goal that eased the anxiety of separation. She also understood that her service to Dave honored her husband and the other soldiers.

The day arrived. Gregg was due to land at 9 p.m., December 27, 2007.

The redeployment process involved a myriad of tasks for returning soldiers. Medical checks, paperwork so they would be paid properly, updating records, and turning in special equipment issued for combat, including all weapons.

Since most soldiers had to travel long distances to their families, unit leadership decided to accelerate the normal processing time and compressed a week-long procedure into two days. Gregg's team decided they'd work all night. The intent was to get the guys home before the New Year holiday since they'd missed Christmas. There was no need to let red tape keep them from their families during the holidays. But it was the Army. Certain things had to be done.

As it happened, the baby was sick. Lia decided not to attend the ceremony. She and Gregg devised a plan instead. His brothers, their families, and his parents would be there the next day. They'd have a delayed Christmas with presents and dinner on December 29.

The day before, in the middle of the night, Gregg slipped home for a few hours. They lived a short two miles from the base. He wanted so much to see Lia and the boys. They reunited as a family, then he returned to base.

Military families often make small sacrifices, like celebrating Christmas on a day other than the actual holiday. Gregg and Lia hosted their extended family, including Dave. It was a wonderful reunion. Dave played with the boys, pulling them around the floor. This was the rest of the family's introduction to him. Most had never interacted with a person from the Middle East.

Later in the day, John saw several of his grandchildren march upstairs. Scarves covered their heads and they chanted something that sounded like Arabic. Dave taught them a few Arabic words and the proper way to wear the scarves. Most of the family laughed and smiled, but John glanced at Dave. He thought the Iraqi might be offended that the kids were being sacrilegious. But Dave laughed along with everyone else, and John realized that perhaps Americans had a lot more in common with Iraqis than he had thought.

Joyous and heartwarming, the day was such a contrast to the violence in Iraq, thousands of miles away. It all felt surreal to Gregg, as if he were in a version of a scene from Dicken's *A Christmas Carol.* In a few short days, he'd gone from the constant stress of patrols and interaction with an Iraqi unit infiltrated by JAM to the safety and warmth of his family. After a long, lethal deployment, he was home. It felt too good to be true. He couldn't imagine how Dave felt, leaving his family and culture behind.

The next several weeks, Gregg and his team had a light work schedule due to the holidays and the freedom afforded returned combat veterans. He would frequently stop by Dave's apartment after work. They'd discuss the future and catch up.

"After you left," Gregg said, "we had a lot of problems with the JAM guys. But the other interpreters helped us out."

"Good guys. I'd have felt guilty leaving if I thought that they couldn't do the job."

"Nobody could replace you." Gregg meant it. "But we were able to continue the mission. After I fired Zorro, the other interpreters got the message that we had to stay disciplined. That's part of the reason all of my guys got home safe, and none of the interpreters or their families got killed. I consider that a success."

Dave was glad for the opportunity to express his appreciation face-to-face for all Gregg had done. "I got a job, found a car, got to see places. All because of you and your family."

"Lia loves you like a brother, and the boys miss you. When you left the basement, the baby kept trying to go down and look for you."

"I'm happy to help any time."

"We appreciate that, but you need to focus on the future. A good way to get a degree and become an officer is to apply for ROTC. If you go that route, the Army might pay for some of it."

"Really? How do I do that?"

"One step at a time. We need to get you established with your work and maybe get credit for your university in Iraq if we're able."

"It would be an honor to join the U.S. Army." Like other Iraqis who escaped the violence, Dave had spent a lot of time with soldiers and Marines. He respected the code of honor the men and women lived by. To him, they didn't seem plagued with corruption and basic challenges like many in the Iraqi security forces. U.S. military members embodied an ethos of patriotism toward their country and loyalty to each other. Gregg personified that in many ways. He had the humility to thank Dave for keeping his team alive. Dave had never imagined he would make it to the U.S. Now, he enjoyed a beer with an American friend and contemplated becoming an officer in one of the most respected institutions in the country. His future was bright.

Dave worked for eighteen months at the aircraft parts firm. Most of his duties were manual labor, but it was a path forward. In 2009 he enlisted in the Army. He'd struggled a bit with college and had no luck translating his Iraqi education into meaningful credits in the American system. Dave talked with Gregg about other ways to become an officer. One was to enlist, become an exemplary soldier, and attend Officer Candidate School. It would immerse him in the military and sharpen his English. If all went well, he could apply for OCS or complete his enlistment and sign up for ROTC.

Several Iraqi interpreters from FOB Justice who had made it to the States decided to join the Army. Recruiters scoured the U.S. for Arabic speakers to fill billets in the Army's linguist program. As translators in uniform, these young recruits would fill a vital need and have the opportunity to apply for a security clearance, which was crucial to American efforts. Some of the military guys from Gregg's unit at Fort Riley instructed Dave about how to speak with a recruiter. He signed his Army contract in July 2009.

At the same time, he learned his parents would be emigrating. Life remained dangerous in Iraq. They had applied for U.S. permanent residency after Dave settled in.

The same day Dave signed his Army contract, he drove to Michigan to meet his parents who were landing that evening. Dave would help them get settled until he had to report for basic training in October. He thought it would be harder for them to adjust than for him.

After Dave completed Basic Combat Training, he moved on to Advance Individual Training (AIT) and then was assigned to the 2nd

Brigade, 1ˢᵗ Infantry Division, based in Fort Riley, Kansas. It was the same unit he supported as a translator in Iraq years earlier. He found it ironic that he would deploy with the unit in November 2011 for a year.

After completing his four-year enlistment, Dave went to work for a defense contractor. He was posted overseas, for a time in Iraq and later Guantanamo, Cuba. He met and married a woman in Michigan and decided to leave the military and contracting in order to raise a family. He settled in Michigan near his parents.

Dave didn't hear much from Gregg over the years since the Haley family was assigned to Germany. Then one day in 2014, Gregg sent Dave an email.

> *Hey brother,*
>
> *It's been a while. I hope you and the family are well. Lia, the boys and I moved back from Germany to Fort Polk, Louisiana, about a month ago. I'm getting ready to take command of a battalion next month. I'm pretty sure you're still up in Michigan, so no expectation that you'd be able to make it to the change in command ceremony. However, I wanted to let you know that you were invited. Please give my best to your family. We all miss you.*
>
> *Gregg*

Dave responded that evening. He scoffed at the notion of missing such an important accomplishment in his American brother's career. He and his wife would attend.

The following month, Gregg's father, John, drove down to Fort Polk. His mother couldn't attend due to poor health. Gregg and Lia went through the logistics of housing family and helping them navigate the military protocols and base procedures. John was on hand to support his son's professional achievement. Dave and his wife would be there, too. He'd been to Fort Polk during his enlisted time and was familiar with the base.

As various family members arrived, they reunited at Gregg and Lia's new home. Outside on the patio, Dave and John chatted. "I can't believe you and your wife drove all this way to attend the ceremony," John said.

"Major Haley kept us all alive when we were in a really dangerous environment. I'm serious when I say he's like my brother, and I'm grateful to be invited."

"We're sure proud of him. I only wish his mother could be here with us."

The morning of the change of command, the family arrived thirty minutes early. As VIPs, they sat under an awning that shielded them from the elements. Dave and his wife joined them.

Change of command ceremonies are a time-honored military tradition. They are meant to send off the outgoing commander and provide an opportunity for the incoming commander to conduct his or her first inspection of the troops. The ceremony involves a lot of pomp and circumstance with a military marching band, speeches, and other rituals. They follow a script, but some deviations are allowed depending on the commanders and the climate of the higher headquarters. For example, commanders' spouses generally receive a bouquet of roses, paid for by the commanders to honor their sacrifice as the senior family advisor in the formation. Commanders also recognized their children, presenting gifts of military significance or family meaning. The Army had integrated families throughout its culture in historic ways during the wars.

Protocol dictates that the incoming commander keep his comments short. Soldiers standing in formation no doubt hoped Gregg would be brief, but he resolved he would acknowledge Dave with the rest of his family. His soldiers needed to hear him speak about this brotherhood forged in Iraq. His remarks would be a first glimpse to help them know the man who would lead them for the next couple of years.

Gregg thanked senior leadership for entrusting him with the opportunity and responsibility to lead America's sons and daughters. Then he thanked Lia and their two sons. A young sergeant presented her a bouquet of flowers and welcomed her to the battalion. The sergeant presented each of Gregg's sons with a battalion coin. The new commander then thanked his parents, expressing regret his mother was unable to attend due to illness. Several other guests were acknowledged, and lastly, he turned to Dave.

"I know it's important to keep this short," he said, "but I need to point out another special guest." He asked Dave to stand. He stood and gripped his wife's shoulder. Gregg cleared his throat and described how the two of them had kept each other alive in combat in Baghdad at the height of sectarian violence in 2007. He told the story of helping Dave get out of Iraq on the Baghdad Underground Railroad and that Dave had served a tour of duty as a U.S. soldier. Gregg spoke a few words of thanks in Arabic. He wanted to convey to the soldiers his focus on understanding other cultures.

That evening, the Haleys hosted a huge party in their backyard, complete with DJ, catered Cajun food, games, dancing, and plenty of booze. Later, guests bid farewell, the party thinned, and Dave located Gregg in a quiet corner.

Dave said, "I want to give you a gift."

"You don't need to do that."

"I couldn't let my brother celebrate such an important event without giving you something."

Under a patio light in the backyard, they sat in lawn chairs. Gregg opened a box and found a six-inch knife and sheath inside. Filled with gratitude, he looked up and wiped an unexpected tear.

"Check out the inscription," Dave said.

Unsheathing the knife, Gregg read, *Allah bukhayr* on one side of the blade, referring to their old running joke of Gregg's misinterpretation of the Arabic saying, "by the goodness of God."

Then Gregg flipped the knife and laughed. Engraved on the opposite side was, *Pull up a chair*.

"You being here really means a lot to me," Gregg said. "You and your wife didn't need to make the trip all the way down here."

"Are you kidding me?" Dave responded. "You're family. I couldn't miss an important day like this."

Dave had adjusted to life at the last stop on the Baghdad Underground Railroad, but some Iraqis had yet to begin the journey. Iraq was still dangerous, although the security situation had improved from the bloody days of 2006-2007. Thousands would never pierce the veil of bureaucracy to have a chance at the perilous journey. As I prepared to deploy to Iraq for the third time, many of our Iraqi partners remained in limbo.

Chapter Fourteen

Iraq Redux

"You're off to Great Places!
Today is your day!
Your mountain is waiting,
So…get on your way!"

~ Dr. Seuss, *Oh the Places You'll Go*

I DEPLOYED TO Iraq as commander of Task Force 1-2, the Black Scarves, in November 2008. Ronnie would again enter my life. Several months into the deployment, Task Force Black Scarves moved to Diwaniyah and Najaf provinces. Our primary base was FOB Echo in the city of Diwaniyah and positioned a company, Charlie Company, in Najaf Province. Najaf was the heart of Shia theological interpretation in Islam and attracted huge numbers of Shia tourists to visit the holy shrine of the Imam Ali. With that religious significance, both Najaf and Diwaniyah had overtones of the sensitivity we experienced in Khadamiyah. While we learned the ropes, I received an email from an old friend.

Hey, sir,

*I heard you were in Iraq. Welcome back from my job in the
Green Zone.*

Respectfully, Ronnie

He was still here? That was a surprise. I knew it was a great risk
for him to remain in Baghdad. I typed a response.

*What are you still doing in Baghdad? We need to connect.
Would love for you to come work with me in Diwaniyah.
Let's chat on the phone.*

Ronnie called. "How have you been, sir?"

"Sounds like you've had more adventures than me," I said.

"I had to add a few more stops on the Underground Railroad. I
didn't want it to be easy or anything. I was rooming with an American
officer, Captain Felix."

Ronnie explained that he wanted to save more money before
immigrating to the U.S. Working as an interpreter in the Green Zone,
he'd put away over ten thousand dollars, then disaster struck. His room
inside Saddam's old palace caught fire. Everything was lost. Ronnie
didn't have a savings account. Iraq functioned as a cash-based society.
His entire cash savings literally went up in smoke. Worse, his passport,
identification, and visa paperwork, which represented his golden ticket
to safety, were all lost. It was a devastating stroke of bad luck.

"I used some connections and paid to get my Iraqi identification
remade. Otherwise, I couldn't get a new passport. It cost me three
thousand dollars and only because another terp's dad had connections.
I'm still waiting on the visa."

"Come work in Diwaniyah with me," I said. "I'll write a letter to
get you transferred."

"I'd love that, sir."

Ronnie had reached out, not to complain or ask for help, but to
keep me informed. He made plans to visit and possibly be reassigned
to my unit. I informed Command Sergeant Major (CSM) Noe Salinas.
He thought I was somewhat crazy, communicating with a local
interpreter who worked with me in Baghdad on my last tour like we

were long lost buddies. Noe told the boys why we were going to get this interpreter. I signed a letter that requested Ronnie by name and sent it to his unit. A few weeks later, the Army and the contracting firm that employed him granted the transfer.

Ronnie caught a ride to FOB Kalsu, the base in Babil Province we had vacated a few months before. From there, we picked him up and had an easy drive north up the main supply route, avoiding a trip all the way into Baghdad. Ronnie still had long hair and a beard, and despite all that had happened, the same rakish, upbeat smile.

"It is very good to see you, sir," he said.

The soldiers eyed us with a little suspicion, casting sidelong glances at each other. The men considered me a leader who had gone native. It was an image we used at times to have fun. For Memorial Day, I dressed in traditional sheik garb I'd received as a gift. CSM Salinas escorted me around the base to see the soldiers, many of whom thought I was an Iraqi. Now, I'd brought some strange local into our patrol.

Early in his new assignment, Ronnie accompanied us on a visit to the governor of Diwaniyah Province. Joseph, our Lebanese-American interpreter with a security clearance, joined me in the meeting. Ronnie remained outside with the soldiers to educate them and allow them to interact with any Iraqis who approached.

CSM Salinas was surveying the security situation in the provincial government building when an Iraqi security guard attempted to communicate with him. He called to Ronnie for help.

"I think he might be joking, although I heard this in Baghdad too," Ronnie said. "He heard that your sunglasses give you x-ray vision so you can see through the women's burkas."

Noe laughed and offered to trade his sunglasses with the Iraqi guard, who declined.

Until Ronnie arrived, Salinas didn't have a nickname. Most of the soldiers were afraid of him, which was common. The CSM, as the senior noncommissioned officer, was responsible for good order and discipline in the ranks and played bad cop more often than not.

Ronnie keyed in on the soldiers' fear and used it to show them his worth as an interpreter. Because Ronnie was not a soldier, he didn't need to be overly deferential to the CSM. He was polite, but he also took the liberty of pushing Noe's buttons. One day on patrol, not long after his arrival, Ronnie discussed over the open microphone whether Papa Smurf was an appropriate nickname for the CSM.

"Hey guys," Ronnie said. "What do you think about Sergeant Major's nickname?"

"Watch it, Ronnie," Noe keyed in over the air as we departed the base.

"I'm serious. I don't think Papa Smurf really does Sergeant Major right. I think we should come up with another nickname."

"I can still have you thrown off the FOB," Salinas said.

"You better watch it," Jon Byrom piped in. "The Sergeant Major knows where you live." Byrom, a major, was the operations officer for the battalion, an even-keeled, thoughtful leader. He and Salinas had a strained relationship because the CSM had no problem telling majors and captains what to do.

"I'm not scared of him," Ronnie said on the radio. In the confines of the vehicle, only the driver, gunner, Ronnie, Byrom, and I could hear the discussion. When a person keyed the mic, it broadcast to the entire patrol. We operated on dual frequencies to enable better communications. It allowed the operations officer a quick switch to the battalion tactical operations center to coordinate fire support or conduct other business. When we passed into a different unit's area of operations, we checked in on their command network for a situation report. The sitrep provided an update on any enemy activity, whether or not routes were closed for an emergency, and other vital information. This was routine procedure, part of the discipline we rehearsed to keep each other sharp and adhere to standard procedures.

Ronnie keyed the mic and transmitted to the entire patrol. "I think that maybe Gargamel is more appropriate than Papa Smurf. What do you guys think?"

Raucous laughter erupted in my vehicle. Gargamel, for those who haven't seen *The Smurfs*, was the evil character always out to get the Smurfs. I suspected the other vehicles had similar reactions, maybe with the exception of Command Sergeant Major Salinas's truck. I imagined a hushed silence in his vehicle, with suppressed laughter as the soldiers' eyes widened.

"Ronnie," Salinas threatened. "Not only do I know where you live, but I have your money." After Ronnie lost his money in the fire that destroyed his quarters, he asked Noe to store his cash in a footlocker.

"He's got you there," Specialist Woods said. There was still a lot of laughter and Byrom slapped his thighs thinking about the new nickname. Ronnie, however, believed he hadn't pushed the boundaries enough.

"Where is Asreal?" Ronnie said over the patrol net. Asreal was the name of Gargamel's black cat in the Smurf cartoon. This caused new waves of riotous amusement and even the other noncommissioned officers joined the fun.

"Oh snap," Staff Sergeant Snader called from the trail vehicle. He had been my Bradley gunner as a corporal when I first took over the battalion. A chain-smoking over-achiever, he quickly rose in rank.

"That's it, Serpico," Noe said. He'd decided to nickname Ronnie after the 1970's New York City cop-whistleblower played by Al Pacino. Ronnie kind of resembled Pacino's character in the movie. "I was only gonna take a ten percent cut as my management fee, now, I don't remember you giving me any money."

"He's got you there, Ronnie," said Byrom. "Guess you better forget about the good ol' U.S. of A. You're gonna be here forever."

"Ronnie, you're in for it now," I said. "Noe is gonna have your ass when we get back."

"I'm not scared of Gargamel," Ronnie said. "I'll just get the other smurfs to gang up on him."

For the remainder of the patrol, we laughed about Noe's new nickname. Each time we thought the laughter had subsided, someone, usually Ronnie, would riff off the Gargamel theme and the jokes fired up. Most of the time it happened over the open mic. That ensured all the soldiers joined the fun.

When we arrived at the next base, Noe and Ronnie had words, but it was all in good fun. Noe couldn't allow the soldiers to believe they could get away with that, so he gave the ruse of coming down hard on Ronnie. But everyone knew the CSM enjoyed the attention.

When Ronnie was approved for the Special Immigrant Visa (SIV), I was happy. Now he wouldn't suffer the same fates as Jack or Nadal. America had thrown him a lifeline, and we had helped him reach for it. Many of the soldiers, while glad for his good fortune, knew they would miss the wild-haired team member's humor and good nature, and his innate sense of the culture. Who could replace him?

Ronnie had experienced more combat than any soldier in the task force. He'd lived in a combat zone his entire adult life. He'd developed a great sense of humor as a defense mechanism for his own psychological well-being and loved to make people laugh. Ronnie infused others with his energy and enthusiasm, which defused tension. He served American soldiers in a much greater capacity than by simply interpreting a foreign language. He demonstrated a level of resilience rather than claim victimhood from a hard life. Ronnie refused to let his spirit wane and lifted the spirits of others. We would sorely miss his presence.

In mid-2009, for the second time, the State Department informed Ronnie of his acceptance for the SIV. He was approved to travel to Amman, but the risk was high. His work with Americans made him a target. Also, there was no guarantee he could stay in Amman and keep his appointment at the U.S. Embassy. Twice, customs officials had sent him right back to Baghdad. The first time, he had no idea why, and the terrifying return trip left him shaken. The second rejection, his SIV paperwork listed a different passport number than the one he carried. That was a result of the fire and new papers. He was escorted onto a plane home while his luggage stayed in Amman. Ronnie was disheartened. He didn't know what to do. He'd given away all of his possessions to friends and family, including his car. He'd said goodbye, prepared to never see relatives again, then he was back. The third time, he took nothing for granted.

Ronnie wanted to say goodbye to his parents again. It was dangerous for them and him. Two close friends offered to smuggle him into his neighborhood. One of them, an Iraqi Army captain, drove while Ronnie ducked down in the back as they entered the neighborhood. The car stopped outside his parents' house, and the officer offered Ronnie his 9mm.

"My dad has an AK in the house, and I've been really careful," Ronnie said.

"I'll pick you up in two weeks. Let me know if anything changes. Don't go outside. Nobody needs to know you're here."

Ronnie pulled a hoodie over his head, exited the car and entered his home. His father rushed and hugged him as his mother ran into the room. Ronnie told them he was leaving again. His mom begged him to stay. She couldn't bear the thought of losing her son to such a distant land. His father explained that Iraq was too dangerous. Ronnie had to leave.

One day during Ronnie's staycation, his cousin visited. The two men chatted for ten minutes, and the cousin didn't recognize him. His beard and long hair gave him a totally different appearance. Ronnie and his brother enjoyed teasing their cousin when they told him who he was.

The Iraqi captain returned on the designated evening and drove Ronnie to the airport. As an Army officer, he faced threats of insurgent assassination and militia extortion attempts, but he had more freedom of movement than the average citizen. However, it was a necessity that he exercise extreme caution and always carry a weapon.

Ronnie had purchased a round-trip ticket to give the impression that he planned to return to Baghdad. At the airport he walked to security and was searched by the guards. As they frisked him and examined his papers, he glanced at the separate American entrance to the airport and wished he could use it. Cleared, Ronnie boarded a bus to the civilian terminal. He was the only passenger. It was a quick trip as cars weren't allowed. Officials exercised intense security protocols at the airport because of the high number of car bombs.

At the terminal, Ronnie exited the bus and entered the main passenger building. He was hyper alert for JAM members. He watched people coming and going as he checked his suitcase and moved to another security checkpoint. He stood in line and felt as if he were being torn in two. His brain moved him forward, his soul longed to remain in Baghdad with people who loved him.

Somebody called Ronnie's Iraqi name. He felt the hair on his neck bristle. No one ever recognized him in his Serpico guise. If someone did, his life, and his family's, would be at risk. Everyone knew the militia had eyes at the airport.

"It's been a long time." An Iraqi man, Ronnie's age, in airport uniform approached him in the line.

Ronnie recognized him from high school. He greeted him, trying to guess his intention. "I see you got a good job," he said. He remembered the guy had been a troublemaker. He was the tallest boy in class and drew caricatures on classroom walls of himself flexing his arms and teasing the other kids. What was he doing with a job at the airport?

"Allah has blessed me. Where are you heading?"

Ronnie sweated. What if this guy worked for JAM? "Amman," he said. "On business."

"Let me help you." It was more command than question.

"Great." Ronnie attempted to sound confident. Then the guy's name popped into his head. "Haven't seen you since high school, Hussein."

"I was different back then," he said.

"We all were." Ronnie was starting to think maybe he should have risked the highway of death through Anbar Province to get to Jordan.

Hussein accompanied him to the departure gate. Ronnie was convinced Hussein surmised he was involved in something risky. Most Iraqis mistook Ronnie for a foreigner, given his attire and grooming, and his old schoolmate reacted as if the look had some purpose.

"Let's have a cup of chai and get caught up," Hussein said. "My treat."

The two men spent the next hour together. They'd been only casual acquaintances in high school. At times, the conversation lagged, and Ronnie's brain raced. How had this guy recognized him? Much to Ronnie's relief, Hussein avoided asking anything about his business in Jordan or what he'd done with his life.

"Goodbye and good luck," Hussein said as Ronnie boarded the plane.

"*Inshallah*. And thank you."

Like other interpreters who transited via the Baghdad Underground Railroad, Ronnie spent anxious days in the Jordanian capital because he didn't fully believe he'd get to America. While in Amman, he reconnected with an Iraqi friend, which lowered his stress levels.

On the next leg of his journey, Ronnie flew from Amman to Chicago. At O'Hare International he processed through immigration after several hours of filling out forms. Finally released, Ronnie wanted his first beer in the United States. This was common with many Iraqi interpreters. They raised a beer in a toast and shot a selfie in the airport bar. Ronnie emailed his photo to his American soldier friends who were not allowed to drink in combat.

Ronnie gathered his gear and made his way through the airport for his next flight to Tucson where Captain Felix's mother, his official sponsor, would meet him.

He felt as if he were in a surreal dream and attempted to contain a mixture of excitement and anxiety. After all he had been through, he couldn't quite believe that he had made it to America. For such a long time he had resigned himself to the notion that getting out of Iraq to the safety of the U.S. was a distant dream, that it was something only a few select Iraqis would get to enjoy. On the flight to Tucson, he pinched himself to ensure it was all real.

While he knew Captain Felix's mom would pick him up, he'd never seen a photo that would help him recognize her. As he walked off the plane, Ronnie had no idea that he'd left one conflict behind for another. He would transition from fighting insurgents to battling bureaucrats to establish his life in a foreign country.

Chapter Fifteen

Madonna
"My American Mom"

"The happiest people I have known have been those who gave themselves no concern about their own souls, but did their uttermost to mitigate the miseries of others."

~ Elizabeth Cady Stanton, *History of Woman Suffrage*

MADONNA FELIX'S HUSBAND died in 2003. Soon after, her only son, Jason, deployed on his first combat tour. She epitomized the Spartan spouse, a woman who has borne the anguish of losing her husband at an early age as she sent her son to war. She endured years of anxiety as her son deployed four times to Iraq.

Captain Jason Felix met Ronnie on his third deployment. He told Madonna that his interpreter was like a brother to him, how he was fearless and had a vibrant sense of humor. Madonna sensed that her son trusted Ronnie. When Jason asked if she would be Ronnie's sponsor, she agreed.

At work, Madonna mentioned the developments to a colleague. The woman's response was one of confusion and worry. Madonna appreciated the concern but said, "My son wouldn't ask me to do something dangerous."

That evening, she was out for drinks with friends who expressed similar apprehension. One friend said, "Honey, you're a single woman living alone. You're going to bring a strange Arab man into your home? You sure that's wise?"

"Jason would never put me in danger," she reiterated and suppressed her own anxieties. He'd always been protective and wouldn't send someone to live with his mother unless he trusted that person. Granted, it was an unorthodox situation, but desperate times called for people to step forward.

In 2008, when CPT Felix met Ronnie, the situation in Iraq for interpreters was dire. He told Madonna that because Ronnie worked with Americans, he would be killed if he stayed. Jason was determined to get Ronnie out and his mother would play an instrumental role.

Several years later when I talked with Madonna, she vividly remembered picking Ronnie up at the Tucson airport. After she agreed to sponsor Ronnie, her excitement mixed with fear of the unknown. Madonna knew she'd joined the war effort, albeit from the relative safety of her home. It was her contribution to a little-known network of sponsors who supported former interpreters.

It was about 9 p.m. at the Tucson airport. Madonna had a photo of Ronnie. A lanky young man carrying a backpack rode down the escalator and entered baggage claim. He saw an American woman watching him, guessed it was Jason's mom and called out, "Mrs. Felix?"

"Ronnie? It's such a pleasure to finally meet you." She hugged him and showered him with questions. "How's Jason? How was your flight? Did they give you a hard time at customs? Are you hungry? Do you want to get something to eat?"

Ronnie said, "No, thank you. I ate back in Chicago."

"How many bags do you have?"

"Just one, plus my backpack here."

"You speak very good English. I can't imagine I could ever learn Arabic that well." Madonna felt an immediate connection with him and understood why her son had trusted this person with his life, and by extension, her life. "How'd you learn to speak it so well?"

"I served with many American units in Iraq since 2003. And I watched a lot of movies and TV. Iraqis love American television. Plus, my dad was an English teacher." They waited for his luggage for fifteen minutes and Ronnie wondered if the questions would ever stop. He was by nature a talkative guy but sensed that his new life would be peppered with these basic questions for a long time. He'd need to get used to it.

Baggage dropped onto the carousel. He reached for an old, tired suitcase.

"Wonderful," Madonna said. "I'm always nervous that my bags will get lost when I travel."

Ronnie recalled what Captain Felix had told him. "My mom worries an awful lot. Maybe it's because I'm an only child, but she'll take care of *everything* for you."

Madonna wondered if Ronnie was scared. What would he do when she left for work in the morning? She thought about telling him to stay inside until she got home. The thought of their late-night arrival followed by her early morning departure made her nervous. At least her parents lived nearby, about a mile down the road.

"Ma'am, I really appreciate everything you and Captain Felix are doing for me," Ronnie said.

He'd interrupted her worrying. "It's our pleasure," she said. "You've been through so much. I don't know if I could've survived that." It wasn't a conscious choice, but she spoke to him slowly, as if to a kindergartener. She had no clue to his English proficiency until they met.

"Sure you're not hungry? We can get something to eat for the ride home."

"I just want to take a shower and get some sleep. It's been a long day."

"I prepared some snacks for you at home if you get hungry," she said, as they walked to the car.

They drove in silence. Madonna needed to navigate the route and Ronnie was taking in his new surroundings, still pinching himself.

The contrast with Iraq and Jordan was incredible. He stared out the window at the modern buildings. Neon signs showcased business names. Streetlamps lit wide avenues and manicured parking areas. The cars on the road were in pristine condition, not like on the streets of Baghdad. Even Amman paled in comparison to the opulence that Ronnie saw on that first drive.

"We can stop for a bite, or I have plenty in the refrigerator when we get home. Just let me know what you want." Madonna couldn't help repeating herself, partly due to her maternal instincts and partly wondering if he was telling her the truth, not wanting to be a burden.

"Thank you. That's so kind of you. I don't want you to think that I am ungrateful. I ate a big meal in Chicago and then had some more snacks on the plane. I'm pretty stuffed right now." He smiled.

"We'll be there in about five minutes. Then you can take a long, hot shower and get some sleep." She continued to chatter. "I have to work in the morning, but I'll show you where everything is tonight. That way, you can get coffee and breakfast. You don't need to worry about anything."

But Madonna worried. She worried that some of the neighbors might not be as open-minded as she was. That some Americans might assume Ronnie was a terrorist. The post 9/11 hysteria in the U.S. ebbed and flowed with media coverage with anti-Muslim sentiment flaring from time-to-time. That thought added to her long list of worries about her mission to sponsor this young man who'd experienced so much trauma. She also worried that Ronnie didn't have a driver's license and would depend on her and her dad to get around.

They pulled into the driveway and eased into the garage. Ronnie lugged his suitcase with his backpack slung over a shoulder. Madonna showed him to his new room. She sensed that he was tired, even though excitement spiked his energy level.

"I laid out fresh towels and a washcloth in the bathroom," Madonna said. "I don't get home from work until 5 p.m. Are you sure you'll be okay?"

"Yes, ma'am."

Madonna's house was great for guests. Ronnie's room was on the other side of her single-story home. It was near the kitchen and he had his own bathroom, which was cleaner and more modern than any he'd seen in Iraq, even in the Green Zone palace rooms where the Americans stayed. Everything felt like a dream. The towels were soft. Crisp sheets, soft pillow. After taking a luxurious shower, he fell asleep with the lights on.

At work, it was difficult for Madonna to focus. Thoughts of Ronnie interrupted her routine. She left twenty minutes early for home. Madonna wasn't sure if her boss was in the camp of people who thought she was crazy or understood the sacrifice and lengths a mother would go to for her only son. She had no idea how this adventure would play out, nor could she anticipate how difficult even routine things would be for Ronnie in the coming months.

His first full day in the U.S., Ronnie woke up around 11 a.m. He hadn't slept that soundly since before the war. It felt as if one minute he pulled the covers up, the next, it was morning. Most nights in Iraq, and even in Jordan, he was jolted awake several times by dreams of militias breaking into his room. They'd accuse him of being a traitor and colluding with the infidel Americans. Sometimes the nightmares were about people arresting and imprisoning his family because of his employment. He couldn't remember the last good night's rest he'd had.

His first day in Tucson, Ronnie gazed out the window at the mountain beyond the backyard. His dad would love this. What an amazing place. So far, he'd seen airports, highways and new cars. Ronnie felt as if he'd teleported into the future. He wanted to share all of it with his dad; to let him be proud that his investment of teaching his son English had paid off.

Ronnie, who loved to cook, found eggs and bread and prepared breakfast. He explored Madonna's kitchen then walked into the backyard and breathed the fresh desert air. He'd never felt so alive.

After work, Madonna found him planted on the living room couch, glued to the television. The couch became a favorite place in the months ahead. It was where he continued his Hollywood education, which was augmented with heavy doses of the reality of American life.

"How'd you sleep last night?" she said.

"Great, ma'am. It was the best sleep of my life."

"Are you up for meeting some friends of mine?"

"Absolutely," he said. "I've been looking forward to meeting civilian Americans to see if they're any different than all the soldiers I've met."

Madonna and several friends met once a week at a local bar. They shared the ups and downs of motherhood, commiserated about life challenges, gossiped, and enjoyed each other's company. Their latest buzz was Madonna's crazy adventure of rescuing an Iraqi man who had worked with her son. Introducing her friends to Ronnie would reassure them that she hadn't made an error in judgment. True, she didn't know Ronnie well, but her mother's intuition had been validated when she met him at the airport. Over the phone Jason had said, "Mom, he gets it." Madonna understood in her first ten minutes with Ronnie. He had an easy air, was confident and respectful. He'd shown a sense of humor and a willingness to have conversations in English. After months of doubt, her friends would see everything was okay.

Ronnie changed clothes. Madonna noted that he wore slacks, a collared shirt and dress shoes with a matching belt. She caught a whiff of cologne. She freshened up in her bathroom and wore her business clothes.

At the bar, Madonna's friends were old enough to be his mother. Ronnie chatted and joked with them, almost to the point of flirting, but he never crossed the line and showed great deference to their years and experience.

"What's Iraq like now?" one said.

"Without the Americans, it would be a mess. Iraqi politicians have messed it up. The militias and insurgents have badly injured the people. But al Qaeda has been pushed out of most areas. Things are improving."

"Were you ever shot at?"

"Yes. I also got blown up. Sometimes I felt like I was in a spy movie. I saw a lot of messed up things, but my American friends kept me out of trouble. They really want to help people, so I worked with them for six years."

Madonna watched as each of her friends asked him questions. One by one they whispered how remarkable Ronnie's English was or how approachable he was. They were impressed by his easy-going nature, more striking for all the hardship he had endured. Some of them asked if he was really an Iraqi.

"He gets it," one said. Madonna felt satisfied that their confidence in her judgment was restored.

One joked, "Are you sure he's not related to Jason? They could be brothers."

Madonna smiled. Now her friends were starting to get it, too.

A couple hours later they moved to a nearby restaurant for dinner. Madonna wanted to make sure Ronnie ate well and experienced American culture.

In the car she said, "What did you think of my friends?"

"I really enjoyed the discussion. They asked a lot of the same questions, but I guess I'll get more of that until people get to know me."

"They all had a lot of concerns about me becoming your sponsor without another man in the house. I guess that wouldn't be allowed in your culture."

"No. Women are supposed to stay covered and only go out with a man from their own family until they are married. Of course, depending on where you are, those rules can either be strict or not enforced at all. The militias really set things back for us culturally. Before they got powerful, Baghdad used to be pretty Westernized. Now the militias go around and enforce these rules on the people, whether they want them or not."

Ronnie was overwhelmed by the restaurant and the huge menu. He ordered steak but was surprised that the waiter had more questions. How would you like the steak cooked? What type of dressing would you like on your salad? Would you like cheese, bacon, chives on your baked potato? He wasn't sure how to answer and deferred to the wisdom of his dinner companion. Medium, blue cheese, everything on the potato.

Ronnie and Madonna talked long into the evening. Such conversations would become a cornerstone of their relationship. He explained what was going on in Iraq, how things had changed for better or worse. Madonna came to cherish those discussions as they provided some insight into Jason's experiences. Families were starved for information when military members deployed to combat. In Ronnie, Madonna had a friend who shared stories about experiences with her son. He also explained contemporary challenges in the Middle East and news reports they saw on television.

The next day she took Ronnie to meet her parents. Her dad, who'd been a soldier in the Army's 10th Mountain Division, had committed to help him learn about the U.S. and adapt to life in America, including getting his driver's license. He'd been a large part of Jason's inspiration to become an officer.

Madonna had no idea how difficult routine things would be for a new immigrant. Ronnie had hungered to make it to America. His hopes had been dashed several times, but he always bounced back. Now that he had arrived, he couldn't wait to get settled into his new life. He was the type of person who needed to stay busy. In his first week, Ronnie applied for his green card then got behind the wheel of a car and began the process of earning his license.

Madonna lent him her 1979 two-door Mercedes. It was a heavy car with heavy doors. She thought it was a good starter vehicle for someone learning to drive. Their relationship blossomed as she helped him work through bureaucracies like Arizona's Motor Vehicle Department.

Everything seemed difficult for Ronnie, as it would for any immigrant. He studied for his license and passed the written test but failed the behind-the-wheel exam. He'd driven almost every day in Iraq, but the American rules were alien. Madonna felt he got a raw deal and had been assigned a difficult examiner. That led to a long discussion about luck and how it could play a role in their fortunes.

"Have you thought about a job?" Madonna said after he'd been in America two weeks.

"I'm going to enlist in the Army."

"What?"

"I worked alongside Americans in Iraq," he said. "They are at the top of society. Before the U.S. soldiers came, the public held the Iraqi Army at the pinnacle. As an interpreter, I was always considered near the bottom of the pyramid. Very few people respected the terps. Even people who hated the Americans respected the power they wielded. Now, I have the chance to jump to the top for respect. I want to be like Jason."

Madonna was touched.

When Ronnie went to enlist in the Army, the recruiter was brand new. He had no idea how to handle an immigrant, especially an Iraqi with a green card. Ronnie and Madonna exercised a high degree of patience as they peeled back layers of the system to understand how it worked. They asked questions, had conversations, researched. They developed a process of discovering and learning that became routine as he navigated the complexities of assimilation. Ronnie had a vast head start compared to many immigrants, yet the experience challenged him well beyond what he envisioned.

Ronnie signed his Army contract in December 2009, but he wouldn't report to basic training until May 2010. To stay busy, he took a job as a role player at a nearby military base. Four other interpreters he knew from FOB Justice in Baghdad had the same job. Role players were paid actors who performed in military training exercises. They pretended to be sheiks, police chiefs, or indigenous people on the streets. American units would conduct scenarios to ensure they could deal with various situations while deployed in Iraq or Afghanistan. Mistakes would be made which became teachable moments.

Ronnie had seen his fair share of errors in combat. He was a natural role player. It was easy for him to replicate the crazy scenarios he had lived. They were moments the best fiction writers couldn't conjure. Writers like Rajiv Chandrasrkaran in *Imperial Life in the Emerald City: inside Iraq's green zone,* and George Packer in *The Assassin's Gate: America in Iraq* catalogued the wacky situations troops encountered in Iraq. For Ronnie, who had lived the majority of his life in crazy conditions, being a role player was easy and fun. He couldn't believe he was paid for it.

In one scenario, he played the police chief in charge of a detention center. In another he was the most disruptive detainee in the facility. As a natural jokester, it was not out of character for him to mess around with the troops. The instructors told role players to give the female soldiers a difficult time. The stated rationale was that it helped the women adjust to the male-dominated culture they would experience in Iraq. One of the female soldiers was particularly attractive.

"Women aren't allowed in a male facility," Ronnie said, trying to goad her into slipups.

Specialist Smith said, "American soldiers go where the mission calls." Her expression was stern, demeanor calm.

"You Americans think you can impose your values and culture on us, but you're wrong." Ronnie worked hard to keep a straight face. Even with her hair pulled back in the traditional tight bun that most female soldiers wore, he was attracted to her. Her blue eyes sparkled, framed by angular cheekbones. She wore the loose-fitting, standard-issue Army combat uniform, but it was obvious she was fit.

"We are here at the request of your government to perform a mission," Specialist Smith said. She remained calm and didn't take his bait.

Ronnie tried another tack. "Out of role."

"What does that mean?"

"It means we're dropping the exercise and addressing a real issue," Ronnie said. "What's your first name?"

"What does that have to do with this training?"

"It wouldn't be appropriate for me to ask for your number if I don't know your name." Ronnie waited. He tried to keep a straight face but failed to conceal the wry smile that tweaked the corners of his lips.

"I'm trying to focus on my job," Smith said. "There is no way you're gonna get my number."

"Out of role. Just give me your number, and we can get back to business and not disrupt the training. I might even go easier on you," he said with an almost imperceptible wink.

"Stay in role and be professional." Specialist Smith was not happy. "I guess I shouldn't expect you to maintain the same level of professionalism as an American soldier, but I have a mission."

Ronnie was stung but refused to take no for an answer. "If you give me your number, I'll be the most well-behaved detainee and help move things along."

Specialist Smith appeared resigned to this aspect of male interaction and remained silent.

"Okay, you win," said Ronnie. "But after the exercise is over, we should get together and you can decide 'out of role' whether you'd like to give me your number. At least tell me your name."

"Jessica."

Triumphant, Ronnie switched back to character. He shouted, "Guard. Guard. This woman is attempting to humiliate me. This is like Abu Ghraib all over again."

Specialist Smith rolled her eyes. Ronnie smiled.

It was May. Ronnie was due to report to basic training in a couple days. One evening, Madonna came home from work, unlocked the door and entered her living room. She saw a strange man, bald and gangly, on the couch. She shrieked, thinking a homeless person had broken into her house.

"What's the matter?" Ronnie said.

Madonna's eyes bugged. "Oh my God." She regained her composure. "I didn't recognize you. Why'd you shave your beard and hair?"

"I'm not going to give the Army the satisfaction of taking something from me," Ronnie said. "So, I shaved my beard and got a haircut to stop anyone from thinking they were humiliating me in basic training."

The shock of his new appearance made his imminent departure real.

"You're leaving in three days." Madonna wiped a tear and sat, but a new anxiety began to percolate. She would miss Ronnie. His presence filled a void created when Jason joined the Army. As a widow with her only child serving overseas, she experienced loneliness, worry, and a low-grade, ever-present fear. The danger was real for Jason, and the thought of losing her one-and-only made her cringe.

Ronnie's presence was the best change in her life in years. He was funny and enjoyable. She doted on him like a son. Now, he too, was leaving her.

"I can't wait to get there," Ronnie said. "I've wanted to become a soldier for a long time, but never thought I'd do it."

Madonna wanted to mirror his excitement but felt dread. "You could've waited another day to cut your hair."

"Truth is, the long hair and beard were always a way for me to protect my identity. As an American soldier, I want everyone to know who I am."

Madonna sensed his excitement and took some comfort knowing the Army could be a positive experience for him, as it had been for Jason. She knew it was the right path for Ronnie. It was almost all he talked about and focused on, besides girls. "I am so proud of you." She hugged him. "You'll be a great soldier."

"And I'll probably be able to meet more women this way."

Madonna laughed, shook her head, and hoped he hadn't seen the tear sliding down her cheek. She was a bit embarrassed about her fear but knew Ronnie would miss her too.

"I started making dinner," he said. "I figured you could use a good meal after a long day at work."

"Wonderful." She was surprised. "Let me freshen up." She walked to her bedroom to hide her tears.

They had a pleasant conversation at dinner. Animated, Ronnie told her about his barbershop experience and the shock of seeing his old self. He prattled on about basic training and wondered how tough it would be. He was so enthusiastic about the plans he'd made. Madonna did a mother's best to empathize and not dampen his passion.

After they cleared the table and washed dishes, Ronnie announced he was going out.

"Where?"

"I have to conduct an experiment." He grinned.

Madonna raised her eyebrows. "What experiment is that?"

"To see if American women will date me now that I have no hair."

Madonna laughed. "The Army's going to whip you into shape."

"Don't wait up," he said. "I might be out late. I got some new clothes today, too." He showed off. "Do I look like a straight guy?"

She shook her head and rolled her eyes. "What am I going to do without you?" She grabbed him for a last hug. "You look great."

"Good. I was worried that I might buy the wrong clothes. The soldiers in Baghdad teased me about Iraqi sheiks and other men always kissing on the cheek and holding hands."

That evening in a bar, Ronnie met a girl. Despite his frustration that English did not have the richness of Arabic for flirting, the woman seemed interested. He was amazed that she could look beyond his awkward appearance and spend time with him in public.

Chapter Sixteen

Basic Training

"Humor is just another defense against the universe."

~ Mel Brooks

RONNIE REPORTED TO basic training with a level of experience many soldiers never achieve. He had, in essence, been in combat his entire adult life. He scored 99 percent on his English language proficiency test. Other new linguists failed and were required to attend language classes.

When some of the silly things began to happen, like drill sergeants yelling, dropping recruits for pushups, and other methods to break down inductees, Ronnie took it all in stride. Sometimes he had to fight the urge to laugh. It all seemed ludicrous and wonderful at the same time. He'd grown up in a poor Baghdad neighborhood, gone to college, but had been trapped by war. He'd watched American movies to escape his harsh reality. Now, Ronnie was a character in the Hollywood movie that played in his mind, a recruit for the most professional military force in the world. He wondered if he would wake up.

"Ronnie, Max, Muhammed, Ahmed, report to the front of the formation," bellowed Sergeant First Class (SFC) Johnson, the senior drill sergeant.

"Yes, drill sergeant!" Ronnie shouted. The others echoed him and ran toward the front of the formation. They stood in a line facing SFC Johnson, their backs to the rest of the young troopers. Each man called was a designated military linguist or Zero Nine Lima (09L) in military jargon. That meant their job was to translate for the military. They were all natives of Iraq or Afghanistan.

"About face," said SFC Johnson. The four linguists turned and looked at the formation of soldiers. Johnson was well-respected. He had served in Iraq and Afghanistan and wore a combat patch from the famed 82nd Airborne Division. Johnson was the company first sergeant, or senior noncommissioned officer, for more than one hundred brand new soldiers. He was responsible for the training and administrative needs of the entire formation.

"You see these men, trainees?" He said it at the top of his voice, so every recruit was able to hear.

"Yes, drill sergeant."

"These men have more experience in combat than you will ever get. They've been to war and seen horrible things. Many of them probably have families in hiding because they decided to help us. One of my interpreters saved my life. They are national treasures. I do not want to hear any racist comments about these guys. I will not tolerate any type of harassment. You will respect the fact that they have been to war and know more than you. Learn from them. Do I make myself clear?"

"Yes, drill sergeant."

"Sergeant Jones, march the troops to the chow hall for dinner."

After dinner Ronnie noticed the other soldiers avoided him. He could tell they were frightened of him because the first sergeant, who was only a step or two below God, had elevated Ronnie to a pedestal that many of them might never achieve.

He knocked on the first sergeant's office door. SFC Johnson was occupied with paperwork. Ronnie cleared his throat and said, "First sergeant?"

Johnson was surprised to see Ronnie. It was rare for any recruit to visit the first sergeant on their own initiative. "What can I do for you?"

"First sergeant, I want to thank you for what you did today, for us 09Limas. We appreciate the respect. That was very nice. But now, all the other guys are kind of scared because you singled us out. We just want to be treated like any other soldier. No special treatment, you know?"

Johnson stared back. "That took courage to come in here and tell me that. Is that how the other 09 Limas feel?"

"Yes. They just want to be treated like the other guys. We already have a lot of things that make us stand out, like nicknames and not understanding the culture. We wanna be as normal as possible and learn to be good soldiers."

Johnson thought about it and said, "The Army is clueless about how good a deal they're getting with you guys. I will instruct the rest of the cadre not to single you out."

"It'll mean a lot to us."

"You're dismissed, soldier."

Mission accomplished. Ronnie knew he had to fix the issue with his fellow recruits. There were about forty trainees in his platoon who thought Ronnie had demanded some sort of special treatment. None of them dared risk the ire of the First Sergeant after they received his direct order.

Ronnie returned to the platoon bay, which were World War II-era, two-story wood buildings, eighty feet long, thirty wide, lined with bunks. All forty soldiers lived in the building. Each had a locker against a wall and a footlocker at the end of their bunks. Rain or shine, hot or cold, they had to leave the building to use the bathroom. Latrines were located several buildings over. The recruits slept with their gear, but weapons hadn't been issued. Those were kept in the company arms room.

Ronnie walked to the center of the long room. "Guys, can I talk to you all for a little bit?"

Given his elevated stature, the soldiers gathered around. Ronnie scanned the faces, noting the diverse mix of America. "I want you to know, I'm just another soldier. The First Sergeant meant well today by calling us out in front of the formation. However, I'm just another soldier like you. I want the chance to know each of you better. I thought I knew a lot about American culture because I hung out with a bunch of Americans in Iraq, but I know you guys will teach me much more. My dream is to become an American citizen. Please treat me like everybody else."

The soldiers looked at Ronnie. They seemed slightly dumbfounded that this scrawny-looking recruit was telling them to keep things in perspective. After all, it was their senior noncommissioned officer, the most important, influential person in their immediate existence, who said he was way above their level.

"I've essentially been deployed my entire life," Ronnie said. "I've been blown up and shot at. But that doesn't make me any better than any of you. I want to get to know you more and maybe I can teach you a thing or two. Just like you'll teach me. Let me start with some rap. Did I ever tell you I know a lot about American rap music?"

Some of the trainees chuckled.

"I like big butts." Ronnie sang. "And I cannot lie." He continued the lyrics for a minute or so as the soldiers began to rap with him and break out with some MC Hammer moves.

Ronnie exceeded standards in basic training. He injured his hip but refused to give up. The gas chamber phase of training involved building a recruit's confidence that the protective gear and gas mask would function properly. The final step involved sending a squad into a sealed tent wearing their gas masks and protective suits. Inside, an instructor in full gear released a CS pellet, filling the interior with noxious gas.

"Side straddle hop," the instructor barked through his mask. "One, two, three, four." The count continued as the troops commenced jumping jacks.

"One, drill sergeant," the recruits yelled. "Two, drill sergeant," and so on as sweat built.

After twenty-five, the drill sergeant commanded, "Halt." The troops dropped their arms and took deep breaths. "Now break the seals on your protective masks, recruits."

Another drill sergeant in full gear checked the ranks as trainees lifted their gas masks and removed them. Hit by the effects of the CS gas, they gasped and gagged. Some bent over and puked. Not until Ronnie gagged did the drill sergeant command, "Okay, recruits, you can depart."

Outside, mucus flowed from noses. Eyes watered. Young soldiers coughed the gas out of their systems. They bitched and complained and vowed to never experience that again.

At dinner that evening, Ronnie thought that everything tasted incredible after the gas chamber. He had a greater respect for life and appreciated the very air he breathed.

After he completed Basic Training, Ronnie reported to Advanced Individual Training at Fort Huachuca, Arizona, with the other 09Limas. He found the experience relaxing. Ronnie's job was to learn English, which he already knew well beyond his peers.

Often, the troops were allowed to wear civilian clothes. On long weekends he changed and drove to Madonna's home in Tucson. On base, he made more friends and met a former colleague's younger brother, also in AIT. Some nights, they snuck out. They'd stuff pillows under the blankets on their beds so the sergeant of the guard wouldn't realize they were gone.

Ronnie gained more confidence as he mastered the training. Upon completion, he was assigned to Fort Polk, Louisiana. He was disappointed. His 09Lima friends were headed to units that might be deployed. He wanted to get back into the fight.

He did. Ronnie deployed to Iraq in 2011 as a military linguist. He was assigned to the 1st Cavalry Division. He served with LTC Ed Callahan, a leader he knew from FOB Justice during the worst of the Baghdad fighting in 2007. Callahan had been a major on a transition team assigned to an Iraqi Army Brigade, which was commanded by BG Usaif, partnered with the Dagger Brigade Combat Team.

LTC Callahan heard about the 09Ls. He was a believer in the value of cultural understanding and wanted to select the military interpreter who would work hand in glove with him. He didn't want to leave it to chance. When they arrived, the linguists lined up and were reviewed by Callahan. One of the troops called out.

"Hey sir, remember me?" Ronnie was never shy around leadership.

Ed turned to see who addressed him. He saw a lanky specialist with his soft cap pulled a little too low. "No," said Callahan. "Help me out, soldier. How would I know you?"

"I was one of the FOB Justice interpreters when you were in Baghdad in 2007," Ronnie said.

Callahan had sharp memories of those dangerous days, however, he couldn't place this guy. Ronnie pulled out his cell phone and slid through photos as Ed walked closer. "Here, sir." Ronnie displayed a photo where he'd been blown up by an IED and sat next to the damaged Humvee, pointing at the damage with both index fingers. He had his "Serpico" look and squinted into the camera. It was the portrait of an angry young man. In those days, Ronnie was enraged by the world, furious that he and his family were subjected to the ruthless behavior of the insurgents, militias, and corrupt government officials.

Callahan didn't know the back story, but he recognized Ronnie. "I remember you," the LTC said.

"They called me Ronnie back then. I go by Specialist Joseph now."

"You were pretty fearless, if I remember correctly."

"I suppose, sir. I don't want to die, but there's not much that can scare me anymore. I'm a U.S. soldier. I roll with the baddest military in the world."

"How'd you like to work with me?" Ed said.

Ronnie's battalion was selected to shut the lights off on the U.S. occupation of Iraq. As events came to a close in 2011, he was on the last patrol that drove to the Kuwaiti border. The majority of troops flew to Kuwait, but Ronnie's unit drove from Camp Adder in Nasiriyah. The journalist who met Ronnie in Baghdad in 2007, Greg Jaffe, now with *The Washington Post*, did a front-page story about him in 2011.

The story described how Ronnie started with the Americans in 2003 as an interpreter when troops patrolled his neighborhood. They needed translators with a good command of English. Ronnie never looked back, even as rumors about American soldiers swirled through Iraqi society, such as:

- The Americans are going to turn all of Saddam's palaces into universities.

- American soldiers have a pill that turns water cold as ice.

- There are many Jews mixed in with the Americans. Some of their units are made up of all Jews.

As a U.S. soldier who accompanied the last convoy out of Iraq in December 2011, Ronnie turned the page on another complex chapter of his patriotic love triangle. It was a combination of loyalty to the United States and love for his homeland. Deployment as a soldier changed his status, but Iraq remained a dangerous place. His family and friends were still at risk and he never told them he was in-country as a U.S. soldier. He called them, chatted, told his parents he was busy…which was true. He never hinted or let on that he'd joined the Army and was deployed to Iraq.

Ronnie expressed concern about his family to Jaffe. "I lie to them a lot," he said. "I have no choice. There are things they don't need to know. If anything happened to them, I would never forgive myself." His alibis and aliases characterized the individual precautions many interpreters were forced to use to protect themselves and their families from the dangers associated with knowing Americans. Even as a U.S. soldier, he lived a double life to prevent adversaries from discovering his identity. Those precautions protected his family members from inadvertent disclosure of information to curious neighbors or others who might pose a threat.

"Hi, Madonna," Ronnie said from the AT&T phone bank in Kuwait, where he'd arrived from Iraq the night before.

She was happy to hear from him. "Thanks for letting me know you're safe."

"I'm looking forward to getting back to the States," he said. "We have a few more days here before we redeploy back."

"I can't wait to see you. Maybe we can celebrate if you get the chance to visit?"

"Hope so. I figured you'd want to know that I don't plan to reenlist."

"I'd be happy that at least one of my boys isn't deploying to combat. What are you going to do?"

"Not sure, yet. Being an American soldier has been an honor, but I want to do other things. Plus, it's hard to meet girls when you're always deployed." He imagined Madonna rolling her eyes.

She laughed. "Let me know if I can help. I'm always here for you."

"I know."

While Ronnie was deployed back to Iraq, I worked for the Obama Administration as Director for Iraq with responsibility for the security portfolio. We lost touch. I had no idea he'd joined the Army and served our country again. He and I wouldn't reunite for several years, after I began advocating for the Special Immigrant Visa and other policy options to protect our closest partners in conflict zones.

Chapter Seventeen

Madame Betty
and Mr. George

"Men are what their mothers made them."

~ Ralph Waldo Emerson

IN THE END, I did what a lot of soldiers do—I called mom, who BG Usaif called Madame Betty.

Turkey was intended as an interim location for the brigadier general's family. The country was teeming with refugees, so the Turkish government withheld education and other services, which they believed incentivized the migrants to move on to other countries.

After Arwa Damon helped the general's family escape from Baghdad, we advocated for the next step. Germany had revoked temporary visa status for 7,000 Iraqis in 2007. Plus, why would the Germans let an American bring an Iraqi family into the country? Given the inhospitable environment, BG Usaif opted for the United

States. He assumed it would be easier to find a sponsor. But who could I convince to sponsor an Iraqi family with five kids and two wives?

I was a thirty-nine-year-old Infantry lieutenant colonel in the Army. I called mom for assistance. She agreed to sponsor the family and assist moving them out of Turkey to the United States. Little did either of us comprehend how much of an ask that was. She expected a typical-size family, mother, father, a couple of kids, and swears I never told her how many children were involved. I did mention the two wives. My mother laughed at that and questioned if I was serious. I told her the story of attempting to prevent the general from marrying a second woman. It was a head shaker for her, but Mom assured me she'd work to understand another culture. At the same time, she insisted that no woman would be treated as a second-class citizen in her home.

Betty, my mom, has always been generous. Hailing from a poor blue-collar family on Long Island, she contributes her time and money to help those less fortunate. A registered nurse for thirty years, she excelled at caring for others. She continued that spirit at church and in the community. She was relentless when eyeing an objective. If she believed in a cause, she pursued it with vigor. She had the personality needed to navigate complex and clunky U.S. government systems made even more inefficient by having to comply with the bureaucracy and rules of the United Nations High Commission on Refugees.

In late 2007 she began seeking and finding points of contact at the U.S. State Department, the International Rescue Committee (IRC) and other agencies that would help make sense of the next steps. The Usaif family escaped Baghdad in October 2007 and settled into an anxiety-filled existence similar to many refugee families. A representative at the IRC recommended the family move to Istanbul in order to attend embassy interviews and move the bureaucracy along. Betty also called the office of Congressman Stenny Hoyer, a Maryland Democrat. She asked if his people could help. During that time, Brigadier General Usaif's first wife became ill, and he often called Betty to see if she had updates on their status. Arwa Damon from CNN also made inquiries. Eventually, the family was approved for transit to the United States. However, the general's brother who accompanied them to Istanbul would be delayed another six months after providing inconsistent answers in some of his interviews.

It was May 2008. The phone rang in the Eble household. George, Betty's husband of fifteen years, answered.

"Can I please speak to Mrs. Betty Eble?" said a woman on the line.

"Who's calling?"

"This is Martha from the International Rescue Committee. I have some information for Mrs. Eble."

"One minute." George walked through the house with the cordless phone and found his wife on the living room couch with their Boston terrier, Maximus, on her lap.

After an exchange of hellos, Martha said, "We have good news for you. The family you sponsored has been approved to travel to the United States."

"I was beginning to think it would never happen. When and where do they arrive?"

"The family chose to fly into BWI Airport in Baltimore and will arrive in two days."

That was how the next leg of the journey on the Baghdad Underground Railroad began for the Usaif family. It was the start of an amazing journey for Mom and George.

"We need to pick up the Iraqis at BWI on Wednesday," Betty told George.

"I don't get off work 'til 4:30."

"I won't be able to do it on my own. We need two cars. It's important. Maybe you can take the day off?"

"What time are they supposed to arrive?"

"Around lunchtime."

"You take your car. I'll take the old one. We should be able to fit them all in. How many are there?"

"Eight.

"So many?"

"There's the Iraqi general, his two wives, and five kids. I still can't believe Steven didn't tell me they have five kids."

George continued thinking about how tight it would be with ten people in the two cars. "Let's hope they don't have a lot of luggage."

On Wednesday, George drove his 1993 Camry with over two hundred thousand miles on the odometer. He was proud he'd kept it running. Betty drove their much newer Toyota Avalon with Max the dog perched in the front seat next to her. Yes, space would be at a premium, but Maximus went everywhere with Betty. She doted on him. Max would introduce the Usaif family to the American affinity for pets, something almost nonexistent in Iraqi culture.

George and Betty made the eighty-mile drive to BWI Airport in tandem arriving forty-five minutes early. With Max in the stroller, they made their way to baggage claim, where Betty asked a guard through which door international travelers would arrive. The arrivals board listed the flight as on time. After an hour, the board indicated the flight had landed.

They waited another hour, but no Iraqis emerged. George asked and found all passengers from Istanbul had deplaned. After a four-hour wait, George and Betty returned home with no information and no Iraqis.

Several days later, Betty left for Ireland on a long-planned trip with her church youth group. Five adult chaperones and ten teenagers traveled to southeastern Ireland as part of the Episcopal Church's Journey to Adulthood program.

Betty hadn't received any answers to her inquiries about the Iraqi family, so she decided to go ahead with the trip. She'd made a commitment to chaperone the teens' spiritual exploration of adulthood, and the kids had worked hard to raise funds to cover costs.

With Betty away, George anticipated ten days to himself and a low-key week. He'd been a reluctant partner in the crazy Iraqi adventure. Betty had agreed to it before speaking with him. He and Max dropped her off at the church and waved goodbye as the mission team loaded into a van headed to the airport. Maximus gave Betty a sad look as she left. Many times, during previous absences, Max spent the entire day in the upstairs bedroom on a sofa waiting for her to come home.

Five days later, George enjoyed his alone time and had even bonded a little with Maximus. The dog began to lighten up and relax. The phone rang at 9 p.m. He expected that it might be Betty, but it was Martha from the IRC.

"You and Mrs. Eble are sponsoring the Usaif family from Iraq, correct?"

"Yes."

"The family just landed at BWI Airport," Martha said.

"What? I thought we were going to get some kind of notice."

"Sorry, sir. Sometimes there's a snafu in the information flow between the UNHCR, Catholic Charities, and our organization. We do have transportation arranged, but the driver is asking for $500 in cash when he drops the family off. Just keep track of the receipt and you'll be reimbursed."

George didn't have $500 in the house. He wasn't sure if an ATM would allow a withdrawal of that amount. "Okay." What else could he say?

"Thank you so much, sir. We're very sorry for the inconvenience." She didn't sound sorry. "I'm sure the Usaif family will appreciate your generosity."

George hung up, suddenly wishing Betty wasn't out of the country.

It was after midnight when headlights turned into the driveway of the Eble residence. George pushed the button on the automatic garage door opener and walked up to the ten-passenger van. A slender Arab man hopped out of the passenger side and extended his right hand.

"My name is Mohammed Usaif."

"I'm George Eble." He shook the Iraqi general's hand.

"Thank you very, very much, Mr. George," Mohammed said in his broken English. "I cannot believe we are here. We spent much time in Turkey. Too much time."

"I'm glad you're here." George was cordial. He knew Betty would have been enthusiastic.

"Where is Madame Betty?" Mohammed said. The general stressed the second syllable of the word "madame," which contributed to the overall surrealism.

"She won't be home for about a week," he said. "Let's get your family inside and get them settled in."

"Okay, okay, Mr. George. Thank you so very much. We are very, very happy to be here."

"Hey, sir," said the van driver, a large man. "That IRC lady said you'd pay me when we got here."

"I don't have $500 cash. I can write you a check."

"Can't take personal checks. Got a credit card?"

George handed over a card. He'd never heard of the van company and wondered if it was a scam. Five excited children ages nine to sixteen tumbled out of the vehicle followed by two women. One wore a traditional burka and stood next to the younger kids. The other woman wore Western clothing and seemed more poised and confidant. She was at Mohammed's side. The kids spoke animated Arabic and eyed their new surroundings.

Luggage was piled up on the driveway, then the van left. George, convinced he his blood pressure rising, didn't have a clue where any of this was headed and wondered for the umpteenth time why Betty had agreed to do this.

George looked at Mohammed. "Follow me." He led the family into the house.

George hoped to settle them upstairs so everyone could get some sleep. He wasn't sure that was possible. The little ones looked as if they'd awakened from a long nap full of energy. The older children and adults were tired but happy as they dragged baggage into the house.

George noticed that the family removed their shoes as they entered. That was a custom he and Betty followed. George had served in the Navy in Japan, and Betty liked a tidy home. Max greeted the new arrivals by barking and wagging his tail. The Western-dressed woman froze when she saw him. The children fell in behind her.

George scooped up Max and stroked his head. The family huddled in the kitchen, wary of the dog.

"This is Maximus," George said. "You don't need to be afraid of him. He's our pet."

"Thank you, thank you, Mr. George." Mohammed then spoke to his family in Arabic. They relaxed but remained suspicious.

George and Betty had a comfortable home in southern Maryland, but they didn't have six additional bedrooms. Betty had purchased cots for the kids. Added to beds in the three guestrooms, everyone had a place to sleep.

George led everyone upstairs. Mohammed was followed by the woman in the burka, the children in descending order of size, and last was the wife in Western clothes. George showed them the three rooms and removed a cot from a shipping box. "You'll have to set these up for the kids."

"Thank you very much, Mr. George," Mohammed said. "This is very good. Very good. We will be fine. We will be fine." After nine months in Turkey, their welcome to America seemed almost surreal. His first wife, the woman in traditional garb, had almost died in Istanbul. As refugees, they had little access to health care and had to rely on the Red Crescent and international NGOs for doctors. The U.S. had seemed like a fantasy when he first contemplated emigrating during the height of sectarian violence in Baghdad. The dream seemed farther away during their time in Turkey, but here they were. Everybody went to bed.

George didn't sleep well but woke the next morning at his usual 5 a.m. He made coffee with the French press. He'd followed the same ritual for years until Betty read an article that said French press coffee was thought to be less healthy than other methods due to higher levels of cafestol. From that day, she wouldn't let him use the French press unless they had guests. Betty decided he could splurge on those days. When they had company, he made two pots, one decaf, and stored the coffee in thermal containers that kept it hot all day. That way the guests could have a cup whenever they wanted. And George, too.

George was working on his third mug when Mohammed entered the kitchen. It was late morning.

"Hello, Mr. George."

"Good morning."

"We would like to thank you for letting us stay in your home. The women would like to cook you a nice meal."

George wasn't expecting that. "Uh, I guess that's okay."

"Good. Where can we find market or store to purchase food?"

"We have plenty of food here."

"We want to cook Iraqi food. We think you will like it. Don't worry, Miska used to eat it all the time. It is very good."

"Okay." George didn't know what to think of this new development. His peaceful week with Max had turned into a full-throttled journey into the unknown.

"How do we get to the market?" Mohammed said.

"I'll take you."

Mohammed and George entered the supermarket. BG Usaif was amazed. It was his first-ever look at a sprawling, bright, fully stocked American grocery store. "There is so much stuff," he said. Even during his trip to Germany ten years before, he hadn't seen anything like that. It overflowed with limitless choice. Mohammed and George pushed a cart through the meat department, then the produce area. They explored the aisles of shelves, found a large bag of rice and spices.

At the checkout, Mohammed stood by the conveyor belt. It was obvious he was uncomfortable. He reached into his pocket and extracted a wad of cash.

The cashier said, "That will be $86.78." Mohammed started to count his money.

"You are our guests," said George. He paid with a credit card.

"Thank you, thank you. I shall repay you."

"Not necessary."

They drove the ten minutes home and found the children and women sitting at the kitchen table.

"Mr. George and I are back from the market," Mohammed said in English then he broke into Arabic. The Western-dressed woman chatted with him as he gave directions. The other wife, still dressed in a burka, unbagged the groceries. Mohammed signaled the children to follow him outside. Meal prep began.

George hiked upstairs. He hadn't seen Max. He checked rooms and found the dog hiding in Betty's closet. George tried to coax him out, but Max refused to budge.

A couple hours later pleasant smells wafted from the kitchen. George had stayed away as the Iraqi women searched for pots and pans. The eldest daughter helped and the three carried on a quiet conversation as they washed, peeled, chopped and cooked.

Mohammed tracked down George in the garage. His garage was a stand-alone structure on the other side of the driveway. He and Betty built it to give him a private place for his hobbies. "My wives have prepared for you a pleasing meal. We hope you will find it acceptable."

George stopped work on his old pickup truck. "Let me clean up and I'll be there in a second." He wondered what was in store. George walked to the house and entered the kitchen. On the way to the bathroom, he noticed the five children stood and waited. For food? For the adults?

George came out of the bathroom and found the entire Iraqi family anxious for his return. The women were nervous, and the kids hovered at the edge of the table. A wonderful, spicy aroma filled the house. George and Mohammed sat.

"Mr. George," Mohammed said. "Is it okay for children to join us at the table?"

"Yes, of course," George said. "We can all eat in the dining room since that table has more seats."

"No, no. We do not want to ruin the special place. That is for very special guests. Yes? We will eat here."

Mohammed signaled the children to join and they crowded around the table. The twins sat on the same chair. The boy grabbed the chair from a nearby desk and rolled it next to his oldest sister. The middle daughter sat on another kitchen chair while the women brought the food. They heaped a mountain of rice onto a serving platter. George saw vegetables, raisins, almonds, and spices in the rice, which was covered with pieces of chicken. The woman in traditional garb prepared a plate and handed it to him.

"Thank you," George said. She did not make eye contact or respond.

Mohammed said, "My wives are happy to have the honor of serving you, Mr. George. We are all very thankful to you and Madame Betty for helping us get to America."

"We're glad that you're safe." George realized that the entire family might have been dead had they stayed in Iraq.

"Eat, Mr. George," Mohammed said. "We are honored to be guests in your wonderful home. The women will serve us while we eat."

That was different. George was about to invite the women to sit, but Mohammed said, "Eat."

George dug into the chicken and rice. "This is really good." He had almost finished his plate.

"You honor us by eating so much," Mohammed said. "Please have more." George watched as Mohammed grabbed a piece of chicken with a bare hand and placed it on his plate. He scooped more rice with another piece of chicken and placed that on George's plate, too. Mohammed then served himself more food. He motioned for the kids to have more. They took turns and dug into the rice and chicken with their hands. George feigned nonchalance. This was going to be interesting until Betty came home.

"I am sorry, Mr. George, that we only have chicken tonight," Mohammed said. "Maybe tomorrow or the next day, I find sheep or goat. We should celebrate by slaughtering a sheep and making you more Iraqi food."

"Uh, okay." George pictured Mohammed chasing a sheep around a barnyard.

The women cleaned up. George and Mohammed retired to the living room. George turned on the television and asked Mohammed what he preferred to watch.

"I am your guest. Please put on what you wish."

The meal routine repeated itself for the week. By the time Betty was slated to return, George and the Usaif family had settled into a schedule that revolved around mealtimes, trips to the supermarket, and short escapes from the kids. He was glad Betty would soon be back. They'd spoken on the phone a couple of times.

"Which rooms are they sleeping in?" Betty said.

"They all crowded into the guest room across from ours. Except for the boy. They put him in his own room at the end of the hall."

"How do they all fit into one room? Did they get the cots in there? How many people are in there?"

"Mohammed, both wives and the girls."

"Seven people in that one bedroom? Are you sure they're all sleeping in it?"

"Yeah. And I'm pretty sure the boy sneaks in at night."

"I've got to see this. Sorry I laid it all on you, but at least you're eating well.

"I'm surprised at how much I like the food."

George waited in Betty's car at the church. She was due to arrive any minute. He thought whatever adventures she'd experienced on her Ireland trip would pale in comparison to his escapades with the Iraqis. George couldn't imagine spending an entire week with a bunch of teens in a foreign country. As he drummed his fingers on the steering wheel, he would have traded with her. He glanced in the back seat where Max looked out the window. "Mommy's coming. Won't be long now." The little dog wagged his tail and did a little dance. He knew the word "Mommy." Poor thing. He'd spent most of his time in Betty's closet.

Two ten-passenger vans pulled into the church lot. Sleepy kids and adults flowed out. They yawned, clutched pillows or backpacks, and retrieved luggage from the rear of the vans. Betty climbed out, waved to George and spotted a wet nose smushed against the window. "Maximus!" she said.

George opened his door. Max hurdled the seat, raced to Betty and jumped in her arms. "You missed Mommy, didn't you?"

"He was in hiding most of the time," George said. "He was scared of the Iraqis, but they were pretty scared of him, too."

"Really? Why would they be afraid of my Max?"

"They're not used to dogs living in the house. It's not common in their culture."

"We'll have to change that, won't we, Max?" Betty was thrilled to be home.

Before they left the church, Betty spoke with the mother of a boy on the trip. Nadine Hughes taught at a nearby middle school and heard Betty speak at church about the pending arrival of the Iraqi family. Betty had voiced concern about possible culture shock and the language barrier. Nadine, inspired by the film *Pay It Forward* and Betty's willingness to take in this new family, volunteered to teach the Iraqi children English during the summer break.

"Let me come over and help," Nadine said. "You just spent two weeks chaperoning my son."

As George and Betty drove home, she peppered him with questions and rubbed Max's tummy. "Where'd they get the food?"

"Mohammed and I go to the grocery store. He picks it out, I pay for it. He doesn't have enough cash, and he doesn't have a credit card. Probably doesn't have a credit rating at all."

"Steven said he would help us with the expenses. How was the food?"

"Excellent. It's all fresh. Nothing processed. They cut all the vegetables, cook a lot of rice, add meat or chicken. I haven't gone hungry, that's for sure."

"I was worried about how you and Max would manage without me."

"We did okay," George said. "The kids are starting to warm up to Max a bit. They watch me play with him. But the cats are another story. Wilma comes around for dinner. The other one pretty much comes in, scarfs food, then disappears outside or hides in the basement."

"The pets have to get used to them. They have to get used to the pets." Betty also wondered how the general and his wives were faring. There was much to do.

"I took the week off work," said George. That surprised her. He never did that. George told her he was worried that something might happen and the Usaifs wouldn't know what to do. Plus, he didn't know what they'd do if left to their own devices. "I came back from running an errand to find all the windows open and the air conditioning running."

At the house, excitement built. Madame Betty was coming home. The women had heard so much about her. Betty had been their lifeline in Turkey. She and General Mohammed had regular phone calls. He sent her all their paperwork to assist with the refugee process at the UNHCR, the U.S. Department of State, and the nonprofit International Catholic Migration Commission.

Betty walked into her house, excited to welcome her guests. First, she greeted the women. She was surprised to see one dressed in traditional Islamic garb, the other in Western blouse and slacks, her hair done up. She introduced herself.

Mohammed approached. "Madame Betty. Such an honor. We are all very excited that you are home. We want you to have a gift."

"Really?"

"Yes. Iraqi tradition. We offer a gift to someone who is generous like you and Mr. George. We are very grateful for Miska and you. And Mr. George, he has been very kind since we arrived."

"You really don't have to do that."

"No, we must. Please accept this as our appreciation for your tremendous friendship. Your son went to Iraq to help my country. You have opened your home to my family. Please take this." Mohammed extended a small gift bag. He handed a second one to George.

Betty pulled out a small jewelry box. Inside it, she found a 22-karat gold ring with a large, white, round-cut stone sparkling in a four-prong setting. The ring had a band that came adjacent to but did not connect under the setting of the stone, giving it a unique appearance. George found a gold watch in his box.

"Thank you, Mohammed, but you didn't have to do this," Betty said. She took in the smiling faces from the entire family, except for the first wife, whose face was covered and did not make eye contact.

Mohammed said, "Iraqi custom demands we provide gifts to those who help us. We are generous people."

"I can see that," Betty said. "The ring is beautiful." She paused. "Because you are guests in my home, I'm going to cook you dinner tonight."

"Very well, Madame Betty." Mohammed bowed. "But my wives would be happy to prepare the meal."

"No, no. You are our guests. I'm cooking for you."

Jet-lagged due to the long flight from Ireland, Betty decided that they'd use paper plates. That would make cleanup easier. When they had a moment alone in the kitchen, George explained a peculiar dinner time circumstance.

"The family refuses to eat in the dining room," he whispered.

"What? Why?"

"Mohammed says that they only eat in their kitchen in Iraq. We might be able to convince them to eat in the dining room on a holiday or special occasion, but I don't think they're going to do it tonight."

"How do they all fit around the table?"

"They make do. You'll see."

Betty prepared a chicken dinner with mashed potatoes and green beans. She added gravy and dinner rolls with butter.

George noted that the family ate in silence compared to previous meals when they chattered in Arabic and tried out new English words. Every once in a while, Mohammed translated when he felt it was necessary. That night, he did all the talking. His wives and daughters helped serve as Betty prepared the food. They then took seats while the kids squeezed into their normal seating arrangements.

Betty looked around the table, "It's our custom to say grace before dinner," she said.

"We are also thankful to Allah," said Mohammed.

"I'll say something for all of us tonight."

"Thank you, Madame Betty."

"Lord, bless this food and bless this family that has traveled so far to flee violence and danger. Thank you for bringing them safely to America. Also, please bless George and Max, my little angel, for their willingness to help this wonderful family. In your name we pray, Amen."

"Thanks be to God," Mohammed said. The woman and children whispered thanks in Arabic.

"Let's eat," Betty said. "Don't let the food get cold."

"Thank you, Madame Betty. We are very grateful for your hospitality. Are you sure you're not Iraqi?"

She laughed. "I have a lot of different cultures in my background, but I don't think any of them come from the Middle East."

Betty explained that for a normal meal she'd serve the food on dishes with silverware, but she was exhausted from her trip. She showed them paper plates and plastic cutlery, hoped they didn't mind, and told the Usaifs to throw everything in the trash after dinner.

"George, show them what I'm talking about. They can put leftover food in the compost container, the trash in our regular waste, and recyclables in the other container."

He led Mohammed to the different waste bins. Several of the kids followed, full of curiosity.

Mohammed tossed his plate, napkin and plasticware in the trash, then watched TV in the den. The kids chatted in Arabic with each other. As they finished their dinner, each threw paper plates in the trash. The wives followed suit.

The next evening, Betty used real dishes and silverware. A couple pieces of silverware were missing. For several weeks George sifted through the trash after meals. He found plates, knives, forks, and spoons. The Iraqis must have thought these Americans were wealthy beyond their wildest expectations. They threw their plates and silverware away after each meal.

Chapter Eighteen

Trials of Assimilation

"Commitment is an act, not a word."

~ Jean-Paul Sartre

WHEN THE SCHOOL year ended and summer vacation began, Nadine Hughes drove to Betty and George's house. Her son, Chasen, had returned from Ireland with glowing stories that Betty was a great chaperone who ensured the teens were always prepared for the day. They were briefed on their destination, tours, events, and clothing suggestions due to weather. Betty made sure they always had passports and cash and knew where to meet at the end of the day, just in case.

Nadine was excited to begin her stint as a volunteer English teacher but didn't know what to expect with the Iraqi family. Betty told her she'd have five kids, ages nine to sixteen. As the first day of her new adventure drew close, Nadine thought, "What have I got myself into?" As with most Americans, she had no exposure to Middle Easterners and was inundated with media stories about terrorists and bombings. She couldn't remember watching or reading reports about normal, everyday people from that region. How was she going to teach five non-English-speaking kids when she couldn't communicate with them?

At Betty and George's house, Nadine watched as the two Iraqi wives approached her. Betty gestured to the woman in the burka. "This is the mother of the children." She nodded at the western dressed woman. "And this is the general's second wife."

Nadine raised her eyebrows. Betty said, "Yes, you heard that correctly."

Nadine thanked the women for allowing her to assist with the children.

"And these are the little darlings," Betty said as she led Nadine into the living room. The children, dressed in pressed school clothes, sat prim and proper on the couch and chairs. Four had their hands folded in their laps. The boy draped an arm over a chair back. Teens are teens no matter where they're from, Nadine thought.

"Hello, everyone," she said. The children knew that word and responded.

Nadine brought games and kids' books. She imagined how disruptive the move must have been. The oldest girl was the same age as Nadine's daughter Jenna, who rode and groomed horses every day. That's why Nadine was able to find the time to help the Usaifs. She couldn't imagine how her daughter and son would react if they had to flee for their lives to a completely foreign culture.

As a teacher, Nadine believed that hands-on experience reinforced learning. She handed out books in each session and focused on basic words until the children formed sentences. Soon, they walked around the neighborhood during her classes and described birds, trees, homes, and cars. A few times, Nadine organized field trips. The kids visited her daughter, who taught them to groom horses and took them on pony rides. They loved these excursions, and it gave the adults a break.

The teaching and learning weren't limited to Nadine's fieldtrips or classroom instruction. The kids learned the old-fashioned way. They watched TV. Every evening they tuned into a few shows. After, the girls headed upstairs with their mother and the second wife. However, the son would beg Madame Betty to stay up thirty minutes later to watch another show. She'd give in, hop on the computer in an adjacent room to pay bills or catch up on email. One night the son watched a classic detective show in which the villain said "shit" as he realized the detective was closing in. Fast forward a couple of weeks. Betty was on her computer. The son was glued to the tube.

"Oh damn," Betty said. She'd forgotten to order a birthday present for a friend.

The boy jumped up from the couch. "What's wrong, Madame Betty?"

"I forgot to get Marion's birthday present."

"Shit," he said, in an attempt to demonstrate a grown-up level of maturity combined with teenage cool, and his new vocabulary of curse words.

"What did you say?"

He knew from her tone of voice he'd overstepped. Sweat beaded on his brow.

"You are grounded, young man," Betty said. "I may tell your father, too."

"I'm sorry." He couldn't find any other words. Cool became shame in a heartbeat.

"Go to bed. No more staying up late for you. Where'd you hear that?" But he was in retreat, running up the stairs with the hope his father wouldn't appear.

The Usaif family adjusted to Madame Betty and Mr. George over several weeks. Betty and George adapted to the tasks of helping an immigrant family. Basics, like dental and medical care, became major challenges. Betty borrowed a friend's Suburban to transport everyone to appointments. Most doctors and dentists refused to take all five kids at once, so the logistics were complex. As the start of the school year approached, Betty attempted to register the children. They would attend three different schools. The two eldest would be in high school, the middle daughter would attend middle school, and the twins were headed to elementary school. They needed shots. Betty was lucky and found a doctor's office that allowed all five to receive the inoculations required to enroll, but the clinic was ninety minutes away near Baltimore. She loaded up the Suburban with five children and two wives.

The kids were stoic. They didn't know what to expect. Their mother responded with one of the few English phrases she'd learned: "Thank you."

At the clinic, the group piled into the waiting room. A nurse indicated they were ready for the first child. Betty asked their mother if she planned to accompany her children. She refused.

"I'll go in and monitor the shots," Betty said. "You stay here with the others." The mother nodded. The second wife made no effort to assist. Betty assumed she didn't want to overstep her bounds. Maybe it was Iraqi custom for parents not to accompany their children into the doctor's office. Later, Betty learned that Iraqis, especially women, didn't question a doctor's authority.

One by one, the five Usaif children received their shots. They had no records from Iraq and received six shots each to meet school requirements. Betty steered them in and out. "This is the last one," she told the nurse, who appreciated Betty's assistance. The children knew some basic English but felt more comfortable with a familiar face as they stared at needles and other medical equipment.

Putting patients at ease was second nature to Betty, a former nurse. "Come on in, sweetie," she said to the middle daughter. "Sit over there on the examining table." Betty remembered the first night she met the children and wondered how she was ever going to remember all their names.

The nurse swabbed the girl's arm with an alcohol wipe and gave the first shot. A small flinch was the only reaction. She administered the remainder of the shots required by St. Mary's County School District.

Betty sighed, relieved. One more step on the road to independence completed. It was one of many she hadn't anticipated. The amount of work seemed to increase exponentially, and the complex logistical considerations hindered her best efforts to move things along. At least they would be able to start school on time.

The girl stood. She looked at Betty and the color drained from her face. Betty realized too late what was about to happen. She watched the girl's eyes roll back in her head as she dropped to the floor with a thud. On the way down she hit her head near the temple on the corner of the examining table.

The nurse jumped into action. She probed the corner of the girl's head and felt a lump forming. She grabbed a cold pack and held it against the girl's head. Betty sat her up, stroked her hand.

"Can you hear me?" She opened her eyes and focused. "Relax. Take deep breaths. Can we get her some water or juice?"

"Sure." The nurse returned with apple juice.

"*Shukran*," the girl said in Arabic.

"That means thank you," Betty said. "Drink up, sweetie. How are you feeling?"

After a few seconds the girl said, "Okay."

"You gave us a scare. Just when I thought we made it through this adventure without much drama." She nodded thanks to the nurse and gave her a look to say she was trying to remain patient in the face of unexpected events.

"I don't know many people who'd do all this," the nurse said.

"My son asked me to. He said the family would be dead if they'd stayed in Iraq. As much work as it is, I'm a Christian, and it's the right thing to do."

In the parking lot, everyone piled into the Suburban. Relieved that she'd survived the ordeal of five children receiving shots for the first time, Betty drove along a winding road. It would be an hour and a half until they were home. She glanced in the rearview mirror. The mother sat in the middle of the seat.

Suddenly, the mother clamped both hands against her head. She turned pale and stared at Betty in the mirror with a look of distress. Betty glanced back a second time. She saw the mother's eyes roll back in her head. "You okay?" No response.

Betty looked for a place to pull off the narrow road. The mom slumped against her daughter and passed out. The children whimpered.

It seemed like an eternity but it was probably only thirty seconds before Betty found a safe place to pull over. She jumped out and raced to the rear passenger door. The kids were hysterical. Her nursing instincts kicked in. She felt for a pulse. None. She eyed the woman's chest to spot the rise and fall that would indicate she was breathing. Nothing. The teenage son yelled in English, "Do something, Madame Betty." In the back seat, the daughters and second wife cried and hugged. Betty raced to the driver's seat, found her phone, and dialed 911.

"What's your emergency?"

Breathing hard, Betty said, "I have a female aged forty, no pulse, who just lost consciousness in my vehicle. I need an ambulance immediately."

"Please calm down and tell me your location."

"I'm at a convenience store along this winding country road." Betty thought, "Please God, don't let her die. What am I going to do with all these kids?" Then she had another thought. George will leave me if I'm stuck taking care of these kids.

Betty performed chest compressions and mouth to mouth as she waited for the ambulance. The children sobbed as they watched. Just as the EMTs pulled into the parking area, Betty felt a faint pulse. The woman was breathing. She briefed a medic on the details.

"You know if she has a medical history of these incidents?"

"No, they came from Iraq a month ago. Their medical and dental histories probably wouldn't translate well in our system anyway."

The ambulance loaded the woman into the rear. Betty and the rest of the family followed in her car. The kids were crying and speaking to each other in Arabic, their anxiety palpable. They'd been through so much and now faced the possibility of losing their mother.

She called George. "You need to pick up Mohammed from his classes and bring him to Southern Maryland hospital."

At the hospital, things were calm. Betty settled the children and second wife in the waiting area and received permission to see the mother in the emergency room. She brought the oldest daughter, Najla, in case the staff needed an interpreter.

"How are you feeling?" Betty said. The daughter translated. Her mother nodded.

"She blacked out after putting her hands on her head," Betty said to the nurse and a doctor.

"We're doing some tests to see if we can diagnose the problem," the nurse said. "You have any details on her medical history?"

"Nothing. They're from Iraq. I don't think they had access to the best medical care. I suspect she'd never had inoculations. Plus, they were in Turkey the last eight months. The kids weren't allowed to go to school, and they weren't in the best living conditions."

"We took blood samples, and we'll do a urinalysis," said the doctor. "We should be able to get a diagnosis. It may be because she's overwhelmed from all of the change."

The urine sample was purple, which Betty had never seen in her career. The urinalysis results came back inconclusive. The doctors didn't know how to interpret them. They concluded that the shock of a new environment combined with many other significant stressors had overwhelmed her. She was discharged the same day under Betty's care. General Mohammed arrived with George. They were updated, and went to pick up medication from a drug store. The rest of the family headed home with Betty.

Even after the events of the day, the kids still insisted on holding a birthday celebration for the general's second wife. They'd been excited about the prospect of a party all week. Betty used the event as an incentive for them to behave during the clinic visit, but she had misgivings about continuing with the plan. The first wife needed to rest. It didn't seem right that everyone else celebrate while she recovered, but Betty went along with it.

George and Mohammed picked up a cake on the way home. Preparations began, but the general's first wife would not relax until she was allowed to help cook food for the festivities.

Later on, Mohammed, his wives, the five children, George, and Betty gathered to mark the birthday. She blew out the candles. As everyone applauded, Betty wrapped an arm around George's waist and flashed a nervous smile at him. He raised his eyebrows and shrugged, wondering how they'd arrived at their current reality.

After two months in the Ebles' house, the Usaif family moved into their own apartment fifteen minutes away. Betty felt that would create breathing room for everyone as she continued to assist the family to adapt.

A milestone arrived for the children. The first day of school. The two youngest took a fifteen-minute bus ride to elementary school. Their sister walked to the middle school, and the oldest two attended high school.

On the first day of classes, Nadine overheard a teacher mention that a young girl from Iraq had enrolled. Surprised, Nadine stopped by the classroom to welcome her summertime pupil. She saw the young girl at a desk writing.

"I'd like to say hello to your new student," said Nadine. "I helped her learn English this summer and thought she might like to see a familiar face."

The girl heard Nadine's voice and looked up. She beamed, dropped her pen and raced to the classroom door. She threw her arms around Nadine in a warm hug.

"Let's grab some coffee after school today," Nadine said to the teacher. "This little one's had quite an experience."

Nadine's school was touted as a model for students of English as a second language. Over the course of the year, she worked with the ESL instructors because no one spoke Arabic nor had any knowledge of Iraqi culture.

Nadine was part of a rare minority in Saint Mary's County. Americans who not only had met Iraqis but also had a cursory understanding of their cultural differences. The smile she saw on the young girl's face made the summer-time effort to teach English worthwhile. The smiles that came in future years as the kids grew up continued to be a gift. Her children, Chasen and Jenna, went on play dates with the Usaifs and remained friends. The investment Nadine made when she offered a hand blossomed into wonderful relationships and the knowledge that her family had made a difference in the lives of others. It increased her passion for teaching and made her time in the classroom richer and more meaningful. Some nights, Nadine said a prayer and thanked Betty for the courage to sponsor the Iraqis and for asking her to be a part of their American experience.

One night, as Betty slid into bed and pulled up the covers, the phone rang. George brought her the phone. "It's Mohammed." Life was returning to normal and she wondered why he'd be calling so late.

"Madame Betty, the chicken is wet. The chicken is wet." Mohammed was loud and frantic.

"What?"

"The chicken is wet," he said, agitated.

"We'll be right over." She hung up.

"What's wrong?" Said George.

"I didn't understand him. Let's go find out."

When they arrived at the Usaif's apartment, Betty and George stepped into a large puddle of water in the kitchen. Drips streamed down from the ceiling. Betty looked at George.

"Well, the *kitchen* may be soaked but at least no chickens are wet." She laughed. George could only shake his head.

Chapter Nineteen

Looking in the Mirror

*"I keep my ideals, because in spite of everything I still
believe that people are really good at heart."*

~ Anne Frank

TOWARDS THE END of my third combat tour in Iraq, I reminisced with Jon Byrom about Hassan. We started the conversation as we ran around the base perimeter. Jon and I were dressed in PT clothes, and we each carried a 9mm pistol. We finished the run and stretched as steam rose from our shirts.

"You need to write a book, sir," Byrom said.

"Yeah, in my spare time."

"Wait a couple of years, after the NSC. Maybe then you'll have the time." The National Security Council provided the President with policy development and coordination across the executive branch of government. That would be my next assignment.

"I'll think about it. Most people I know who've written books tell me it's the quickest way to ruin your life. Time management goes out the window."

Byrom laughed. "Whatever happened to your primary interpreter from Baghdad? The one that Ronnie talked about all the time."

"Hassan transferred to Taji. He didn't like the command climate of the new unit at FOB Justice. Something about treating him like a second-class citizen."

"That must happen a lot," Jon said.

"He needed the break. He'd been there for two and a half years. The politics and religious dynamics were intense. Now he helps with training and provides insight for American contractors." I thought about all that Hassan and I had been through together. "He probably saved my life more than once. Hassan was always there, to check ideas, like a guardian angel. Our chai drinking sessions kept me from going crazy."

Maybe George Packer saved my life, too. Saved me from the grinding guilt that would have followed me to the grave had I not done something for the Iraqis who risked everything for us. George would never take credit, but his bright, piercing, media spotlight identified a serious problem we had overlooked in our meticulous planning for combat. It's something that haunts many vets with PTSD to this day. Thanks to the Baghdad Underground Railroad, we fought the insurgents, the bureaucracy, the unrelenting chaos of the environment. We saved guys like Ronnie, Mohammed, Dave, and many others.

I reunited with my family in November 2009 in Germany. After three combat deployments to Iraq, we wondered what the transition back to the U.S. would look like. Amy and the kids had lived in Germany for eight years. Our children had grown up there. They had visited the United States but really didn't know our country well. We sought an assignment in Washington, D.C. as the logical place where the kids could have stability while we explored continued military service. I sensed my time in uniform was coming to an end. D.C. was one of the few places I could transfer between assignments without having to move the family, uproot the kids from school and still allow Amy to find a job.

We were nervous about the children. How would they adapt? Both were great students but grew up in a sheltered lifestyle in Bavaria. The atmosphere in Schweinfurt reminded Amy and me of our childhoods on Long Island. Agriculture and tourism. Vineyards and wineries. In Schweinfurt, we walked the dog through farm fields and enjoyed the beautiful farmland surrounded by forests and creeks. Life was idyllic in this small town.

Early during our time in Germany, 2005, Amy said, "We have a problem." We thought we would soon move back to the U.S. We didn't yet know a second Iraq deployment would change our plans.

"What's that?" I said, not certain I wanted to hear the answer. She was not prone to histrionics.

"Rob can't write in English. If we're moving back to the States next year, I'm going to have to homeschool him."

I was dumbfounded. Of course he couldn't write in English. His school in Estenfeld instructed kids in German, with French as the secondary language. What should have been clear to us as parents escaped us because he could speak and read English without a problem. We were so excited that he had the opportunity to attend a German school that we missed the cost.

Amy had worked hard to get him enrolled. The administrators didn't want an American kid. We didn't pay taxes and American military families didn't have the greatest track record of assimilating to German culture. Amy was an elementary school teacher. We decided to homeschool the kids. Next year, the Army extended us due to another Iraq deployment. We moved to Schweinfurt and put the children in the Department of Defense School on base where Amy returned to teaching.

Five years later, we again thought about the transition to the U.S. Our original three-year assignment was extended twice due to combat deployments. At least both of our children could read, speak, and write English. They were excellent students, but we worried (as all parents do) about how life would be for them in Washington.

I had a pretty good idea about mine. I would replace my longtime friend and West Point classmate Charlie Miller as Director for Iraq on the National Security Council. That meant long hours at work and not much help on the parenting side. Amy would teach fulltime, and the kids would adapt to life in the U.S. for the first time in eight years. It was a good time for the transition. It aligned with Rob entering high school as a freshman and Heather starting the seventh grade. But we still worried.

A previous time abroad we had lived in Panama. We loved the lifestyle, became SCUBA divers, and traveled around the Caribbean on dive trips and other explorations. When we returned to the U.S. after three years, we felt culture shock. In Panama, we lived a simple life in a remote village named Gamboa along the Panama Canal. We worked hard and played hard with close friends in the neighborhood. When we returned to the States, we were overwhelmed with the amount of consumer choice in grocery stores, the fast pace of life, the "in-your-face" marketing. How would our children manage their return having left the U.S. at such a young age? How could Iraqis navigate the transition when we, as Americans, struggled with it?

Rob, Lady, our Golden Retriever, and I flew to the U.S. early in May 2010. We were to find a home while Amy finished teaching third grade at the Department of Defense dependent school in Schweinfurt and Heather finished the school year. We bought a house south of Reston, Virginia, and camped in it for a couple of weeks before Amy and Heather joined us. We slept in sleeping bags on air mattresses and grilled our food on the back deck. We stocked bare necessities, towels, and toilet paper in the bathroom. By the time my wife and daughter arrived, the utilities worked, and we were ready to receive a limited supply of household goods. Most of the shipment would take about two months to arrive from Germany.

Amy surveyed our caveman living arrangements. "It's time to buy some furniture," she said. "We're not going to live like college kids until the shipment arrives."

My assignment to the NSC was delayed a year. That was a blessing because I could assist with parenting before the intensity of a government administration job kicked in. I was selected as a Counterterrorism Fellow at the College of International Security Affairs at National Defense University. I began a yearlong academic study of the problem that had so frustrated me in the field in Iraq. Why was the only policy tool available to protect our most trusted partners, the interpreters, so limited in scope? Why weren't there other options besides the Special Immigrant Visa?

Despite my frustration, when I took stock of the accomplishments of Task Force Justice, they were significant in many ways. By the time we left, roughly three dozen interpreters had either been approved or had complete packets submitted to the State Department for consideration. I never received closure on how many of those cases were approved. I know of at least one interpreter who was approved but decided not to leave his family and stayed in Iraq. Ronnie, Dave, George, and at least three others enlisted in the Army or Marines. At least three deployed back to combat as U.S. military members.

It was complicated to find out what had happened with the others. After Baghdad in late 2007, I decompressed with the family over the holidays and immediately prepared to assume command of a battalion task force and return to combat. The assignments required intense focus, and the loose ends of war slipped through my grip like sand. Even the interpreters lost track of each other. When I interviewed several of them for this book, most didn't know what had happened with their Iraqi colleagues. Some kept in touch, like George and Ronnie. Both serve together today. They are employed by a defense contractor that conducts sensitive work that requires a security clearance. Others arrived in the States and focused on their families or adapting to their new life. The time with Task Force Justice became a fleeting memory of a crazy dream we experienced together.

George Packer introduced me to two young men the evening of Kirk Johnson's book launch in Washington, D.C. Kirk had written a book titled, *To Be a Friend is Fatal*. In it, he described how the U.S. abandoned its Iraqi partners. He drew on his experience with USAID, the United States Agency for International Development, in Iraq. Kirk started a nonprofit called the List Project, which he chronicled in his book. The List Project tallied name after name of Iraqis who reached out to the State Department, the military, USAID, or other groups for help. They were fleeing for their lives. Our country seemed to have no response or even care. These were Iraqis who worked closely with Americans and drew the short straw when they realized their new partners might not stick by them.

George introduced the author and explained to the crowd of sixty people why they should read the book and get involved. We were at the home of a wealthy family who hosted the event. Kirk spoke about the List Project and how he hoped more Americans would understand why it was vital that we stand by our closest Iraqi partners. He spoke about how great the need was, and how his list grew exponentially after Iraqis learned about it.

After the pitch, two former Marines, Mike and Jeff, talked about how they came to be at the event.

"I did two tours in Iraq, in 2004 and again in 2006," Mike said as he sipped a glass of wine. "My interpreter saved my ass during the second tour. He got word of an IED on our route and warned us. We called it in over the radio to ensure the battalion alerted other units. But a patrol from another battalion passing through the area wandered right into the kill zone. The bomb killed one guy and wounded three others. That would have been us if not for Ahmed." I'd heard many of these experiences and lived through a few myself.

Mike said, "I'm still in touch with him about every month or so. I thought about the SIV after hearing about it. I mentioned it to Ahmed one time, and he said no way. He couldn't leave his country."

Jeff listened to our discussion as he nursed a beer. "I used to hear from my interpreter about every three weeks or so. But I haven't heard from him lately, so I'm pretty sure he's dead," he said.

We stared at each other for a few seconds.

"Is there anything else we can do for these guys?" Mike said. Jeff held my gaze. They were about the same age and told me earlier in the evening they were starting a business together.

"The SIV is pretty much it," I said. "And if they're lucky enough to get through the process, they need to be prepared for the shock of coming to our country. They think the Hollywood representation is what the typical experience is like. Most Iraqis don't understand how hard it is to find a job and make a living here."

Jeff looked away. The military did a great job of instilling an ethos of "leave no one behind." Yet, nobody told us in training that we would leave our closest partners behind to the brutality of the enemy we fought. And the fact that our country's response was anemic, at best, rubbed salt in the wound.

Early Spring, 2019

I picked up the phone. It was my mom, Madame Betty. "I'm calling to see if you and Amy can visit us this summer."

A lot had happened since Iraq. I retired from the military after twenty-five years. We moved to California to put our kids through college without going bankrupt. Both would attend University of California schools.

"What's the big occasion?"

"We're having a special guest visit and I wanted to celebrate. Najla plans to visit with her new husband." I hadn't seen Najla, the Usaifs' oldest daughter, since she was sixteen. "She wants her husband, Rahim, to meet her American mom. I'm going to host a party and invite everyone who helped her family when they arrived."

I could feel her pride through the phone.

We had a whirlwind summer. Amy's breaks seemed to speed by like an express train that whooshes past the platform without slowing. My nonprofit work often took me to the East Coast. I stayed in contact with family and saw many of our old friends. Amy rarely made it. We decided to spend a week in the area. We'd catch up with friends and cap off the visit at Madame Betty and Mr. George's house for the celebration.

We arrived at my mother's home to hugs and hellos. George was eager to take Rahim and me out on his sailboat. Rahim hadn't spent much time on the water but knew how to swim. I had grown up on the water on Long Island and was eager to spend any time exploring the waves. After a minor adventure of snagging a buoy line on the sailboat's rudder, we powered back to harbor happy from the sea, salt, and sun.

That evening, I met Nadine Hughes for the first time. About a dozen of Mom's friends from church and the community came to celebrate the nurturing and hospitality they provided for Najla and her family. But the big surprise was something none of us had anticipated during the challenging days of 2007 and 2008. There, in a century-old bassinette, Najla laid a month-old baby girl. She had struggled to get pregnant for years. With pride, she held the baby for all to see and graciously allowed many of the guests to hold her.

Dinner was Iraqi food followed by cake for dessert. The mood was merry. Stories flowed, laughter echoed throughout the house, and everywhere Najla brought the baby, people smiled. They had all played a role, some grand and some small, at the last stop along the Baghdad Underground Railroad. Many didn't know there was an effort to help people escape the horrific sectarian violence of Baghdad in 2007. They had simply responded to the call for help when they learned about a family in need. It was a testament to their generosity and hospitality, acts that would be respected throughout the Middle East.

After a few hours, the celebration wound down.

"Well, that was wonderful," Mom said.

"We're really glad we could be here," I said.

"Yes, thank you, Uncle," Najla said. "Rahim and I are honored by your presence." She and some of the other Usaif kids referred to me as uncle since we first met at Mom's house ten years earlier.

As Amy held the baby, Betty said, "Did you know the baby was born on your birthday? We're going to nickname her 'Baby Amy.' That's a beautiful name."

As Amy cradled the baby, Najla and Rahim looked on with Mom, George, and me. We marveled at the life made possible by the incredible journey we had traveled together.

Afterword

In Germany after a combat deployment, I attended a community play performed by our children. The material was so sensitive that Amy and I refused to allow Rob to rehearse in public. He could practice in the privacy of our home but had to keep it down because the neighbors might hear. The play was *And Then They Came For Me,* about the life of Holocaust survivor Eva Gerringer Schloss, whose mother married Anne Frank's father Otto after the war. Rob played a Nazi youth who opened the play with a soliloquy that shocked the audience. He definitely shocked his parents. His words, parsed amidst several "Heil Hitlers," reverberated in the theater as swastikas were projected on a screen behind him. Sounds of Nazi rallies and marches echoed from the sound system as Rob accentuated how the character had been indoctrinated to believe that Jews were the scum of the earth, lower than rats.

Later in the play, Rob described how the Nazis gave each youth a puppy. After six months they were ordered to break their puppy's neck. I was never able to verify the authenticity of the practice by Nazi youth, but its inclusion in the play continued the audience's revulsion about the cruel practices of the Nazi regime. Although we were all familiar with the facts of this history, to review the intentional subjugation of a nation's young, the brainwashing of their malleable minds to further the propaganda and control of a political party, was chilling to contemplate.

I remember thinking about how the play intended to remind audiences all over the world about history, the fact that history could repeat itself. Never forget. That was Eva's legacy, to remind the next generation that we were not out of the woods. It could still happen. I flashed back to Iraq. Genocide played out all around us. We sent soldiers to the sectarian fault lines to prevent the fighting, like referees stepping between boxers. Violence and lack of basic services weathered our men and women at the combat outposts. Those same conditions pummeled the Iraqi civilians. We hadn't empathized with their plight until George Packer wrote *Betrayed*. He forced us to pick our heads up from our own collective misery and realize that others had it worse. Once we trained our eyes to see the horror, we could choose to look away, but we could never say we didn't know. The mirror became a harsh task master.

How did guys like Ronnie, George, and Dave ever muster the courage to leave their families and work alongside us? We were considered heroes at home. Our interpreters were considered traitors in theirs. Iraqi parliamentarians would castigate them, people would spit on them, threaten their families. Yet, Ronnie went on every patrol. Maybe he felt he didn't have a choice?

When I returned to the United States from eight years overseas and three combat deployments to Iraq, civilians in the U.S. would say, "Thank you for your service," when they happened upon a veteran. They didn't know what else to say, and most conversations never progressed beyond that. Most people didn't know how to speak to soldiers. What would they say to someone who abandoned his family and culture to support our cause, who had sacrificed everything to support another country? Would they want to?

The Iraqis who immigrated through the Baghdad Underground Railroad became family, in many ways, to the sponsors who embraced them. Some would enlist in the military and put those very sponsors through the same anxiety that all parents experience when a son or daughter goes into combat. Regardless of the paths they took after arriving in America, the journeys of Ronnie, Dave, and the Usaif family all began with one central woman exhibiting the courage to extend a welcoming hand. If it were not for Madonnna Felix, Betty Eble, or Lia Haley, the Iraqi experiences could have concluded in less positive—and even drastic—ways.

Some recent Afghan arrivals have considered returning to their country though they could be killed by the Taliban. They consider the risk of return preferable to the shame and humiliation of not finding a job and being unable to provide for their family. Even with nonprofits stepping in to fill the void, sponsors play a critical role in the journeys of these heroes.

Many men played pivotal roles, and I don't want to downplay their contributions. Gregg Haley was the key driver in getting Dave out of harm's way and into the United States. John Haley was able to lend Lia a hand during a critical time shortly after Dave's arrival. However, had Lia not exhibited the courage to bring Dave into the Haley home, the initial few weeks could have been different. Many former interpreters who immigrate to the U.S. left their families and cultures behind and found it difficult to adapt. Most are intelligent and willing to work hard, but they lack credit ratings, licenses, and basic fundamentals most Americans take for granted. The support that women like Lia provided at the last stop of the Baghdad Underground Railroad allowed guys like Dave to catch up and eventually compete on a more level playing field.

As a widow, Madonna Felix exercised bravery by bringing Ronnie into her home. She gave him a loving place to start his new life, provided counsel, and convinced her father to assist. Ronnie came to America with a level of confidence and self-sufficiency that exceeded most but benefited beyond measure from Madonna's nurturing. He considers her his "American mom" and is the first to admit her vital role in his early days in the United States.

In my mother's case, she took the organizing burden on her shoulders. She wrangled five children, two wives and a general used to being in charge. She integrated the children into the U.S. health, dental and education systems. Betty didn't do it alone, but she was the driving force. She formed a team that included her husband, George, Nadine Hughes, and others. People at her church volunteered support, inspired by her example. Jimmy Butler, then a Navy captain who was recently promoted to rear admiral, spent hours coaching Mohammed on his resume. Russ Horton, a friend from church who was in his mid-eighties when the Usaif family arrived, provided mandatory Maryland drug and alcohol classes so Mohammed and other family members could apply for a driver's license. Through it all, Mr. George supported Madame Betty's efforts and provided critical assistance. But Betty was the glue that brought the team together. Without her spark, none of the people in her small Southern Maryland community would have had the opportunity to welcome a family from Iraq that would have been killed had they remained in their home country. Betty gave those around her the chance to "pay it forward."

These three women, in various ways, helped to fill a void for assimilation of vulnerable people immigrating to the United States. That void would create enough distress to bring multiple nonprofits, like No One Left Behind and Miry's List, into existence. They provide a systematic approach to the gap that Betty, Madonna, and Lia filled. These organizations aid former interpreters and other refugees with sustainable housing and employment. They help interpreters reconnect with military veterans, as well. Those veterans often volunteer to sponsor interpreters or lend support in other ways. Eventually, the intangibles of feeling welcome and being treated with dignity combine with the realities of work, income and home to integrate these new members. But it is still difficult, as any nonprofit staff member or SIV recipient would be quick to admit.

Another organization, the International Refugee Assistance Project, has also played a fundamental role. Started by a group of Yale law students at the height of sectarian cleansing in Iraq, IRAP has represented thousands of SIV candidates and other vulnerable refugees through a combination of pro bono legal support, graduate law students at college-level chapters, and the savvy of its leader, Becca Heller. Becca has grown the organization to new heights and continues to chart a path for many destitute refugees around the world.

Veterans for American Ideals, a program founded by Scott Cooper at Human Rights First, has also led a charge for advocacy to help SIV recipients. VFAI marshals a network of veterans concerned about the impact to national security for the failure to live up to the values we profess as Americans. Many of these vets, who wish to continue to serve after taking off their uniforms, have championed worthy causes in communities around the country by tapping into citizen desires for nonpartisan leadership on important issues.

Thomas Friedman wrote in his book, *Thank You for Being Late: An Optimist's Guide to Thriving in the Age of Accelerations*, about a conversation he had with Eric "Astro" Tester, the CEO of Google's X research and development lab. Tester tried to explain Moore's law, or the rapid acceleration of technological change, as it relates to societal change. His argument is that social change occurs at a linear pace while technological change happens exponentially. This theoretical construct could help explain the Arab Awakening (or Arab Spring) across the Middle East and North Africa. As technology spreads rapidly, it allows every individual with an iPhone a journalist's capability to report on events in real time. The capacity of governance to respond to the demands of managing new technologies in the hands of a more aware populace has diminished. As a result, people in many Middle Eastern and North African nations have demanded social change that their governments are either unwilling or unable to provide. Thus, we witnessed the cascading effect of governments toppled or lashing out in survival mode as authoritarian leaders suppressed their people in Tunisia, Egypt, Yemen, Syria, and Iraq.

Our government has not been immune to the demands of social change. Example: After experience on the ground in Iraq, other veterans and I returned to the U.S. frustrated by the lack of policy options available to practitioners in the fight. The SIV was important, but it was the only policy the U.S. had. From my research, I would come to think of the SIV as "too little, too late." It provided too little capacity to address the size of the problem, and it was enacted too late to get ahead of U.S. adversaries in their logical campaign to target American soft networks. My argument accelerated and developed beyond the SIV. It was a critical policy tool but should be a policy of last resort, not the only policy in the toolkit. America could better insulate its partners, protecting their identity and relocating them when necessary.

Yet, given Tester's description of social change, it should not surprise anyone that it took our government much too long to adapt to changing realities on the ground. As a result, I needed to take an appetite suppressant with respect to how quickly we could generate awareness and implement new tools for our military and diplomats to insulate our soft networks. Those policies would all revolve around identity protection and, when that failed, relocation.

As a result, I spent a year-long counterterrorism fellowship researching and writing on the subject. More important, I thought about the challenge through different prisms. In every class, whether the topic seemed relevant to my thesis or not, the burning issue would rise in my consciousness. It allowed me to contemplate it from a variety of historical perspectives, including cultural and theoretical. I was able to bounce ideas off classmates and professors, many of whom were from other countries. My experience at the College of International Security Affairs provided a rich and diverse environment from which to dive deep into something that had been a personal struggle since Baghdad in 2007.

During the counterterrorism fellowship, I wrote a 125-page thesis on the problem of failing to protect our most trusted partners in conflict zones. After my assignment at the NSC, I taught at Marine Corps University. I wrote about and advocated on behalf of soft networks. Eventually, I started a project that received a sizeable grant from the Smith Richardson Foundation.

The project to Strategically Protect Soft Networks is a public-private enterprise of partner organizations in academia, government, the think-tank community and private sector. It proactively insulates foreign national partners in conflict zones by combining a research team with a policymaking effort. That coupling works to harvest best practices from nontraditional areas like NGOs in conflict zones, the media, domestic witness security programs, and others. The team has tremendous support from the staff and leadership of the Pacific Council on International Policy led by Jerrold Green. We attempt to infuse creativity into the policymaking effort through new ideas and advocating on behalf of national security interests achieved by adopting stronger practices. Such policy would create more resilient soft networks for U.S. diplomats and military practitioners around the globe.

In 2014, I took students from Marine Corps War College to Florida to learn about the Special Operations Command, Southern Command, and the Joint Interagency Task Force in Key West that coordinates the U.S. counter drug effort in the Caribbean. In Florida, George, Ronnie, and I had dinner. We rejoiced in their exploits, the progress they'd made in the U.S., and adventures yet to come. Later, Ronnie traveled to Morocco to assist a film production team produce a movie about the retaking of Mosul from the Islamic State. A desperate

Hollywood producer had reached out to a military veterans' network and asked if we knew anyone who could fill in for two Iraqi Army officers who failed to arrive on set after their visas were denied in Baghdad. The producers asked for three weeks, which Ronnie's boss granted. The film makers loved Ronnie so much they asked him to extend for ten weeks. I have no idea how he worked that out with his employer. Who else but Ronnie could fulfill that role?

A couple years ago, Hassan came to visit his daughter. She was graduating from a California university. We had a long breakfast together and reminisced about the people and times we shared. He was on his way back to Iraq after visiting his family for ten days. Still at it, the Old Dog had his finger on the pulse of the Iraqis and Americans who worked alongside each other in the still evolving and complex cauldron of Iraq. He remains there to this day, assisting the American effort with invaluable advice to those who operate alongside him.

Chris Hondros was killed in Misrata, Libya, HHe alongside Tim Hetherington. during a regime mortar attack in 2011. Chris had launched from Benghazi with the rebels as they sought to prevent Qaddafi from "not showing any mercy" to the city of over 600,000. I had no doubt at the time that the madman would butcher the city. The rebels expected similar results but benefited from coalition air support that tracked down Qaddafi. Chris had been at the front lines in many conflicts before he covered the rebel defense in the urban environment. His boss and coworkers at Getty Images were devastated when he died. His fiancé and Getty Images began the Chris Hondros Fund Award to promote up-and-coming photojournalists.

At his funeral in Fayetteville, North Carolina, home of my old unit, the famed 82nd Airborne Division, Hondros' colleagues thanked me for making the trip from Washington, D.C. Some of them had also embedded with my unit, though none as often as Chris. They expressed gratitude at my presence, the only person from the military. I valued Chris's service and sacrifice as much as any servicemember in uniform. As a noble champion of the first amendment, he volunteered for combat duty to help tell our story to the American public.

Arwa Damon remains a senior international correspondent for CNN. She also started INARA, a nonprofit that helps children wounded in war find the medical support they need. We had breakfast in L.A. a couple of years ago. She no longer smoked. She wasn't staying long. Uninterested in the trivia the domestic media obsesses over in daily coverage, the front lines called her back to the Middle East.

Michael Holmes anchors for CNN in Atlanta, Georgia. He actively stays on top of issues around interpreters and vulnerable refugees. Want to get the energetic Australian's attention? Tweet to him about a compelling SIV story.

Kristy Palermo lives in Florida with her son, Marcus. Tony's parents get to see their grandson in Maine every summer. Kristy worked in the corporate sector for about ten years after teaching at Embry-Riddle for three years as a ROTC instructor. She has a background in criminal justice from her Military Police time in the Army. She has not remarried and has focused on raising her 14-year-old son. Captain Anthony Palermo is honored with other soldiers in memoriam at Fort Riley, Kansas, home of the Dagger Brigade combat team.

I intentionally omitted or changed the names of the Usaif family. Their future safety still depends on anonymity from many of the actors portrayed in the book. Those actors' names have also been changed to dampen the likelihood of revenge and provide plausible deniability. Like all families, they share challenges and triumphs, big and small. The birth of "Baby Amy" was one such event, celebrated by Americans and Iraqis at Madame Betty's and Mr. George's house. We celebrated a birth that day, but we also celebrated the best of what America can be, a place of hope and inspiration where people can escape persecution and start life afresh. We celebrated a future that may not have come to pass had the courageous members of a little southern Maryland town not shaped it so.

There are things that people can do. There are things you can do. Many soldiers, veterans or their family members step forward as sponsors or remain in contact with former interpreters to help provide a lifeline. You don't have to be someone who served in uniform to help. Some people contact the International Refugee Assistance Project. Others volunteer with No One Left Behind, Miry's List or other nonprofits that help refugees assimilate. Some people open their wallets and help provide the resources that fuel the nonprofits while others educate themselves about national security issues like protecting soft networks, our most vulnerable partners in conflict zones. Many call or write their representatives in Congress to advocate for assistance.

To learn more about this issue, sign up at the Project to Strategically Protect Soft Networks. [https://protectingsoftnetworks.org/] We have a free newsletter and provide information about partner organizations. Our team published a white paper, free for download at the website, that explores the strategic challenge and possible policy options to better insulate our closest partners in conflict zones. Reach out to me personally. I would be happy to provide ideas on how you can help.

To this day, the Iraqi flag, the one that Mark gave me at the farewell party, hangs in my office. Those signatures and the others they represented helped provide the inspiration to keep writing and editing this story, so it could be shared with others.

Acknowledgements
- With Gratitude

Telling this story has been a long journey. There are many people along the way to thank, not least of which are the interpreters, soldiers and families with whom we served. I resisted writing the story for many years, despite encouragement from trusted sources. Maybe I didn't want to resurface old wounds, or maybe I've never been that good at reviewing my own history. If you are one of the many people like Emma Sky, George Packer, and others who encouraged me to write the story, thank you. This experience needs to be shared beyond a military audience. The American people can celebrate alongside the few Iraqis who were fortunate to escape the violence.

To the families of the fallen, Kim Felts Thomas and children, Katharina & Bill Felts, Inge Hondros, Christina Piaia, Jack's family, Nadal's family and many others, my intent with respect to your loved ones in this story was to honor their service and sacrifice. Our country owes you a debt we can never repay. I hope that shedding some light on this time in Bagdad brings some solace in learning how your loved ones impacted those serving with them.

To the intrepid journalists, Chris Hondros, George Packer, Greg Jaffe, Arwa Damon, Michael Holmes, and many, many others, thank you for shining a spotlight on some very dark corners of the human experience in conflict. Many times, a front-page story for *The New York Times* would help accomplish things that no amount of bullets could affect.

To the interpreters, Ronnie, Dave, Mark, and many others, the Usaif Family, sponsors, Madonna, Lia & Gregg, Betty & George, and Kristy Palermo, all who agreed to interviews at risk of opening their own old scars, I am indebted. You did it in the hope that we could impact policy in a way to help others mired in conflict zones around the world. We will continue to spearhead the charge for needed change.

To the readers and reviewers: Ambassador Ryan Crocker, a constant champion for our interpreters; J. Ford Huffman, a fearless advocate in the free press; Ambassador Greta Holtz, who along with Emma Sky, recommended that I work at the NSC following Iraq and have consistently encouraged me in the writing process; Becca Heller, who fearlessly advocates for and alleviates the hurdles for potential SIV candidates at IRAP; Greg Jaffe, never taking his eye off the importance of this issue; General David Petraeus, who joined the cause with Ambassador Crocker and continues advocating with NOLB; and Kevin Anthony, thank you. Ronnie and the general's son provided feedback specifically to ensure that the information in the book would not increase risk levels to some of the characters. Jerrold Green, President of the Pacific Council on International Policy, not only provided enthusiastic feedback for the book but also helped with underlying research for the policy development process. He has been a champion. Special thanks to Seth Freeman, who read two different drafts, provided commentary, and recommended that I apply for the Veterans Writing Project at the Writer's Guild Foundation several years ago. Julie Waxman has been a consistent and trusted confidant, helping me seek out representation and providing thoughtful feedback along the way. I am grateful.

To the many hosts, both friends and coffee establishments run by friends, thank you. Ken Cassine and Janet Rathod, Barbara Ferguson and Tim Kennedy, J.P. McGee, you provided a sanctuary where much of my thinking could take place during D.C. trips. Sarah and Curtis at Zebra House Coffee, Dan and Tai at Jadore, Terry at Café Rae, Jess and Jodi at Rockwell's Bakery, and many others, your hospitality, warmth and friendship have helped bring this story into existence. Much gratitude!

To the publishing team at *Onward Press*, who tackled this project with class and persistence. Your efforts embellish the reputation of the United States Veterans Artists Alliance and support aspiring screenwriters and other veteran artists to achieve their dreams. Thank you for your willingness to serve the veteran and military family community, and thank you for your patience with this author. You have made this work substantially better through your efforts, especially Timothy Wurtz for his mentorship, Christina Hoag for her editorial prowess, and Keith Jeffreys, for leading USVAA. Tremendous thanks to Farahn Morgan, the team publicist who brought strategic vision to the project. To the other writers and actors who populate the table reads on a monthly basis and in the Veterans Writing Project at the Writer's Guild Foundation, thank you. Your insight and suggestions have strengthened the work. Special note of thanks to Jamie Peterson. Your artwork, patience, and ability to shape a non-artist's instinct into something that honors interpreters, amazed me. We are all indebted.

To the Strategically Protecting Soft Networks team, I am indebted to your willingness to dedicate long hours, amazing intellect, and great cheer to some very dark topics. Starting with Jamie Haag, my friend and colleague from CISA (the "First Sergeant"), who helped keep me sane and ran herd on our researcher team: Rebecca Asch, Sam Romano, Jure Erlich, Shalinda Sprehn, Lina Craighill, and Alek Ball. My hope is that this book furthers the research and policy work you have accomplished. Dr. Ami Carpenter, Professor at University of San Diego, consistently encouraged me to partner with her students. Zoe Knepp has joined the book effort to help with the myriad of tasks to publish and promote the work. Special note to Dr. Tammy Schultz, my colleague and boss at Marine Corps University, who first convinced me that research assistants could add tremendous value. Roslyn Warren, who first co-published on soft networks with me and helped get SIV legislation passed in Congress, set the bar amazingly high for future teammates. Marin Strmecki at the Smith Richardson Foundation believed in this effort enough to provide a generous grant. Thank you!

Lastly, I want to thank my family. Some of you had choices like my mother, Madame Betty, yet you stuck by me and committed to endeavors few would ever accept. My children, Rob and Heather, like many other military kids, didn't have a choice about whether Daddy went to war. You dealt with the missed birthdays and holidays with amazing tolerance and style. We tried to make it up when we could. My wife of 29 years, Amy, has stood by me every step of the way, providing subtle guidance and direction when I needed it, and the license to make, and hopefully, learn from my mistakes. I am forever grateful.

Glossary

1SG – First Sergeant

AD – Accidental Discharge

AI – Area of influence, a term describing areas adjacent to or affecting a unit's AO

AIT – Advanced Individual Training

AO – Area of operations, a term used to describe a military unit's area of responsibility

AQI – Al Qaeda in Iraq, the Iraqi affiliate of Osama bin Laden's al Qaeda, precursor to the Islamic State

BIAP – Baghdad International Airport

BG – Brigadier General in military rank (one star)

COL – Colonel in military rank

COP – Combat Outpost, smaller, more austere bases

CPT – Captain in military rank

CSH – Combat Support Hospital (pronounced "cash" in military jargon)

CSM – Command Sergeant Major (senior enlisted in a command billet)

EFP – Explosively Formed Penetrator, a technical IED made with manufacturing technology

EOD – Explosive Ordnance Disposal

FOB – Forward Operating Base, usually large military bases

FPS – Facilities Protection Service, providing guard forces for critical infrastructure

FRG – Family Readiness Group

GEN – General, the highest peacetime rank attainable (four stars)

HMMWV – High Mobility Multipurpose Wheeled Vehicle

IA – Iraqi Army

ICMC – International Catholic Migration Commission

IED – Improvised Explosive Device

IO – Investigating officer

IP – Iraqi Police

IRC – International Rescue Committee

ISF – Iraqi Security Forces

IS/ ISIS – Islamic State also known as the Islamic State of Iraq and al-Sham

IZ – International zone, also referred to as the Green Zone

JAM – Jaysh al Mahdi, also known as the Mahdi Army. A Shiite militia organization run by Moqtada al-Sadr, a Shiite religious figure in Iraq

LT – Lieutenant in military rank

LTC – Lieutenant Colonel in military rank

LTG – Lieutenant General in military rank (three stars)

MAJ – Major in military rank

MG – Major General in military rank (two stars)

MTT – Military transition team

NAC – Neighborhood Advisory Council

NCO – Noncommissioned officer

NGOs – Non-Governmental Organizations

NSC – National Security Council

PIR – Passive infrared

PTSD – Post-traumatic Stress Disorder

QRF – Quick Reaction Force

ROTC – Reserve Officer Training Corps

R&R – Rest and recuperation

Salatia – Restitution payment for injury or death, commonly called "blood money"

SAPI – Small Arms Protective Insert, ceramic plating used in body armor

SFC – Sergeant First Class

SGM – Sergeant Major (staff level senior enlisted)

SOP – Standard operating procedure

SIV – Special Immigrant Visa

SVBIED – Suicide vehicle born improvised explosive device

TAC – Tactical Air Coordinator

TBI – Traumatic Brain Injury

UNHCR – United Nations High Commission for Refugees, the UN Refugee Agency

USAID – United States Agency for International Development

VBIED – Vehicle born improvised explosive device

VFAI – Veterans for American Ideals

Basic Arabic words

Shukran – Thank you

Afwan – You're welcome

As-salamu 'alaykum – Peace be upon you

Allah Bikhayr – God is fine

Gensia – Iraqi identification

baksheesh - bribe

abu Mashakel – "father of trouble" Miska's Iraqi nickname

About the Author

Steve Miska spent twenty-five years in the U.S. Army, including three combat deployments to Iraq and service in the White House as Director for Iraq on the National Security Council. He earned top academic honors as a Counterterrorism Fellow at the College of International Security Affairs and has taught at the United  States Military Academy, West Point. Steve speaks on first amendment issues and soft networks and has addressed DIA, RAND, the Pacific Council on International Policy, the Young Presidents Organization of LA, and numerous media outlets and think tanks. He holds degrees from Cornell University, National Defense University, and West Point. He is the executive director of First Amendment Voice, a nonpartisan effort to reinvigorate civic awareness around free expression, religious liberty, press freedom and other first amendment issues.

About the Publisher

Onward Press (www.onwardpress.org) is the publishing imprint of the United States Veterans' Artists Alliance, Inc. a 501-c-3 educational non-profit (www.usvaa.org). Our mission is to publish well-written, compelling books by military veterans, spouses, military brats and other family members, as well as people who served in other government agencies and their family members.

Onward Press books available at Amazon:

"*Zippo Boys – Serving Gay in Viet Nam*" by Dave Lara

"*Welcome to Blackwater – Mercenaries, Money and Mayhem in Iraq*" by Morgan Lerette

"*Baghdad Underground Railroad – Saving American Allies in Iraq*" by Steve Miska

The United States Veterans' Artists Alliance (USVAA) is an award-winning, multi-disciplinary non-profit arts organization founded in 2004. USVAA provides opportunities for veterans by highlighting their work in the arts, humanities and the entertainment industry. As a voice representing the veterans' community and in our endeavors as artists, the organization strives to address issues of concern to veterans and their families, including the transition from military to civilian life, education, employment, the effects of wartime and military-service injuries, including posttraumatic stress disorder (PTSD), traumatic brain injury (TBI), military sexual trauma (MST) and homelessness.

CPSIA information can be obtained
at www.ICGtesting.com
Printed in the USA
LVHW021021010621
689024LV00037B/2749/J